Woodstock, Vermont

A Treasure in the Mountains

THROUGH TIME

ELIZABETH C. JEWELL

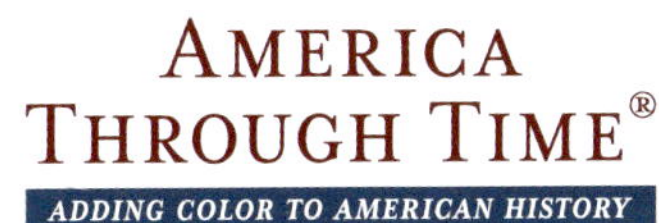

America Through Time is an imprint of Fonthill Media LLC

First published 2016

ISBN 978-1-63500-042-9

Typeset in Mrs Eaves XL Serif Narrow

Published by Arcadia Publishing by arrangement with Fonthill Media LLC
For all general information, please contact Arcadia Publishing:
Telephone: 843-853-2070
Fax: 843-853-0044
E-mail: sales@arcadiapublishing.com
For customer service and orders:
Toll-Free 1-888-313-2665

Visit us on the internet at www.arcadiapublishing.com

INTRODUCTION

Woodstock Through Time is something between a love letter and a thank-you card from me to Woodstock.

I want to give something back to Woodstock in appreciation for all it has given me over the years. The town is full of natural, cultural and historic gems, making it truly, "A Treasure in the Mountains."

I have wonderful memories, beginning when I was very young and my family drove from northern Vermont to picnic on The Green. My first date with my husband was a day trip here. I often brought my children to Woodstock to traverse Middle Bridge, visit Gillingham's, see the raptors, tour the library, and experience all of Woodstock's many wonders.

Woodstock is steeped in history. First settled in 1761, and incorporated in 1837, Woodstock became a Shire Town in 1785 with the most formative period soon after, during the 1800s. Mills sprang up along the Ottaquechee River and the valley prospered. The Woodstock and White River Railroads conjoined in 1875, opening a whole new world of possibilities to the region, which are reflected in the stately homes and dignified public properties located around The Green.

As a result, Woodstock is a small place with a big personality. Nestled between Mount Tom and Mount Peg, Woodstock resides along the Ottaquechee River like an indulged child between doting parents. The surrounding hills and mountains are forested and laced with skiing and hiking trails; picturesque and productive farms occupy the fertile river valley lands.

The allure here is enhanced by the absence of visible electric lines and flashy signage. The downtown and surrounding neighborhoods have been well-preserved.

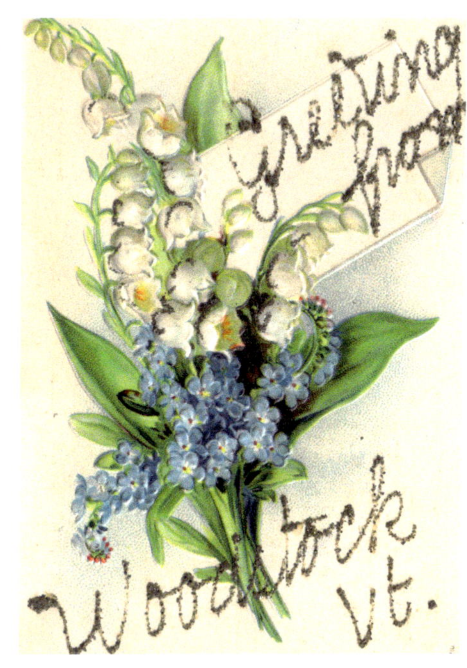

The vintage postcard at right was sent from Woodstock over 100 years ago.

The natural beauty of the region is further enriched by the foresight and wisdom of former and current inhabitants.

Several interesting communities encircle Woodstock protectively like handsome suiters surrounding a poised country dancer. I've included a few of them here. Plymouth, Taftsville, Quechee, South Woodstock, West Woodstock and Bridgewater; while perhaps not the center of attention at the ball, each have separate and interwoven histories and a significant supporting role.

This book begins much like I savor Woodstock. Unless I'm "on a mission," I park and walk around The Green, usually counter-clockwise, getting reacquainted. The images in the book can attest to the timeless quality of this route. But things here do change subtly and constantly. The light softens or sharpens, the air warms and crisps, the shadows lengthen and disappear; new flowers bloom in the many pocket gardens, the leaves change and fall. It's the little things here that make a big difference.

From the initial circumnavigation of The Green, I've arranged the book by related topics. Some topics may belong to more than one category and then, I've had to decide the best position for them. This book is not intended to be a comprehensive history of Woodstock. There are many fine books available which do that very well. This is a collection of interesting places, hopefully enticing you to continue your own exploration.

Please keep in mind as you travel through time in Woodstock with me:

All the "before" images are derived from old postcards or vintage photos loaned by generous people. Then I, or sometimes my brother Jon, photographed the corresponding "after" images. There are a few exceptions when something was too interesting to pass up but didn't have a current or previous partnering image. Then it's been woven into the fabric of the story. When I mention the date of a postmark on a vintage post card, the image was captured before that date.

Travel "Through Time" with me and discover a sampling of this special place for yourself!

On and Around The Green

The Green, or The Common as it was often referred to in days gone by, is an oblong park in the metaphorical center of Woodstock. The rest of the town seems to radiate out around The Green. Much of Woodstock's history is reflected as you stand in the center and look about. The first house was built on The Green, in 1772. By *on it*, in this instance, I mean surrounding the perimeter. There are no buildings actually *on* The Green, except for the information booth. North and South Park Streets surround it and showcase many majestic Georgian and Federal style homes, rubbing shoulders.

Woodstock lives its entire public life on center stage. The library, county courthouse, town hall and inn face one another across The Green.

Originally The Green was triangular shaped. In 1830 it was redesigned by a village committee into the current oval shape. During the Civil War, the space served as a militia training ground. The encircling decorative iron fence was completed in 1878 and continues to embrace the park. Events are held on The Green year round: Bookstock, vintage car shows, chili cook-offs, apple festivals, and Wassail Weekend to name but a few. The Green is quite versatile and whether transformed by a Pentangle Art display or covered by booths during the Farmer's Market, it is welcoming and inviting to locals and visitors alike.

Please journey with me now around The Green as I point out some of the interesting places that elegantly surround the perimeter.

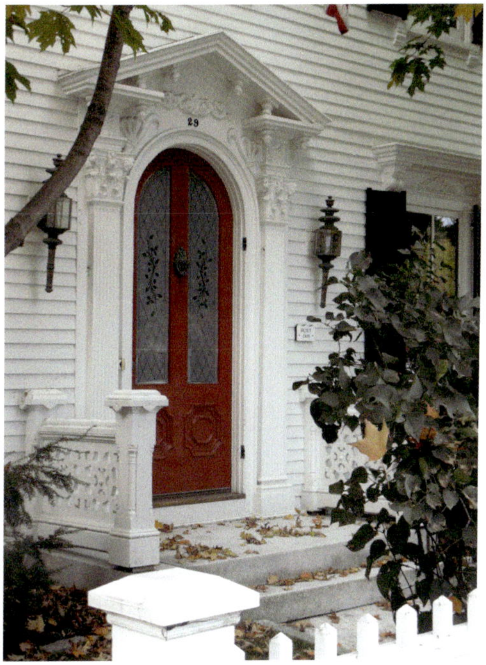

This doorway graces one of the elegant old homes on The Green.

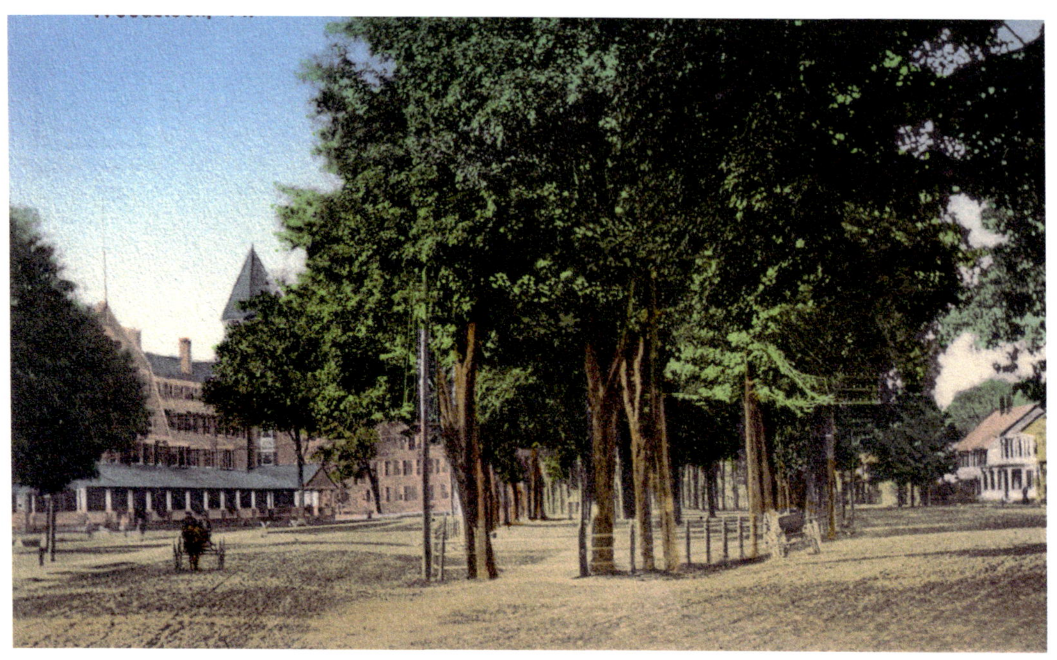

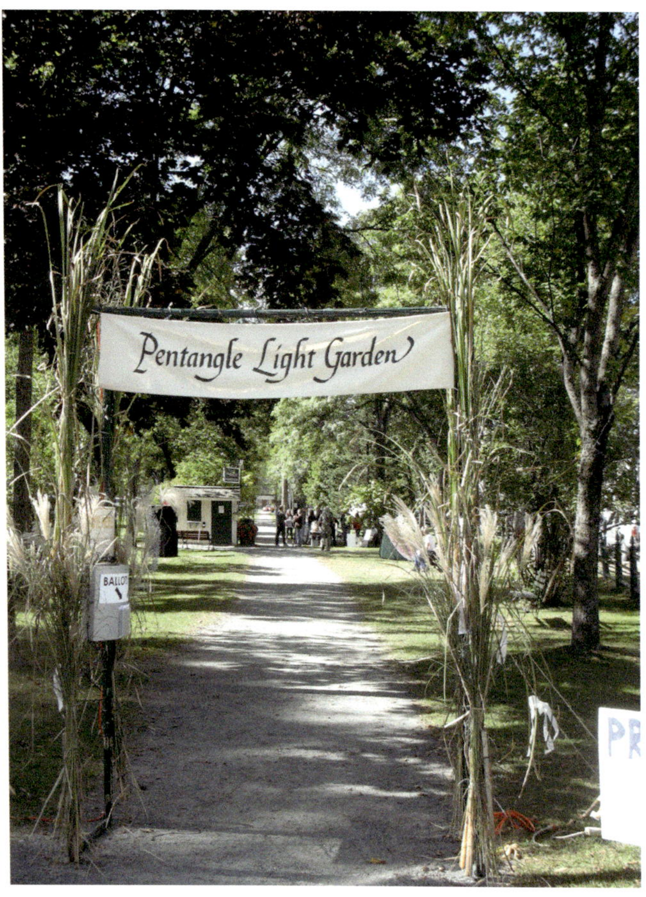

THE EASTERN ENTRANCE TO THE GREEN: Provides a panoramic view of some stately buildings. To the south one can see the bank, stone houses, library, courthouse, front of the inn and the Anderson House. On the north side a row of dignified homes can be seen right down to Mountain Avenue, where Middle Bridge resides. The image above was captured over 100 years ago. Notice the horse-and-buggy mode of travel and the unpaved streets surrounding The Green.

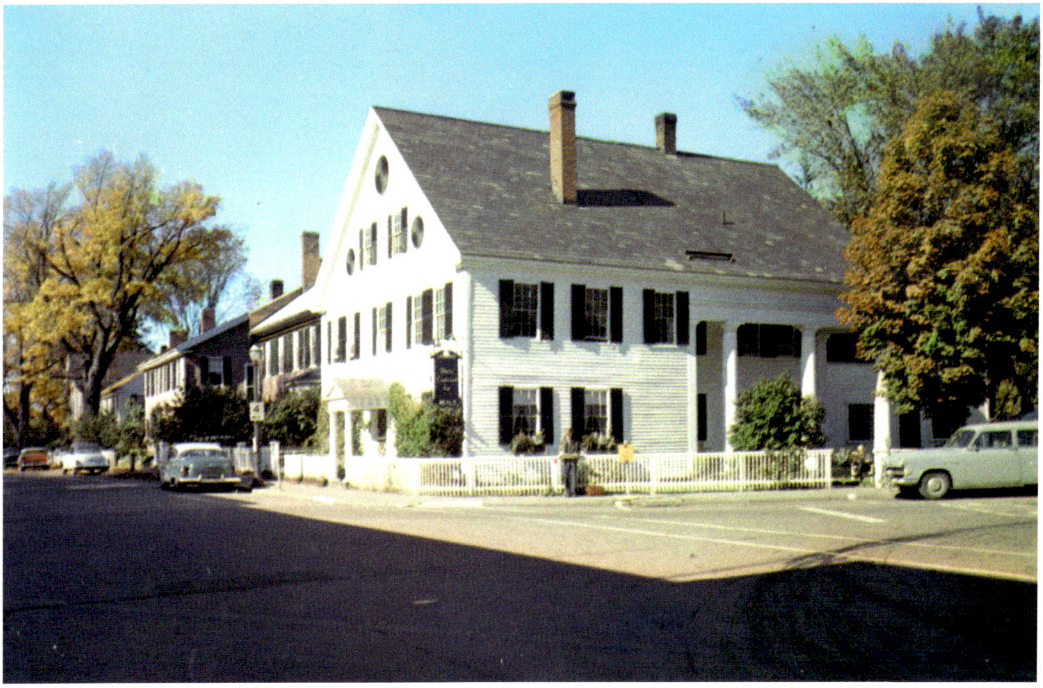

THE TITUS HUTCHINSON HOUSE: Opened as the White Cupboard Inn in 1925, it has been a grocery store, restaurant, soda fountain, and had other commercial applications at various times. The house was built in the late 1790s by Jacob Wilder and later owned and expanded by Titus Hutchinson, Vermont Supreme Court Chief Justice. In the 1800s, this home was a stop on the Underground Railroad. It commands an advantageous site at the intersection of Elm, Central, and Park Streets.

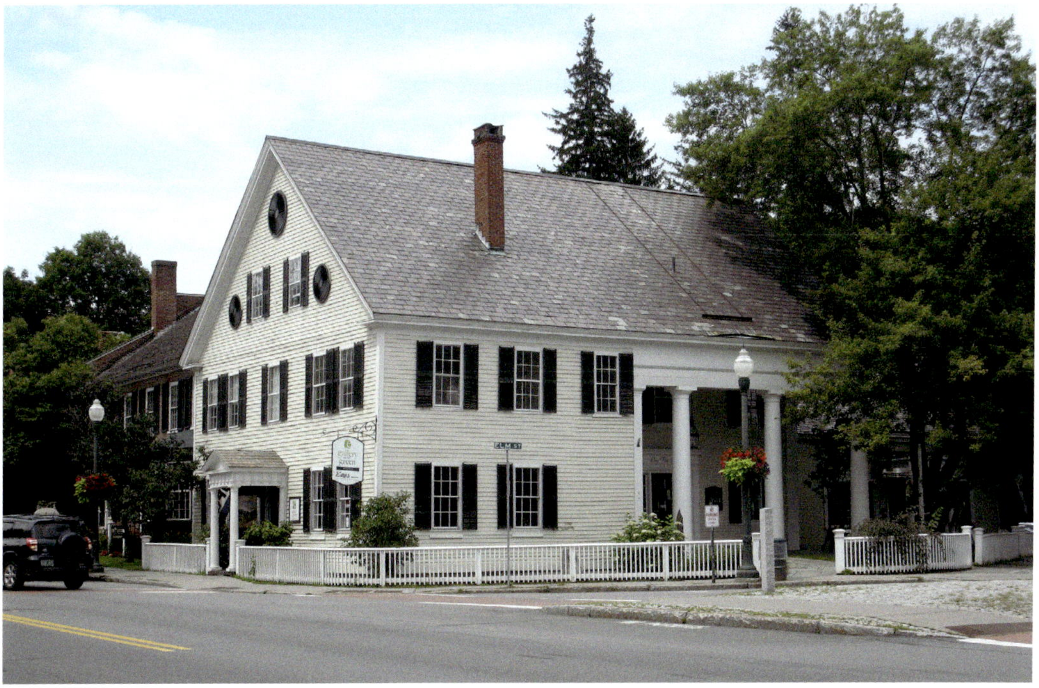

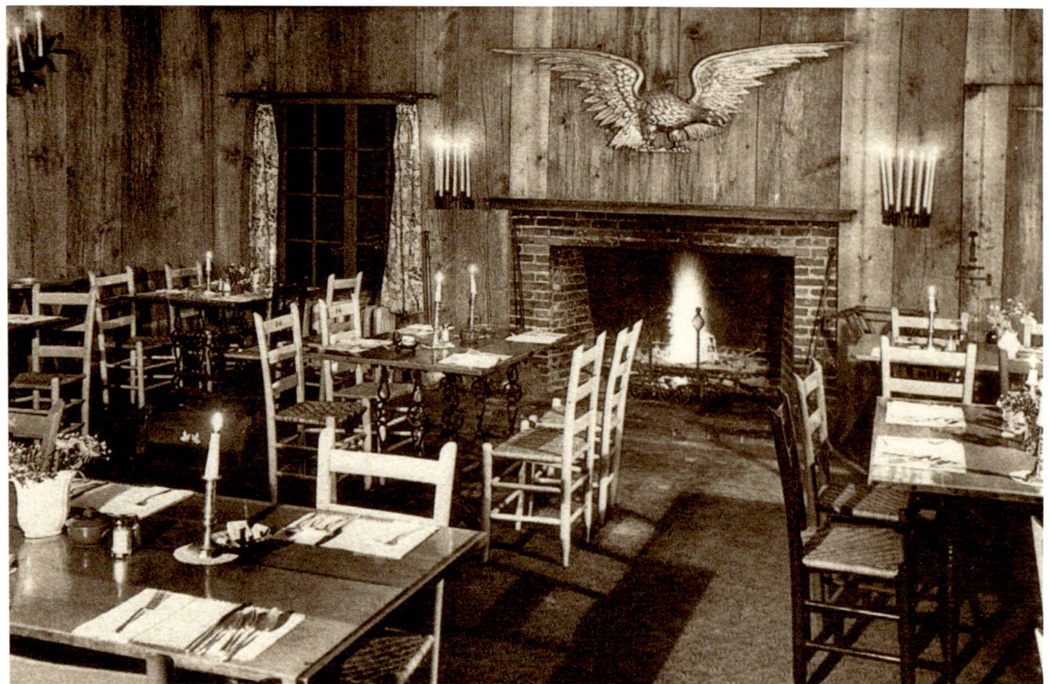

THE WHITE CUPBOARD INN DINING ROOM: When the house was an inn and restaurant, this was one of the dining rooms, above. Notice the changes when the interior was photographed below as an art gallery. This imposing and centrally located property highlights Vermont artists and artisans. It has the very fortunate address: One, The Green. This building still has a rugged slate roof and maintains much of its original exterior appearance.

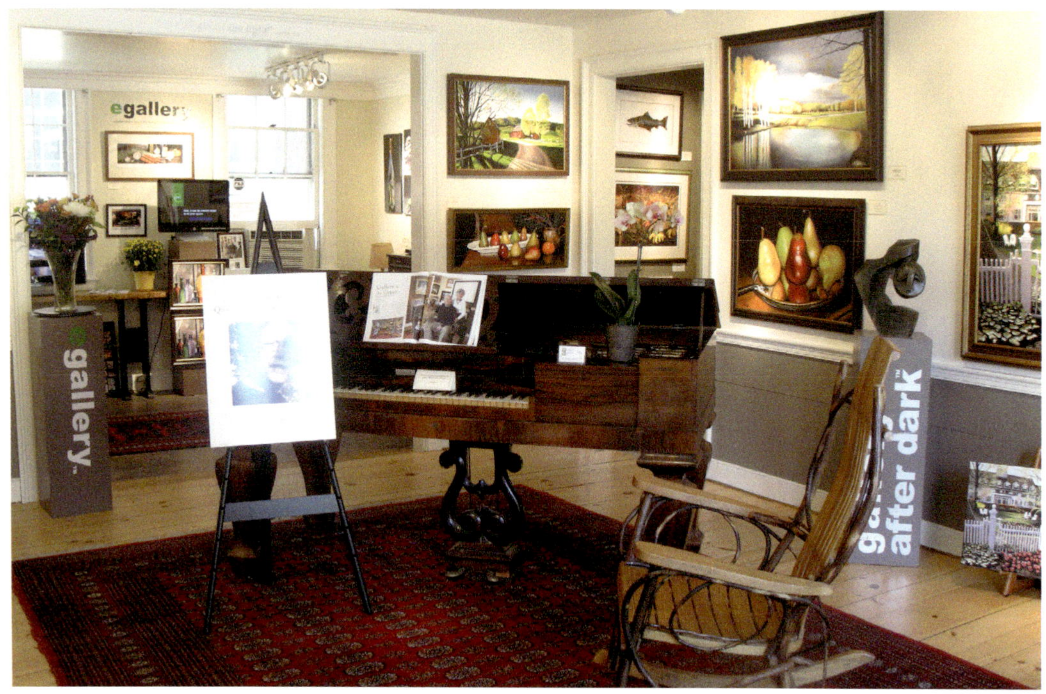

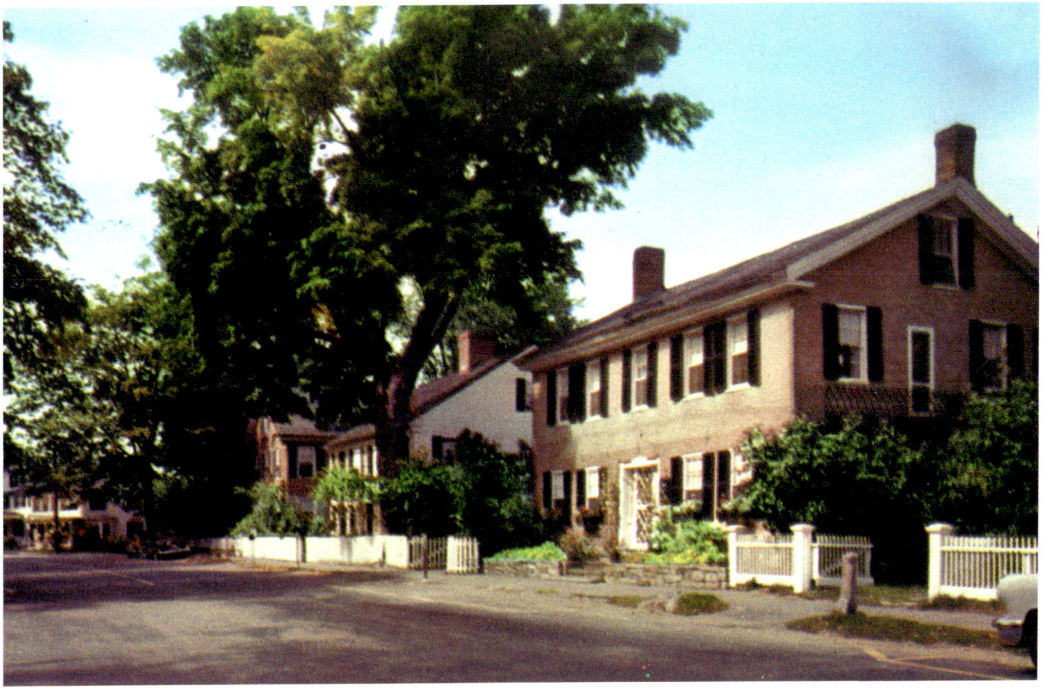

PARK COTTAGE: This house was also known as the Raymond Brothers Building and later as the Park Hotel. It was built of brick in the Federal style in 1807. The main entrance was moved at some point after the structure was completed, from the eastern gable end to the front of the building. That change was well done and is only obvious upon close inspection. This house has been used commercially for many of its years but it's now a well-preserved private residence.

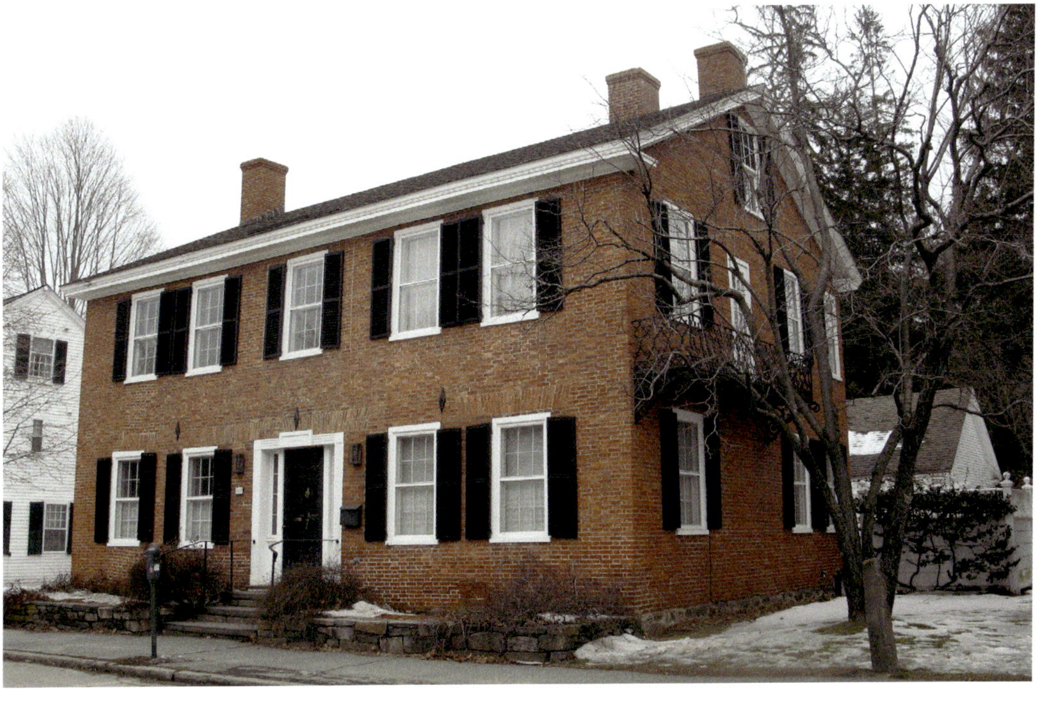

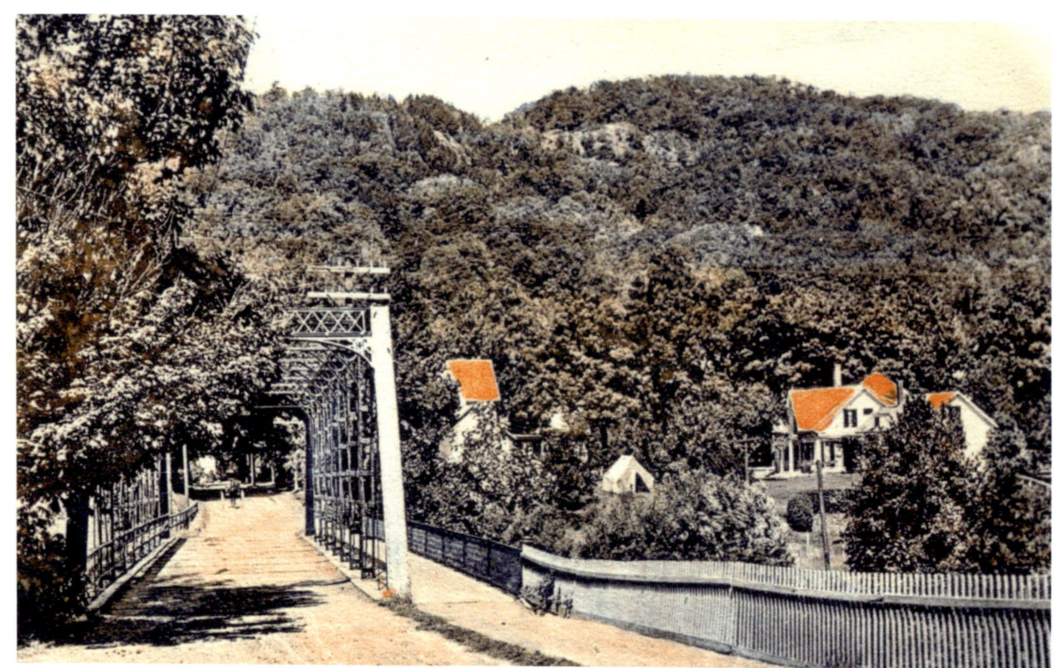

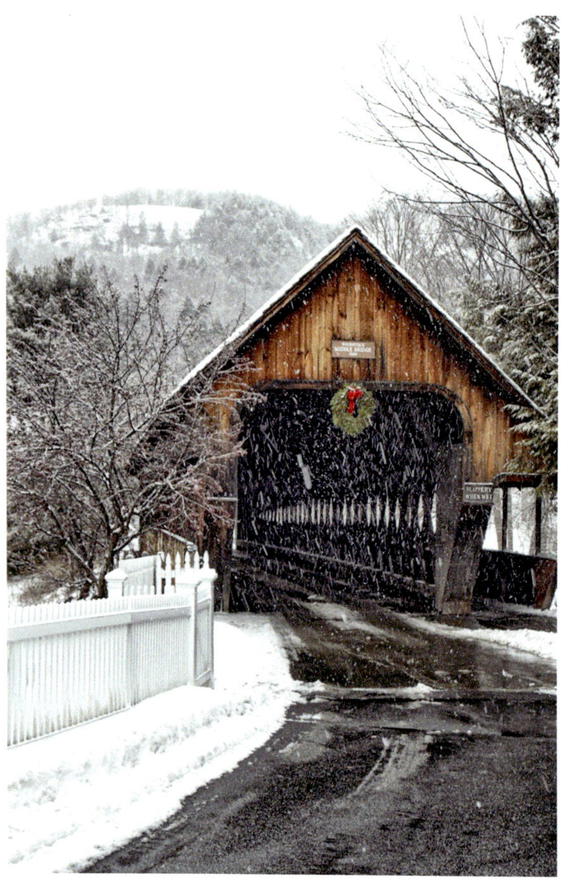

ORIGINAL MIDDLE BRIDGE: Built in 1877, this bridge was made of iron. The postcard image above was postmarked 1947. That bridge was condemned in 1966. It was replaced in 1969 with a wooden covered bridge. When Middle Bridge was reconstructed on Union Street (now called Mountain Avenue), it was pulled across the river with oxen. Mt. Tom seems to watch over Woodstock from behind Middle Bridge like a protective guardian.

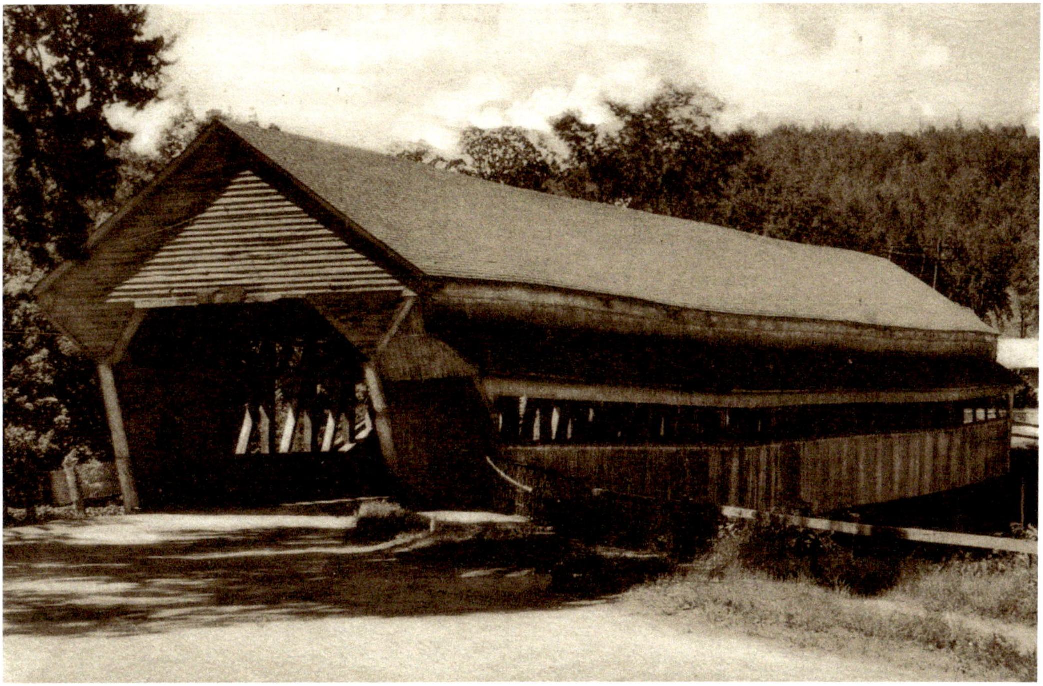

MIDDLE BRIDGE: The image above shows Middle Bridge soon after it was rebuilt of wood and installed in 1969. It was designed by Milton S. Graton and moved into place across the Ottauquechee River by Ben and Jo, a pair of oxen. In 1972, the bridge was tragically the victim of arson. It was extensively damaged but was restored to the original design, below. Middle Bridge is 14.5 feet wide with a 5-foot walkway and runs 150 feet in length.

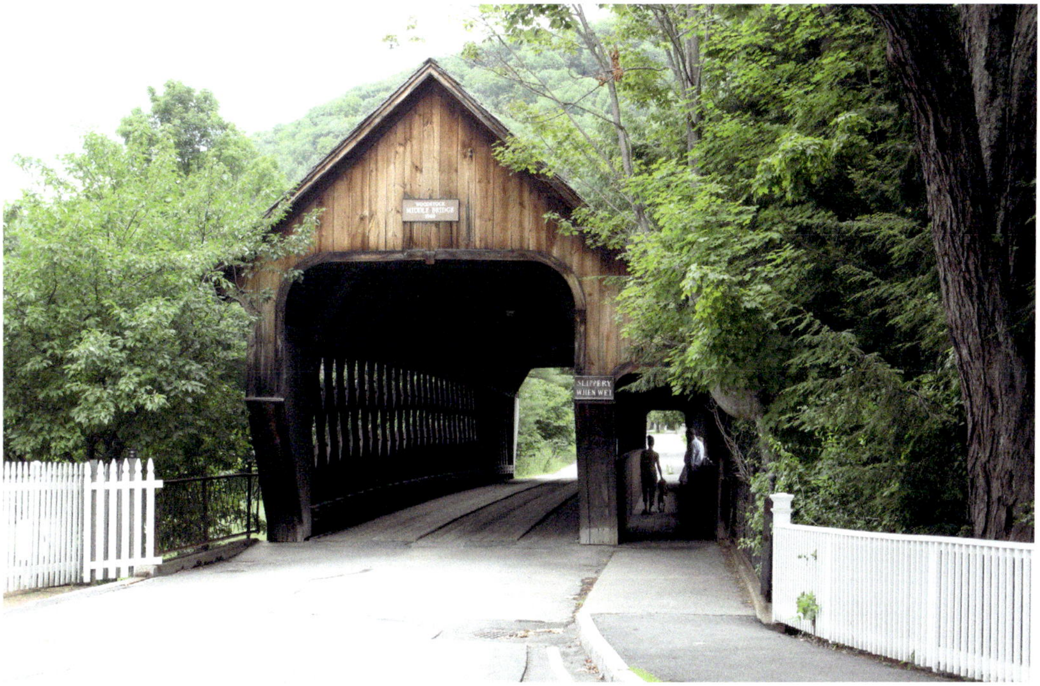

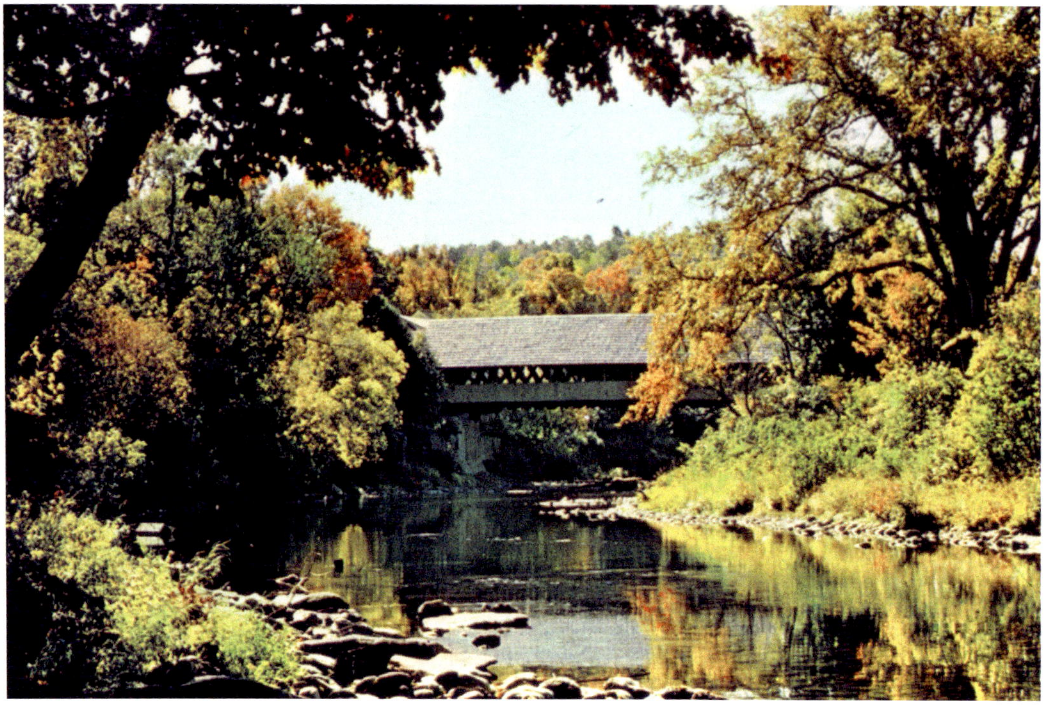

Middle Bridge from Down River: This image of Middle Bridge was taken just a little way downriver and shows the unusual plan with a pedestrian walkway as part of the original design. There is a beautiful lawn, behind the Dana House Museum, extending to the Ottauquechee River. Standing there, you can clearly see the details on the side of the Middle Bridge and the view behind changes with the seasons.

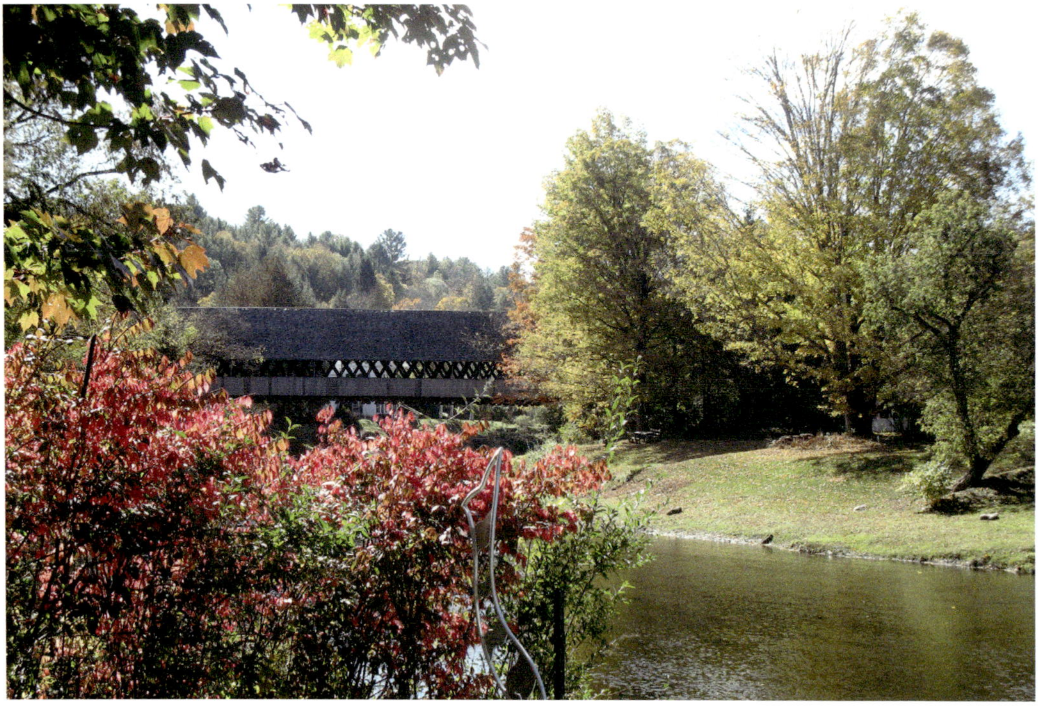

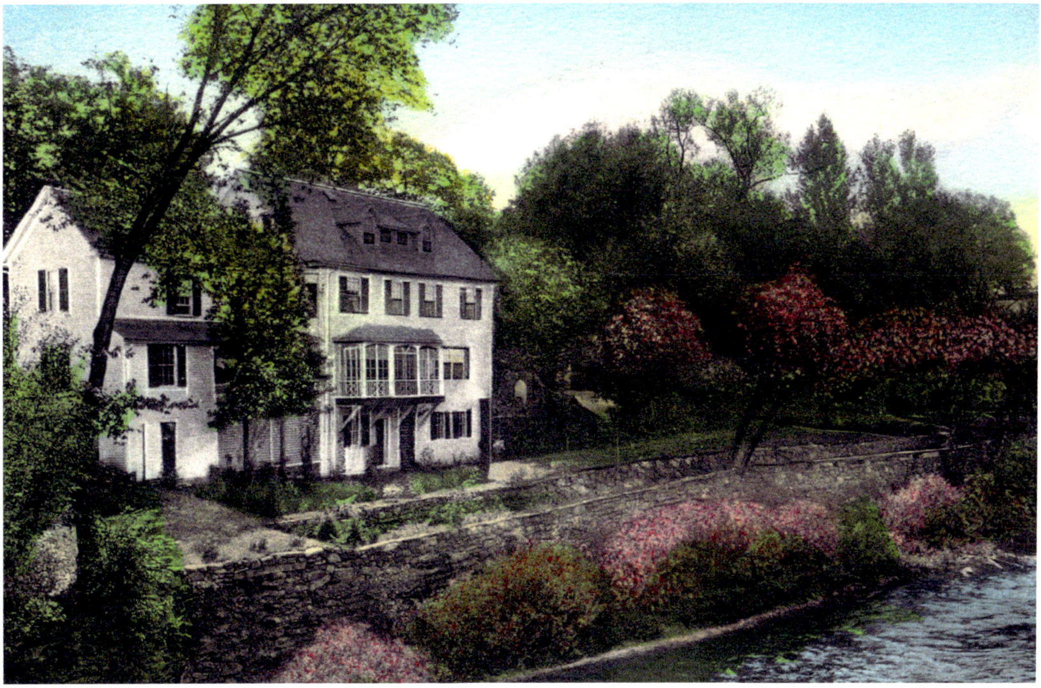

The Back of the Otis Skinner House: This view of a well-known North Park Street residence is from the opposite bank of the Ottauquechee River. The above postcard image is postmarked 1935. The front of the house sits on The Green, see the inset photo. Otis Skinner was a worldly actor born in Massachusetts in 1858. When Skinner retired, he and his wife Maud bought this spacious 1805 home in Woodstock. Skinner continued his interest in acting until he died in 1942.

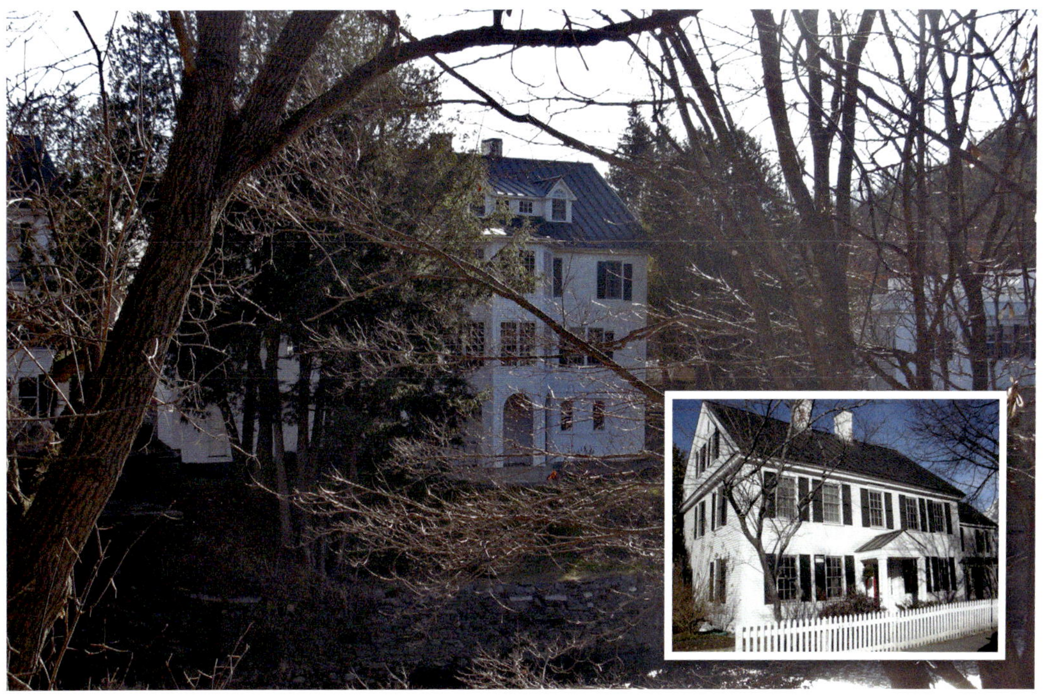

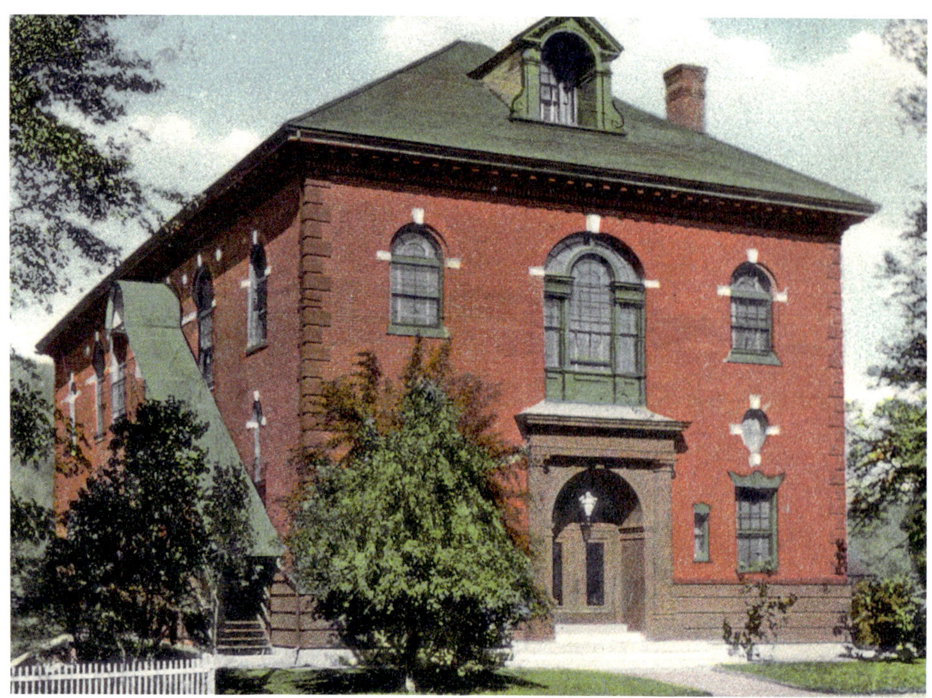

WOODSTOCK'S TOWN HALL: Built in 1899, it barely survived a terrible fire in 1927. After much debate, it was rebuilt in brick in the Classical Revival style. Later remodeling included massive two-story columns across the front. As well as the traditional town offices, the building houses the Pentangle Council for the Arts theatre which hosts regular stage and film performances in the 400-seat venue. The image above is from a postcard postmarked 1948.

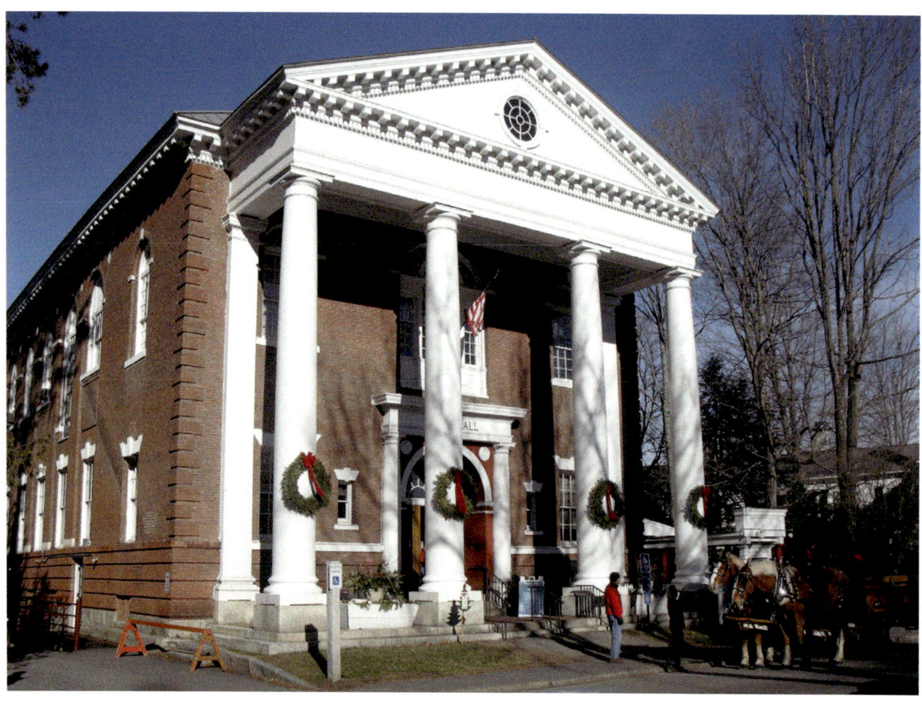

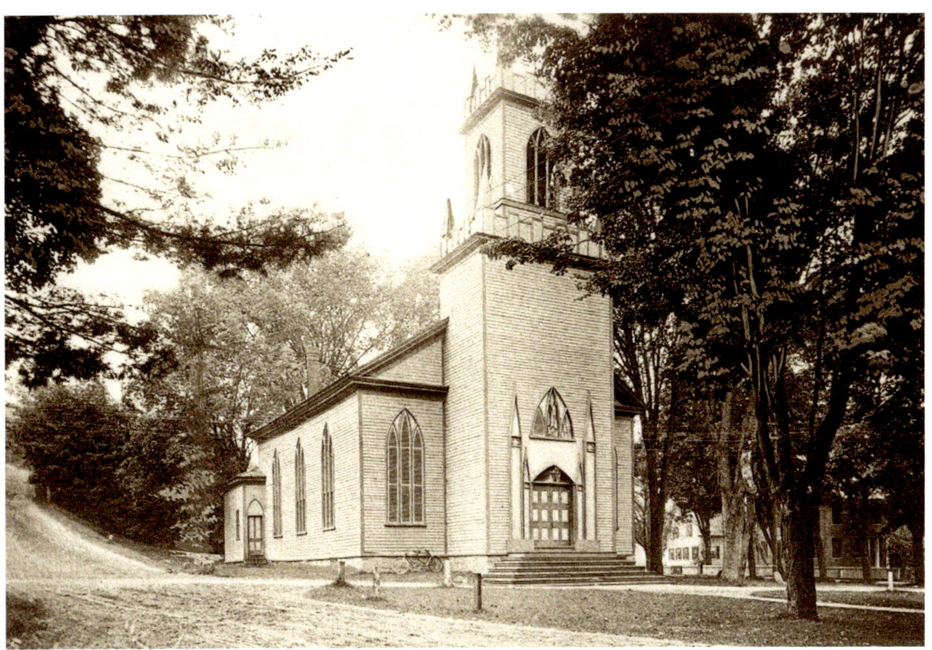

St. James Episcopal Church: Originally planned as a stone building but after stone was quarried and detailed soil tests indicated the site unable to withstand the weight, that plan was reconsidered. In 1827 St. James was built from wood instead, above. Over time, the foundation began to sink due to underground streams, and eventually the structure had to be dismantled. Steps were taken to rebuild, as originally planned, in stone. The current granite church, below, was completed in 1907.

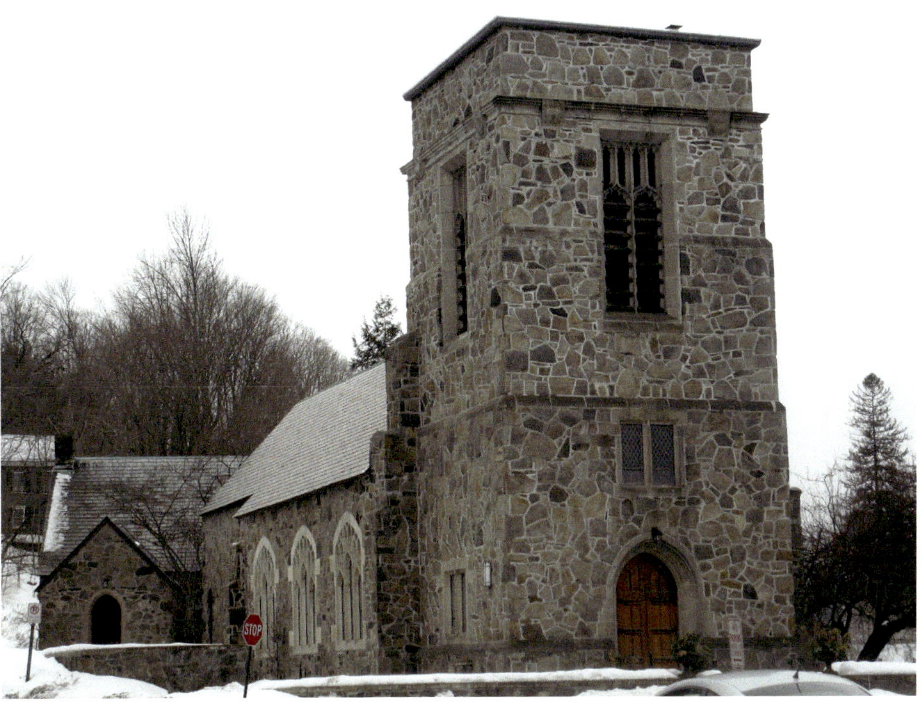

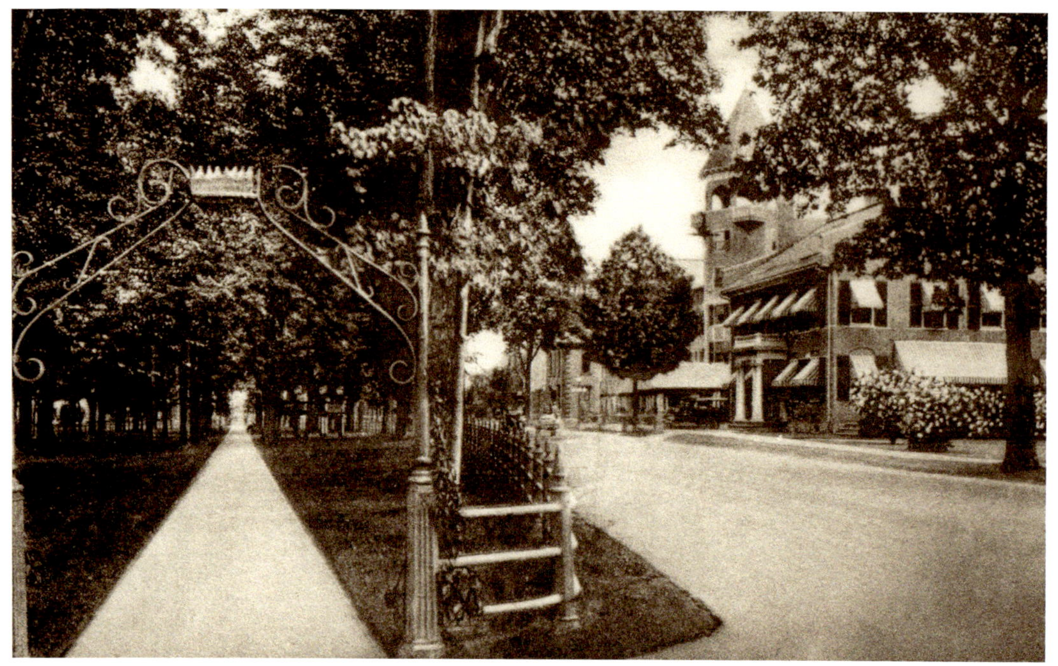

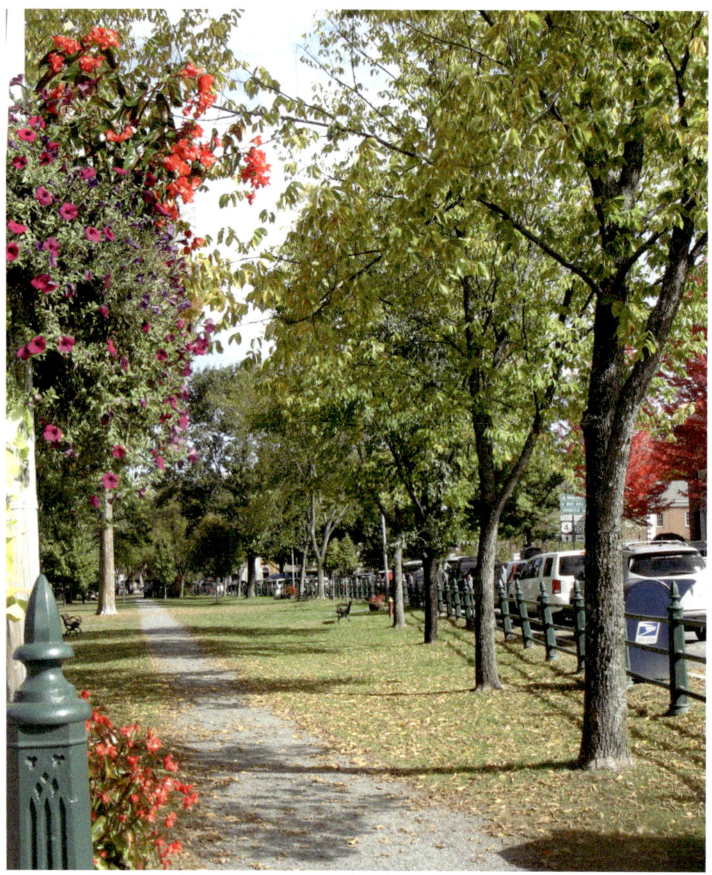

West Entrance to The Green:

Located across from St. James, this entrance to The Green affords an interesting view. The Town Hall sits to the north and Route 100 curves toward West Woodstock and Bridgewater. Prospect Street veers up Church Hill to the south and the DAR House is one of the historic homes to our right. Notice the original Woodstock Inn was still snug to The Green in the above photo. The elegant wrought iron archway attached to the fencing, still surrounds The Green, as seen in the image on the left.

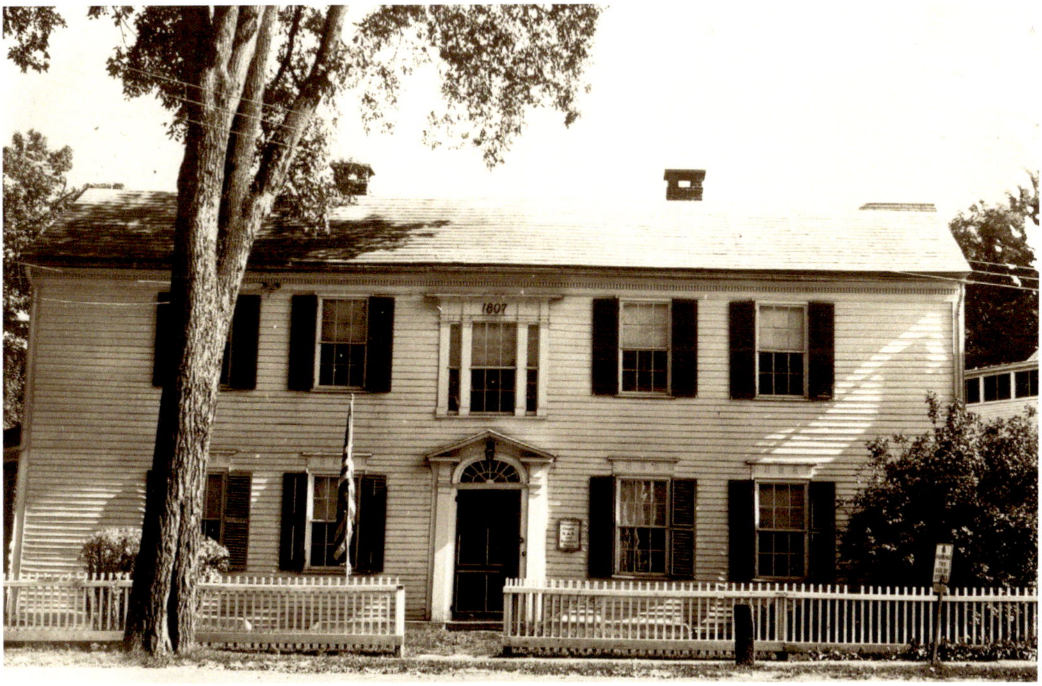

THE DAR HOUSE: To our right as we round the western end of The Green, we see this 1807 house as it appeared in 1948. Originally it was built as a haven for travelling legislators from other Vermont communities, when staying in town. For many years it served as a tavern and then it housed the headquarters of the Ottauquechee Chapter of the Daughters of the American Revolution (DAR). Below, it's a well-preserved private residence but still often referred to as the DAR House.

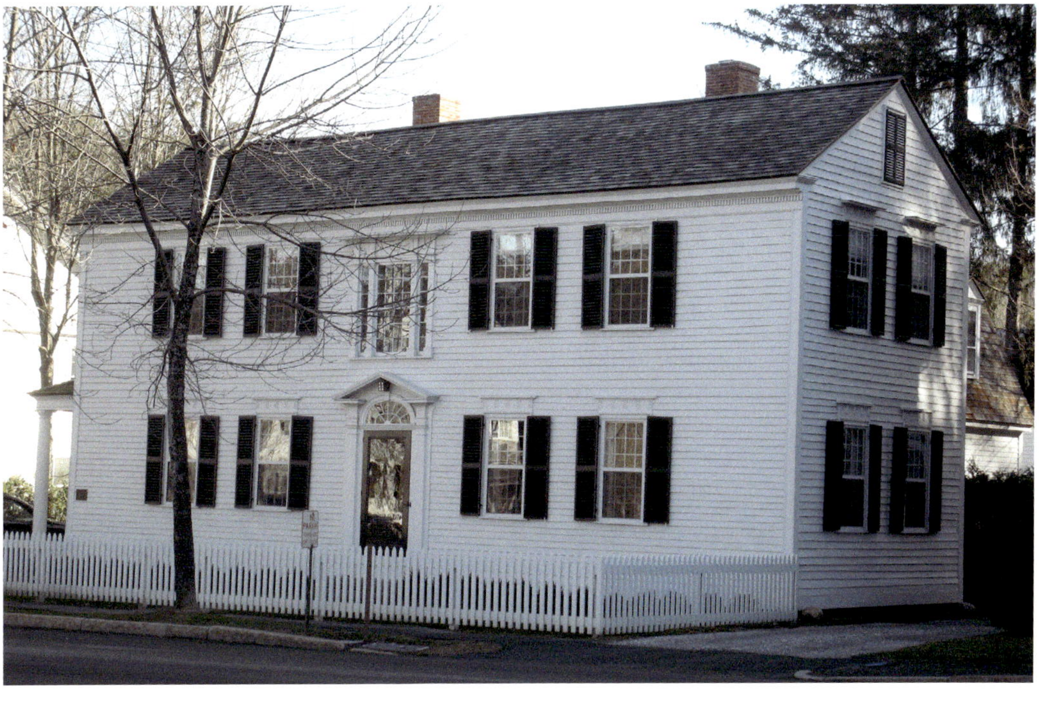

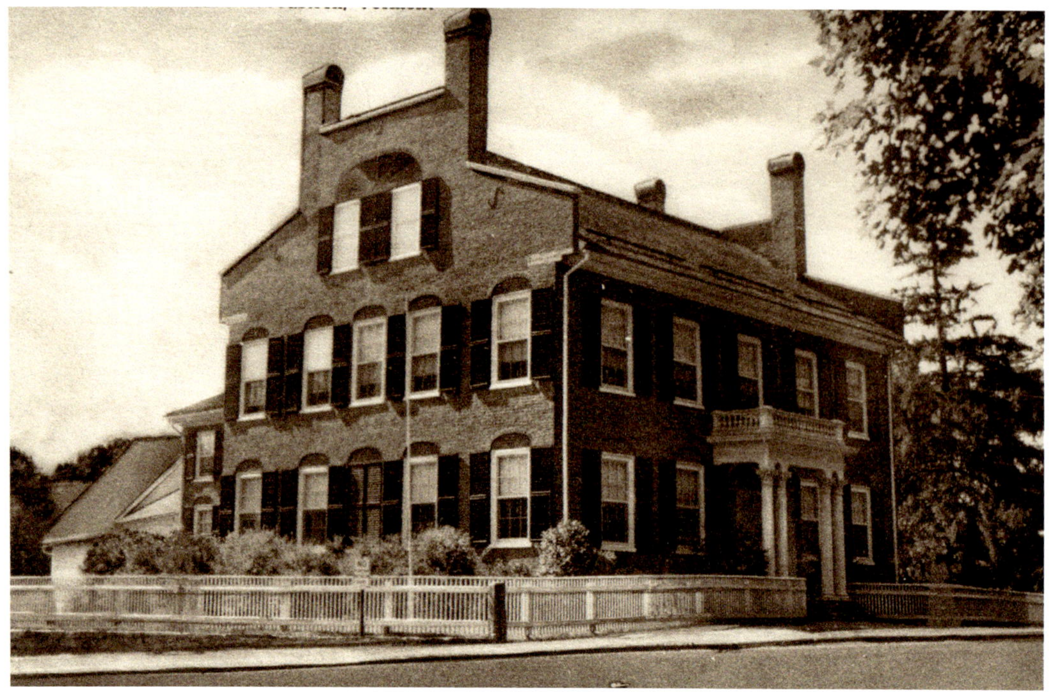

THE GENERAL LYMAN-MOWER HOUSE: Built in 1823 and described as the Anderson residence when this vintage image above was captured. It is an impressive brick house, separated by Church Street from the lot occupied by the Woodstock Inn. In the 1800s, Frederick Billings purchased this home for his parents and younger siblings to live in. It is a two-and-a-half story Federal style home with stepped gabled ends and elegant fanlight windows in the gables, facing east and west.

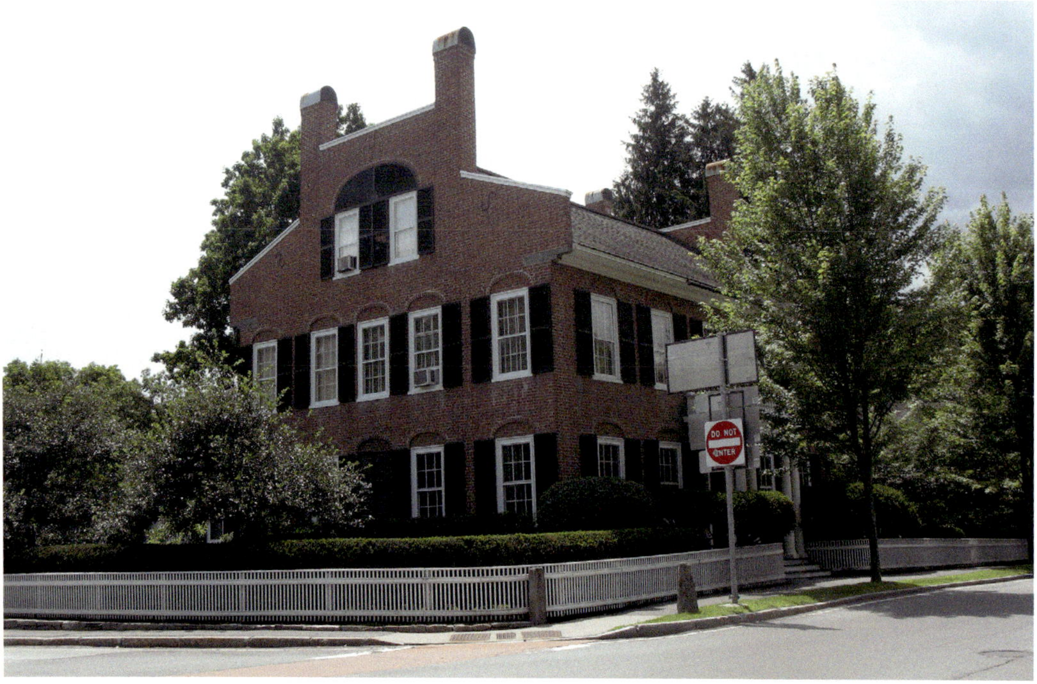

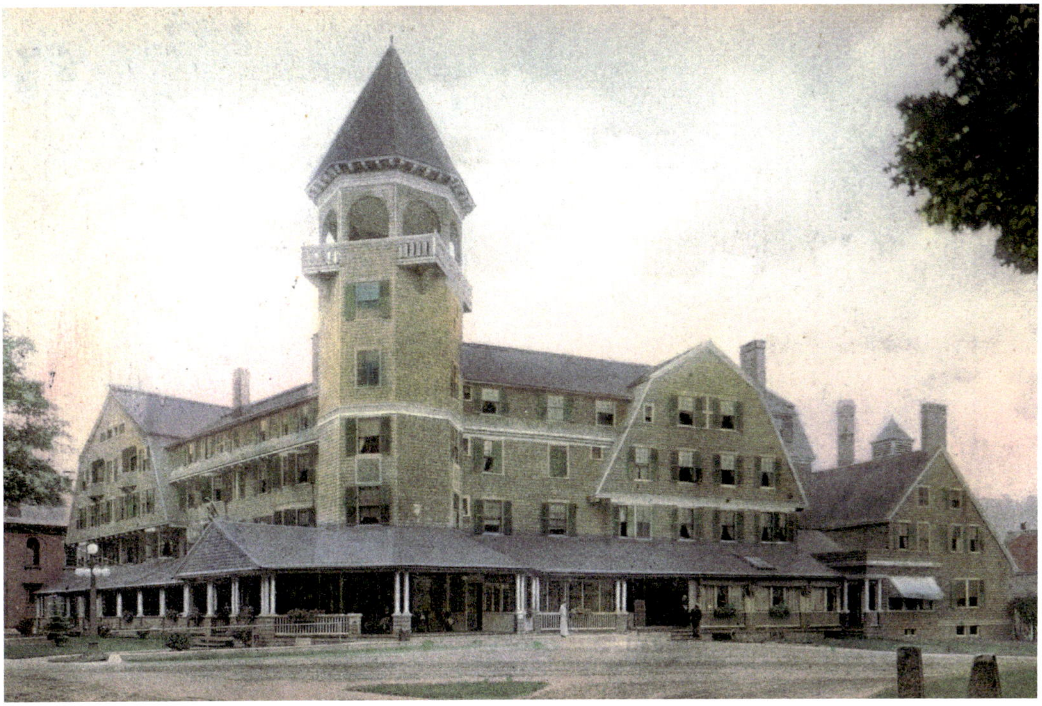

THE WOODSTOCK INN: This graceful lodging surveys The Green from South Park Street with presence and dignity. The inn, opened in 1892, has been a real focal point in Woodstock for over a century and is enjoying its second incarnation. The current inn, seen below, opened in 1969 and sits back on the lot. It replaced the previous Woodstock Inn, shown above, which was located much closer to the edge of the street.

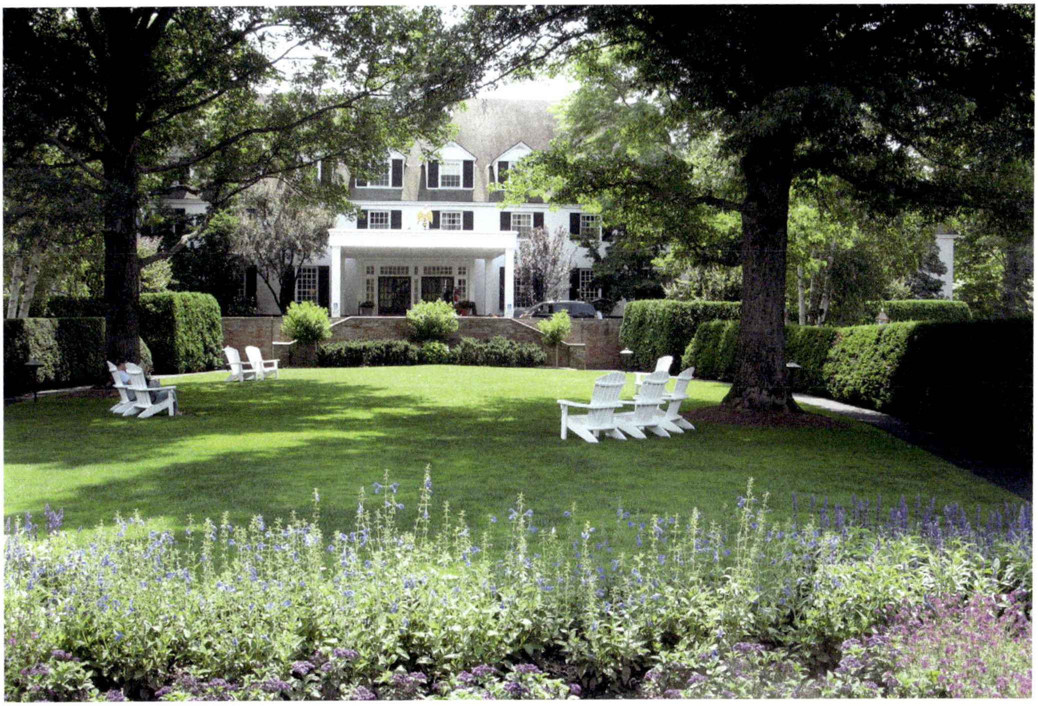

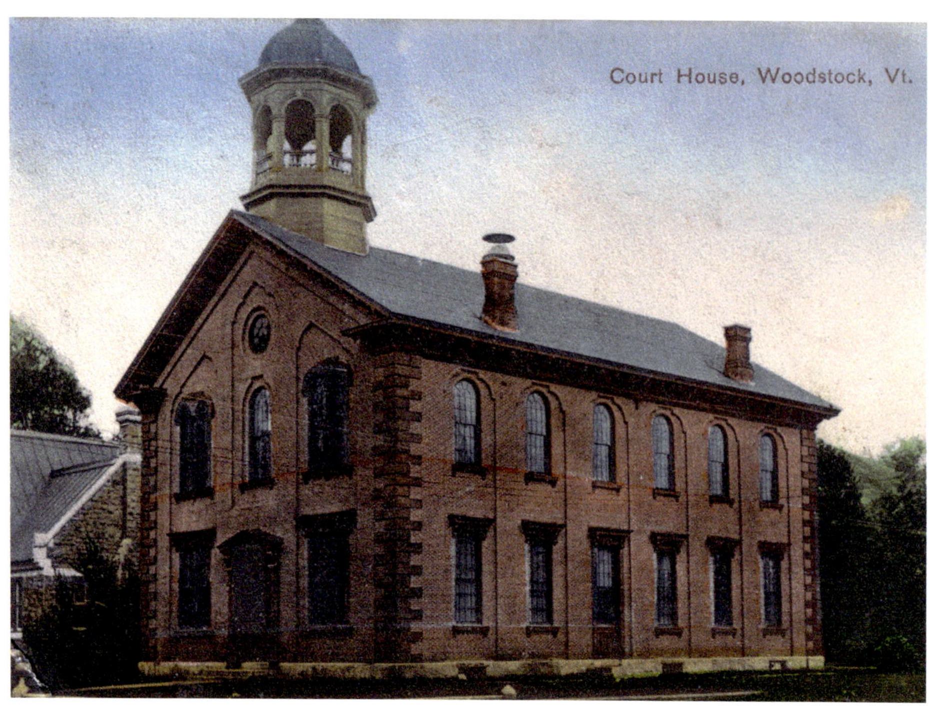

WINDSOR COUNTY COURT HOUSE: As seen above in the postcard postmarked 1909, it is a majestic brick building with corner quoins and an octagonal belfry. It houses the Windsor County Superior Court and is the county seat for Windsor County, Vermont. The previous court house was built in 1793 and was located elsewhere "on" The Green. After that building burned in 1854, the present courthouse was built on the corner of Park and Court Streets in 1855.

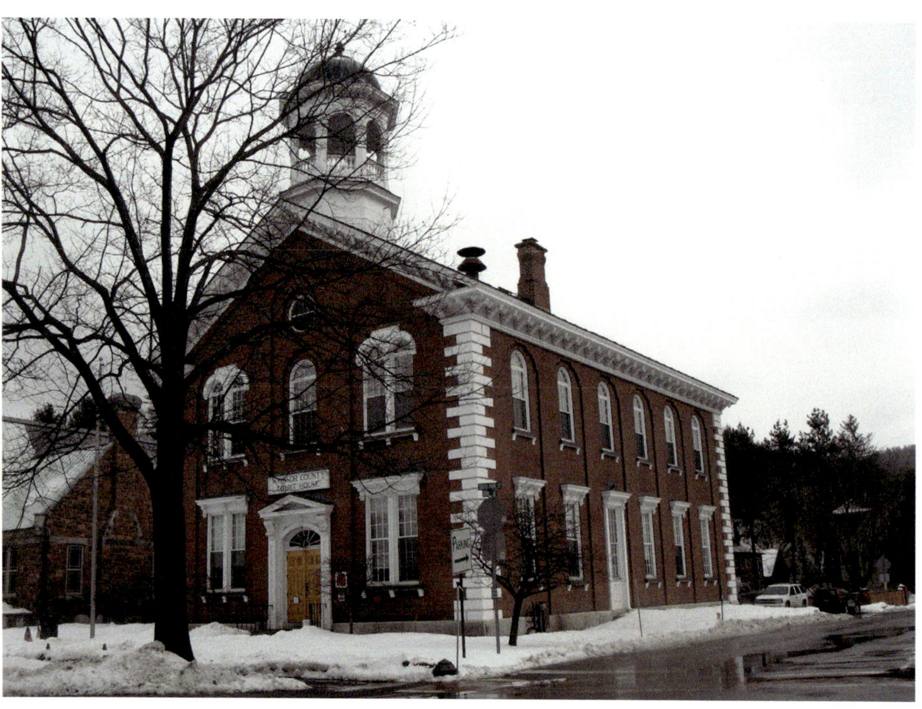

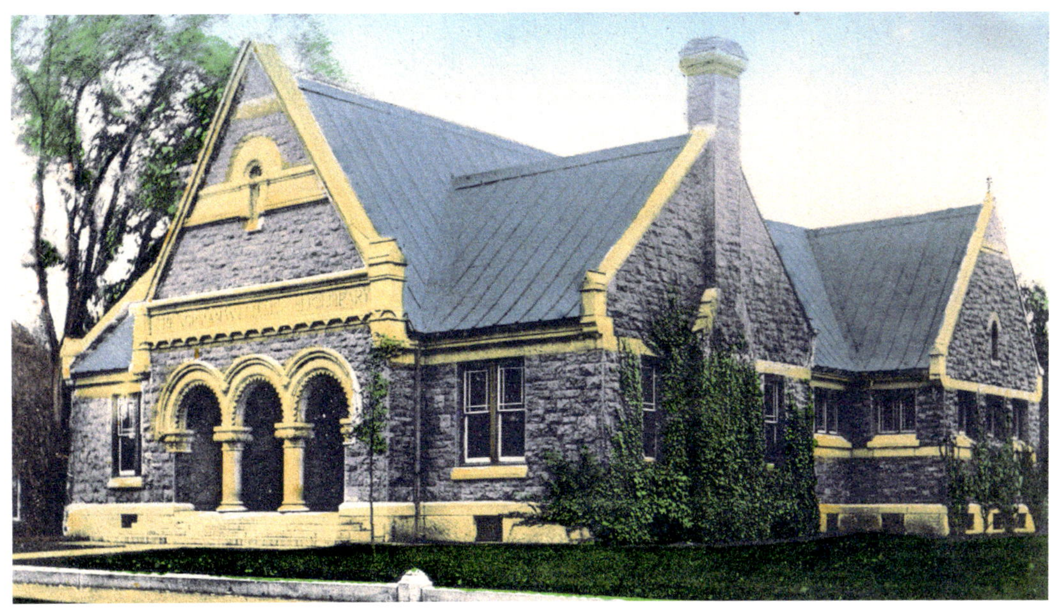

NORMAN WILLIAMS PUBLIC LIBRARY: Built of limestone and granite, the library resides on the site of one of the Williams' family homes, south of and adjacent to The Green. Norman Williams was a Registrar of Probate, Senator from Vermont, and Secretary of State. The Williams' Family donated the land and money to build the library in his name, after the family home built in 1798 was removed. As we continue our journey around The Green we see two very unique houses.

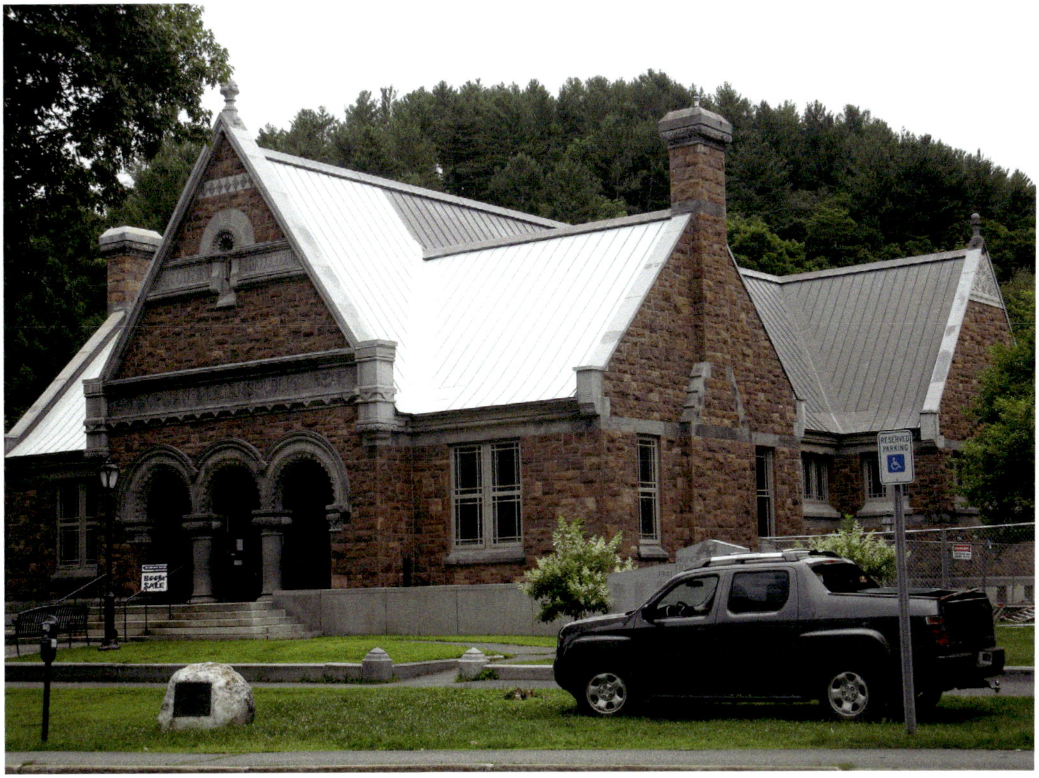

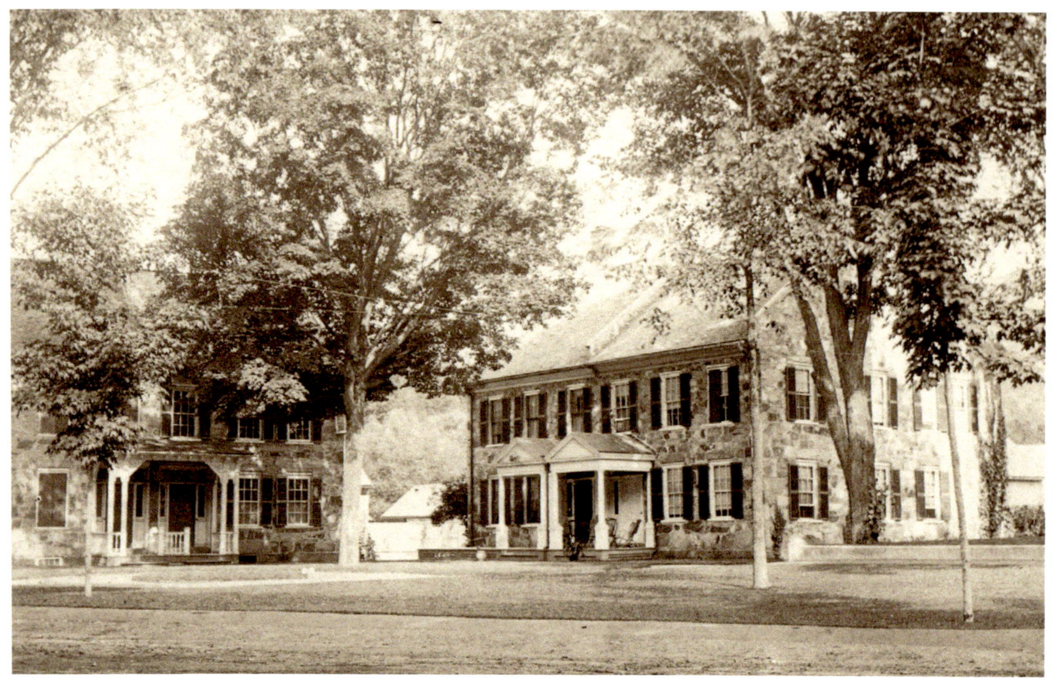

VAIL HOUSE AND T'OTHER HOUSE: Located to the east of the library, at a 90-degree angle to one another, these houses seem to anchor this corner of The Green. They were built in 1827 and 1828 by Sylvester Edson with stones originally quarried for St. James Church. They were initially built as homes, but sometimes were used, at least partially, for commercial purposes. Vail House and T'Other House appear almost to rise from the earth of substantial stone. Some architectural changes have been made over the years.

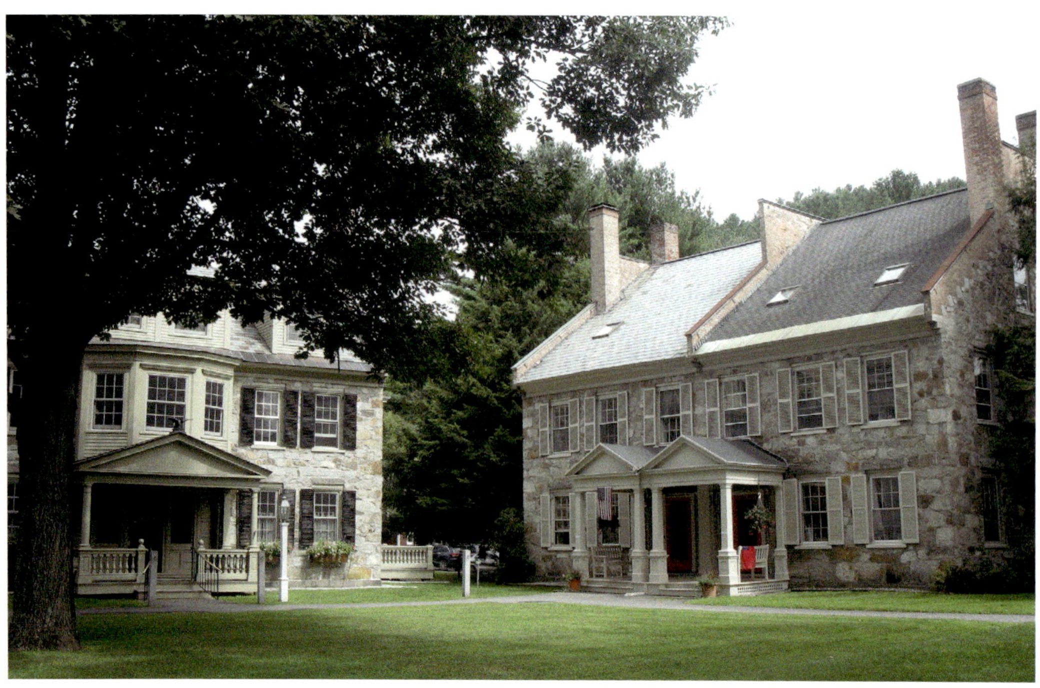

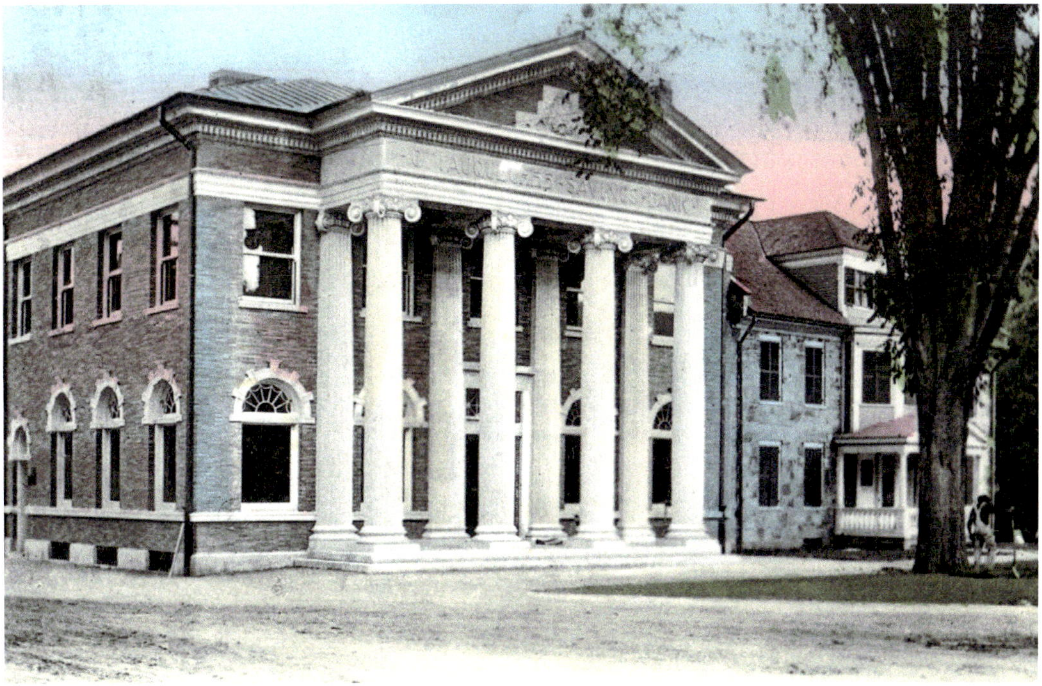

OTTAUQUECHEE BANK: This prestigious building, completed in 1902 in the Classical Revival style with a colonnaded portico, was known as The Ottauquechee Bank in the early 1900s. The bricks are an interesting golden hue. The bank was built on the site of the Churchill House which was built in 1793 and dismantled in 1901. Although it's changed hands and names, the bank's classic exterior architecture remains the same. This completes our trip around The Green, returning us to the east end.

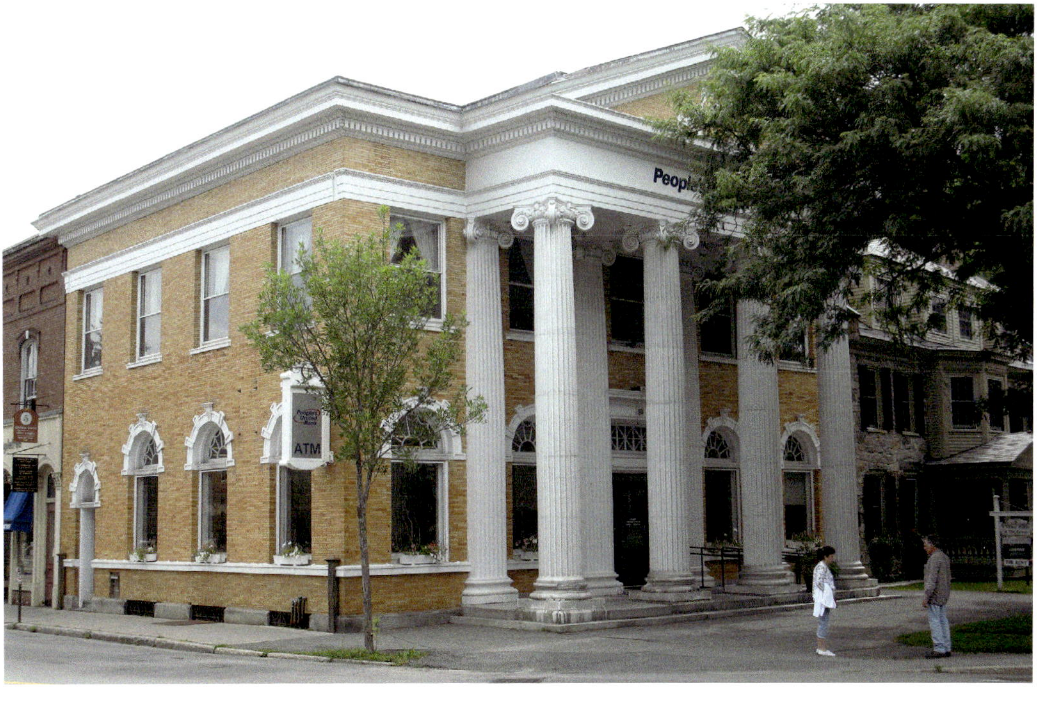

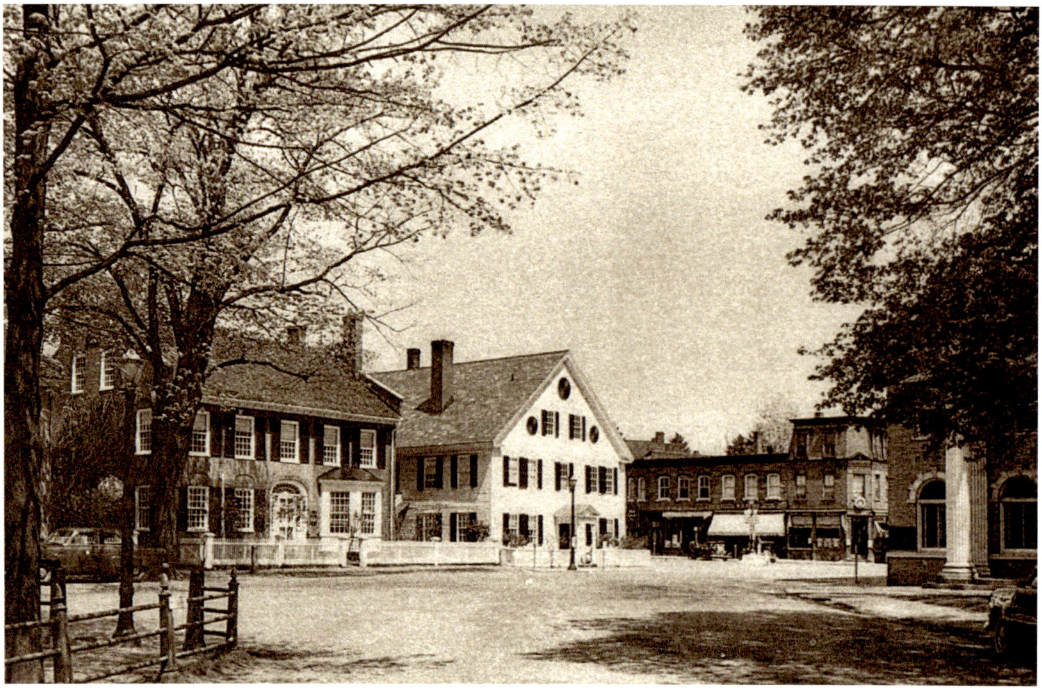

ELM AND CENTRAL STREET INTERSECTION: Looking ahead. Not much has changed in this landscape since the above image was taken in the 1950s. This otherwise seemingly timeless vignette below still shows the bank on our right and the Titus Hutchinson house, most recently an art gallery, to our left. On the triangle between Elm and Central Streets, and the impressive granite Cabot Block; is the lamp post that replaced an 1888 monument commemorating Frank MacKenzie. Let's turn left down Elm Street.

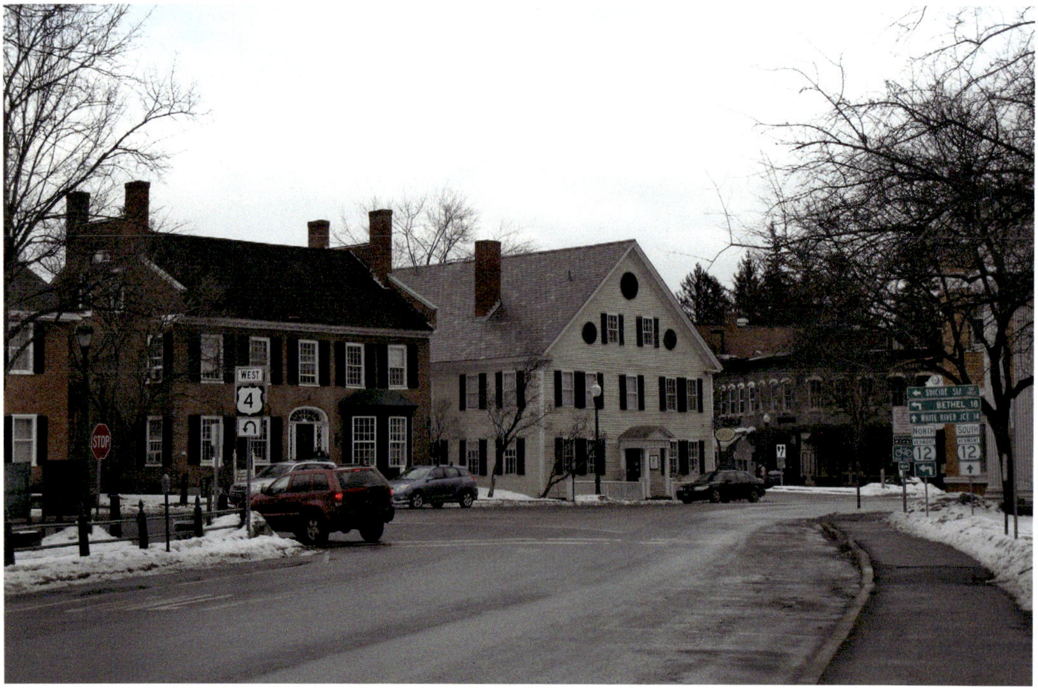

Commerce and Industry

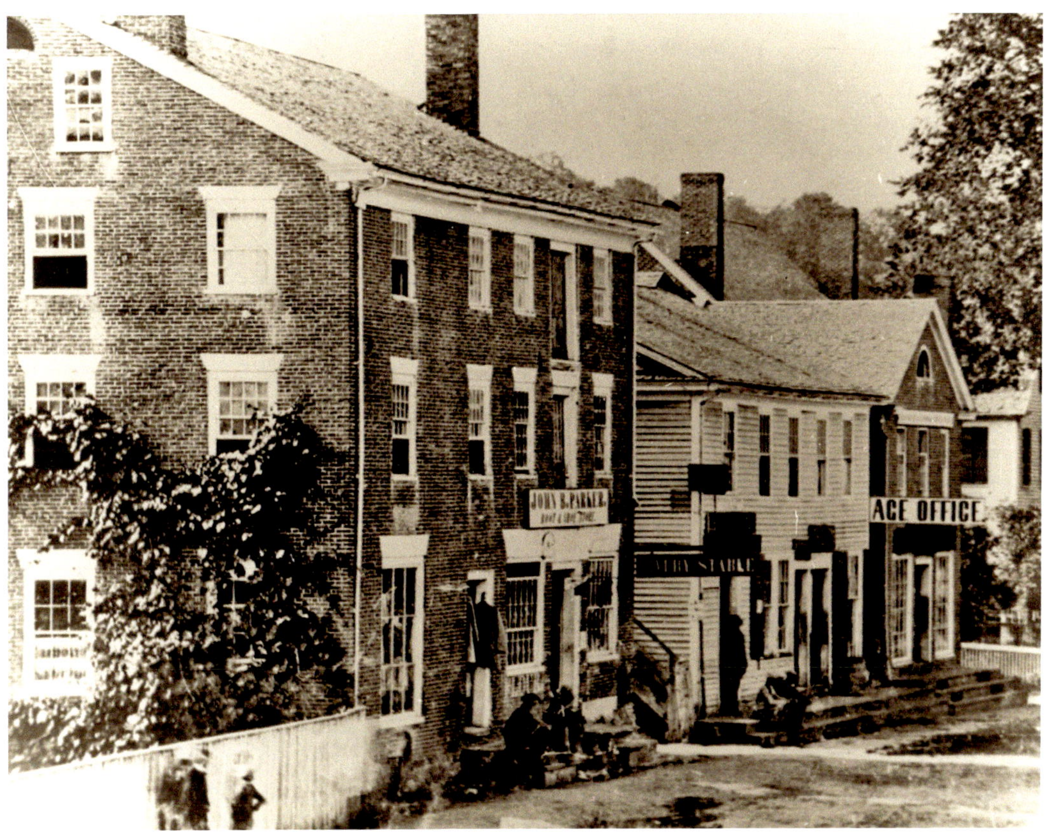

Elm Street: Developed in 1797 by Charles Marsh and Jesse Williams, when they saw the potential in the formerly wooded area. They first cleared lots for building and then planted elm trees along both sides of the street, hence the name. The first section of Elm Street that we'll encounter is the business district, including this interesting and history-filled row of buildings. John B. Parker was a boot and shoe shop. This image dates from the 1850s.

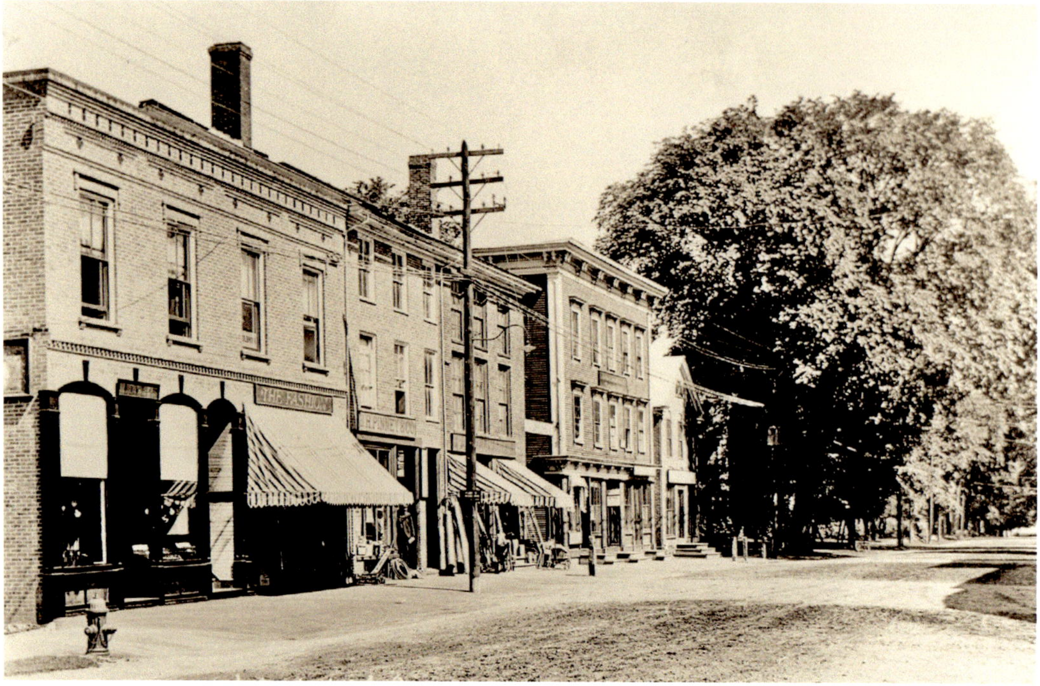

Shops on Elm Street: The face of commerce here has altered over the years, including owners and types of businesses. Note the changes in building styles: some merged; stories added; roof lines, windows, and doorways moved. Gillingham's Grocery building, built in 1810, had a serious fire in 1971 but was repaired and remodeled. In fact, Gillingham's has expanded many times since these images were taken; above in 1895, and below in 1937. The former Dana Store building at the far right still remains.

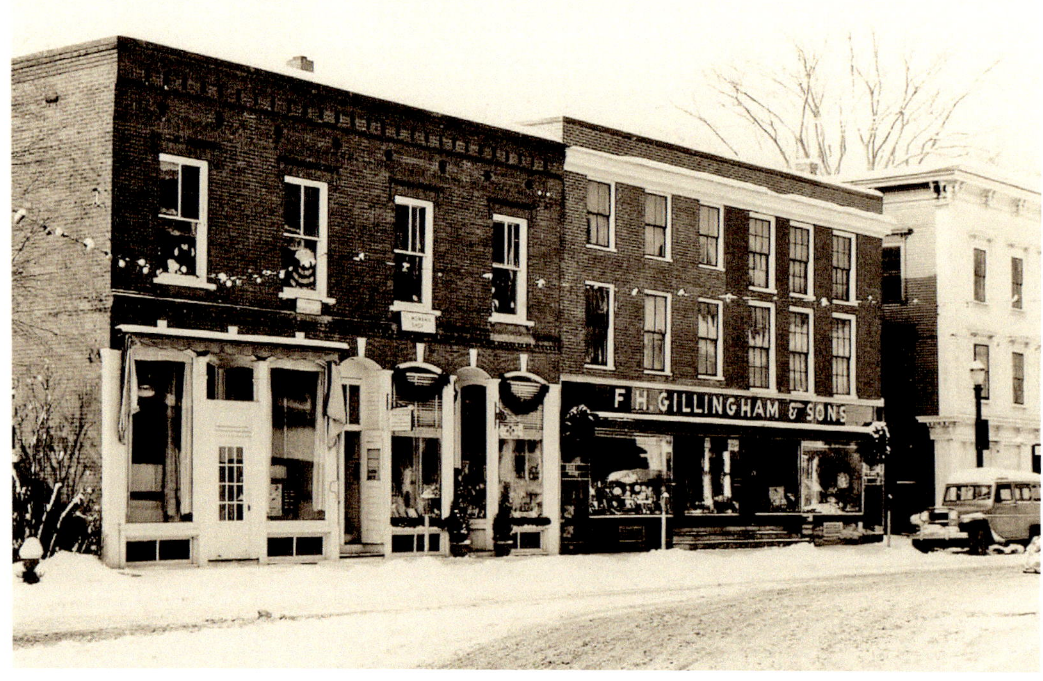

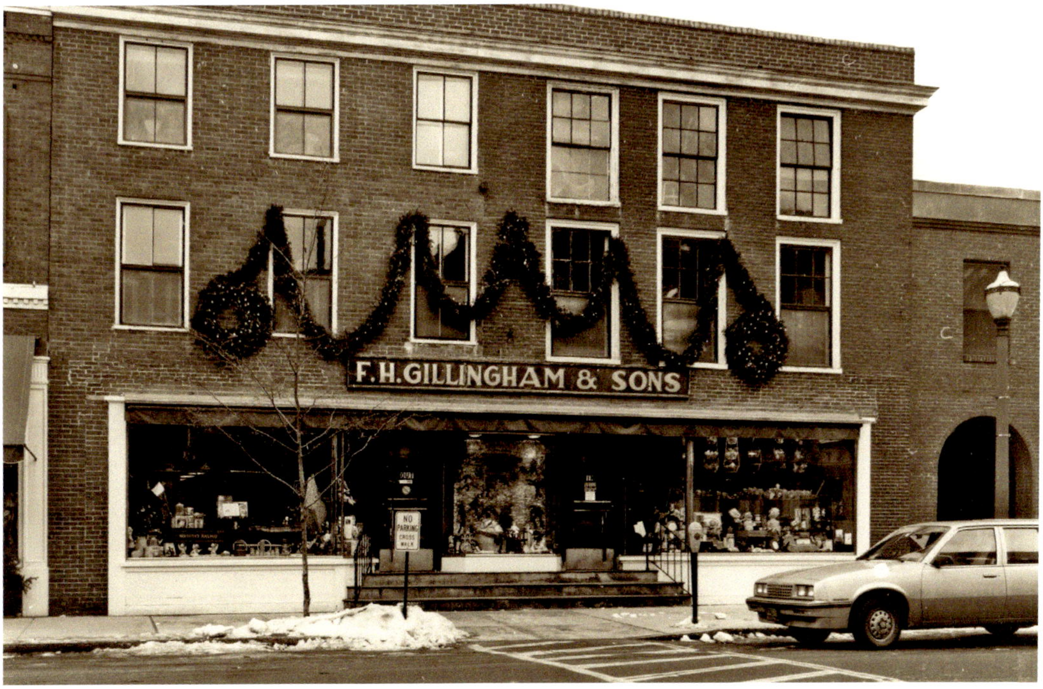

F. H. GILLINGHAM AND SONS GENERAL STORE: Opened in 1886 by Frank Henry Gillingham at the site where it still operates today, and it's run by two of Frank's great grandsons, Jireh and Frank Billings. The Gillingham Store building is shown during the Christmas season in 1986 above and almost thirty years later at Christmas time, below. Gillingham's takes care of their customers and offers an across-the-board, money-back guarantee on everything they sell. And they sell a lot!

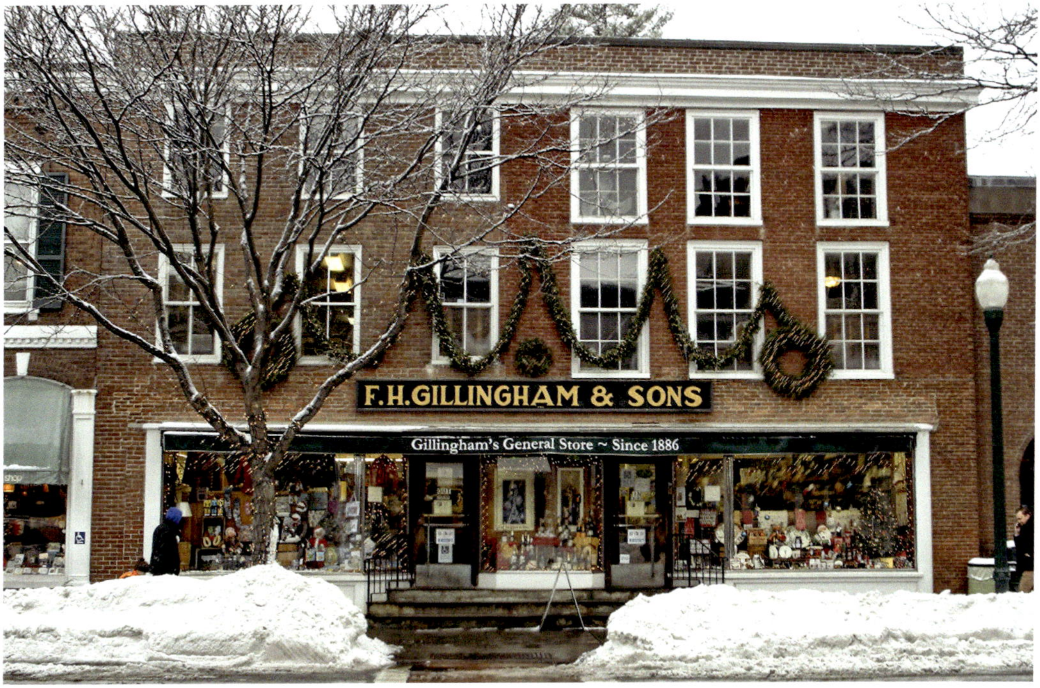

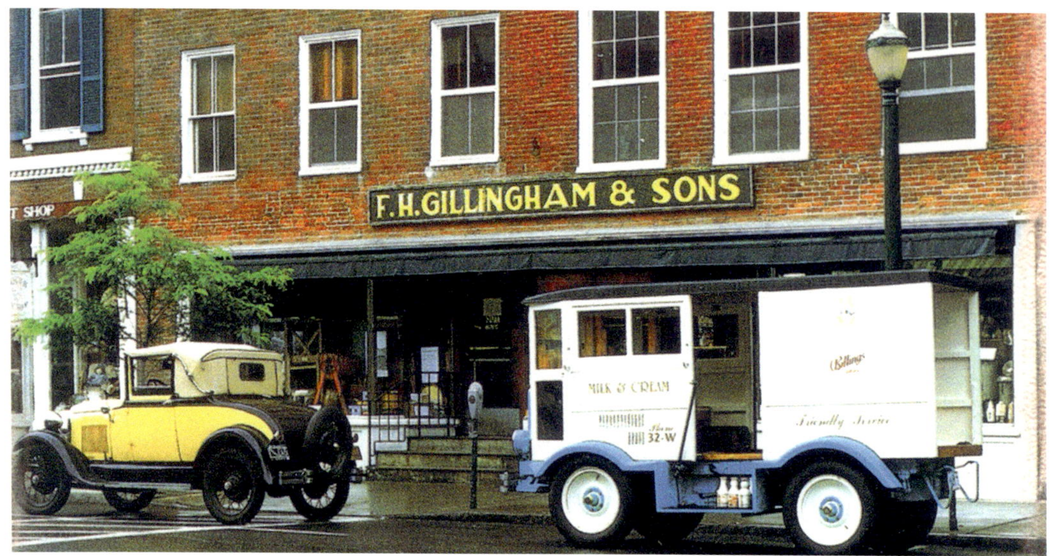

GILLINGHAM'S GROCERY STORE: Family values and traditions continue here. Besides residing in the same physical footprint, something else remains intact at Gillingham's – a strong work ethic and a caring attitude about customer and employee contentment. The original building has been remodeled and expanded, survived a fire and continues to do business as it always has for over 130 years. Things here keep getting better and better with time, like one of the fine wines Gillingham's carries in its dedicated wine room.

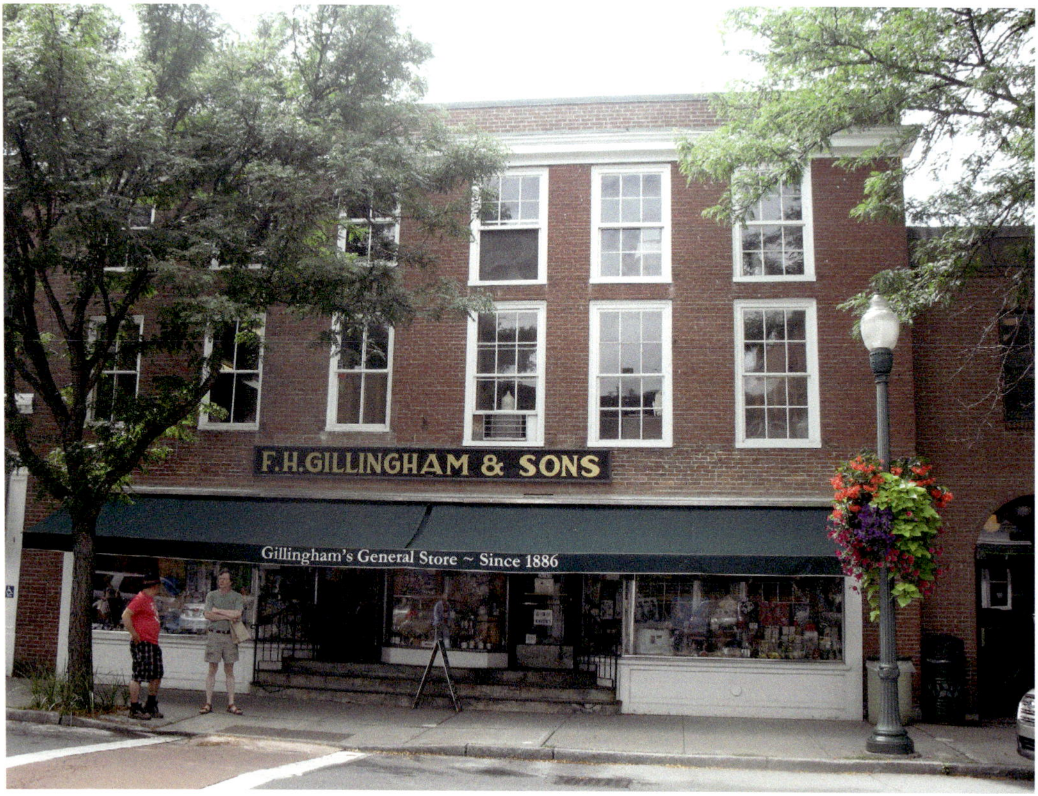

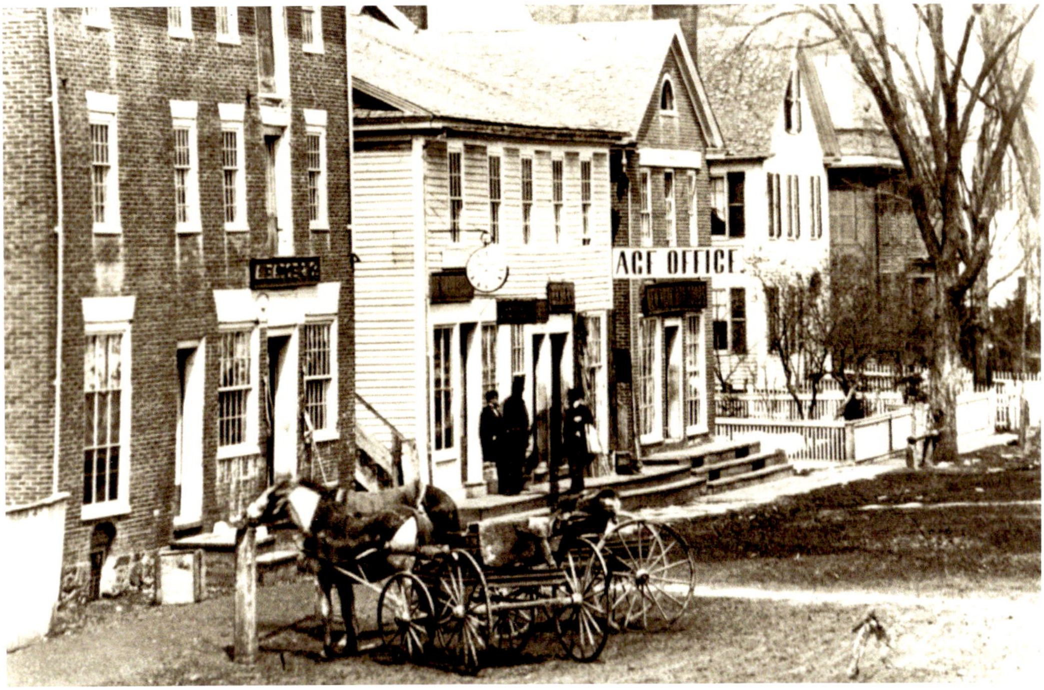

STICKY BUSINESS! The image above dates from the 1860s and shows the Elm Street shops including the Hatch Grocery Store, first building from the left hand side, above. F. H. Gillingham worked at the Hatch Store until buying it out and renaming it Gillingham's in 1886. The image below is dated early 1900s and shows Gillingham employees easing a large molasses barrel into the basement for storage. Despite many changes around Gillingham's, the store remains a fixture in the community.

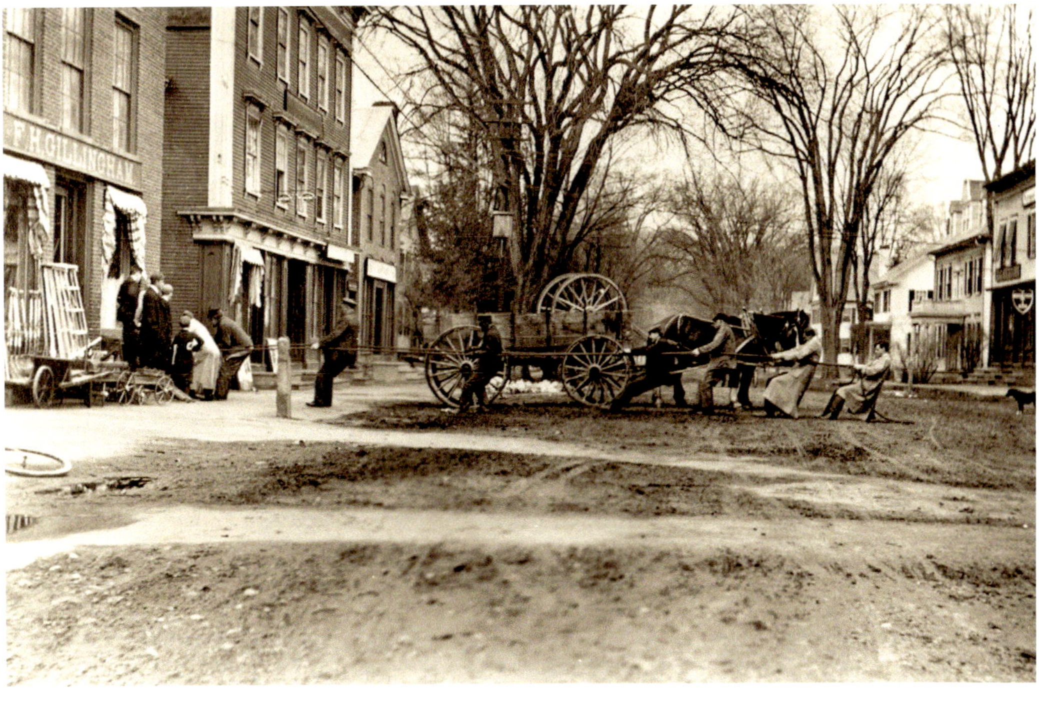

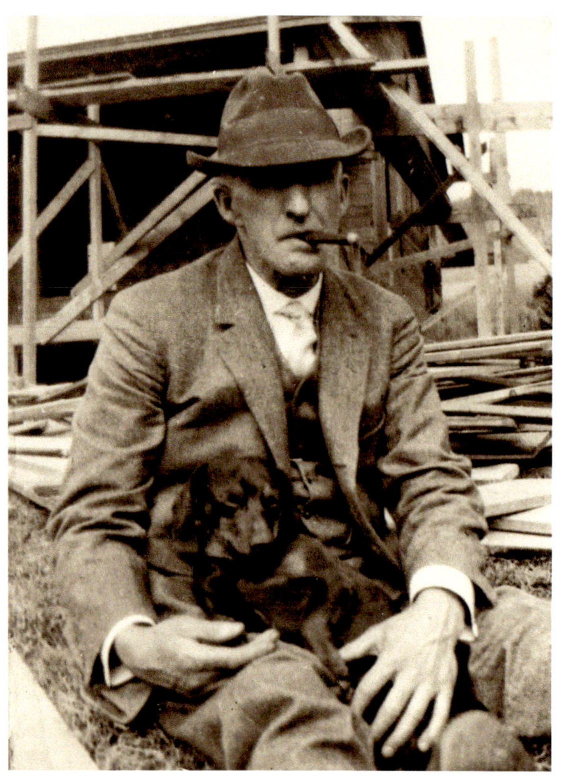

FRANK GILLINGHAM: F. H. as he is affectionately called by his descendants, was a visionary. He built a warehouse at the train station, ensuring a steady supply of staples for customers. F. H. had Gillingham's logo stamped on the lids of his flour barrels so there would be no mistake about the satisfaction guarantee. At left is the only known photo of him, with his dog Dutch at camp in Plymouth, Vermont. The early freight bill below is dated 1887.

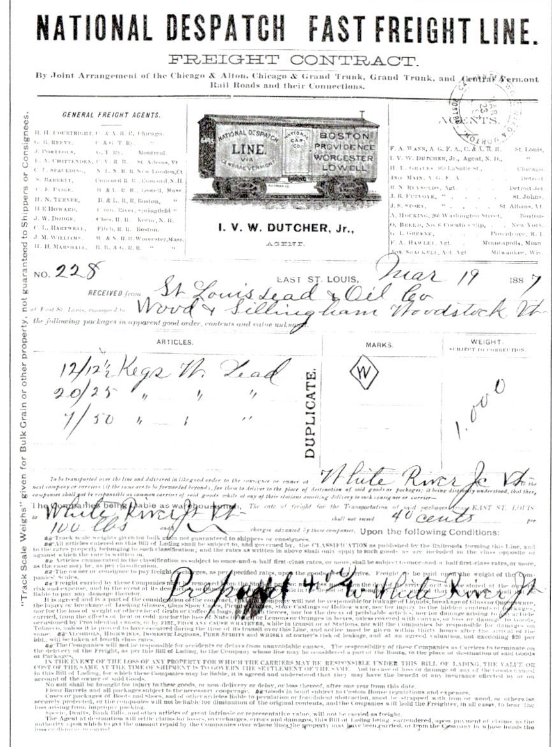

NATIONAL DESPATCH FAST FREIGHT LINE.

FREIGHT CONTRACT.

By Joint Arrangement of the Chicago & Alton, Chicago & Grand Trunk, Grand Trunk, and Central Vermont Rail Roads and their Connections.

GENERAL FREIGHT AGENTS.

AGENTS.

NATIONAL DESPATCH LINE VIA CENTRAL VERMONT — BOSTON PROVIDENCE WORCESTER LOWELL

I. V. W. DUTCHER, Jr.,
AGENT.

NO. 228 EAST ST. LOUIS, Mar 19 1887

RECEIVED from St Louis Lead & Oil Co at East St. Louis, consigned to Wood & Gillingham Woodstock Vt the following packages in apparent good order, contents and value unknown.

ARTICLES.	MARKS.	WEIGHT. SUBJECT TO CORRECTION.
12/12½ Kegs W. Lead 20/25 " " " 7/50 " " "	W	1.000

DUPLICATE.

To be transported over the line and delivered in like good order to the consignee or owner at White River Jc Vt or to the next company or carriers (if the same are to be forwarded beyond), for them to deliver to the place of destination of said goods or packages; it being distinctly understood, that these companies shall not be responsible as common carriers of said goods while at any of their stations awaiting delivery to such consignee or carrier—

The Companies being liable as warehousemen. The rate of freight for the Transportation of said packages from EAST ST. LOUIS to White River Jc Vt shall not exceed 40 cents per 100 lbs and charges advanced by these companies. Upon the following Conditions:

Prepaid 40c White River Jt

"Track Scale Weighs" given for Bulk Grain or other property, not guaranteed to Shippers or Consignees.

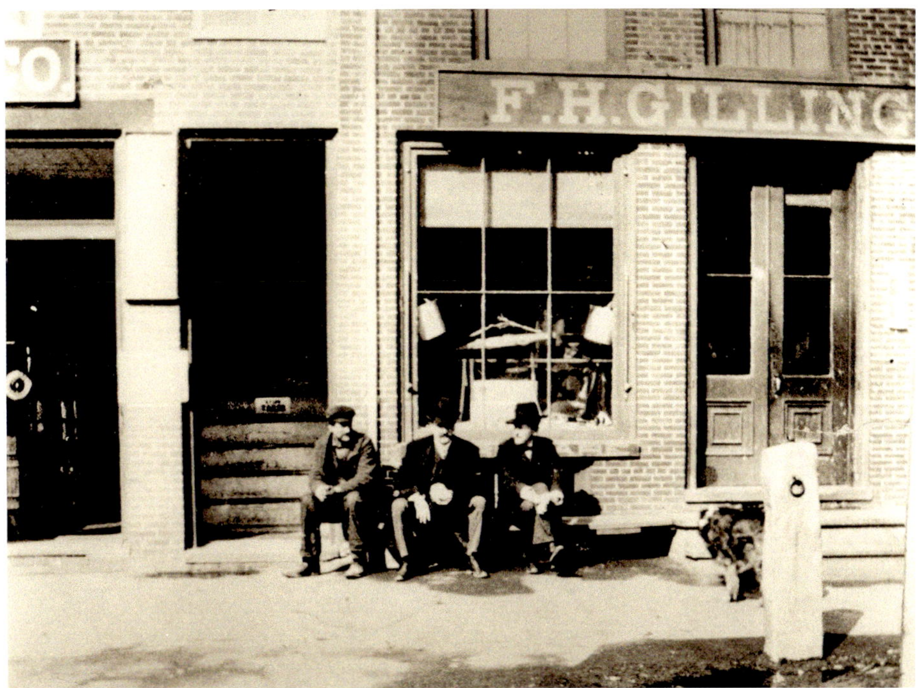

GILLINGHAM'S: Not only a great place to shop, but also a wonderful photo op! Unfortunately, the mens' identities in the photo above are lost forever but the two men in the image below are the great grandsons of F. H. Gillingham, current owners Jireh S. (left) and Frank S. III Billings (right). These two men have a sense of history and dedication to match their great grandfather's, and the determination to continue the legacy of Gillingham's into the future.

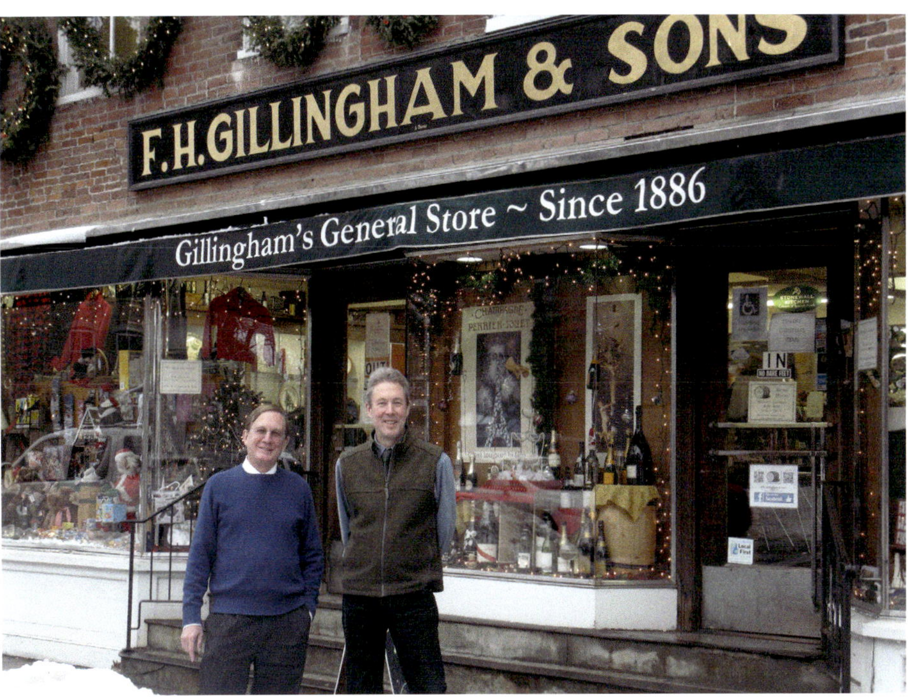

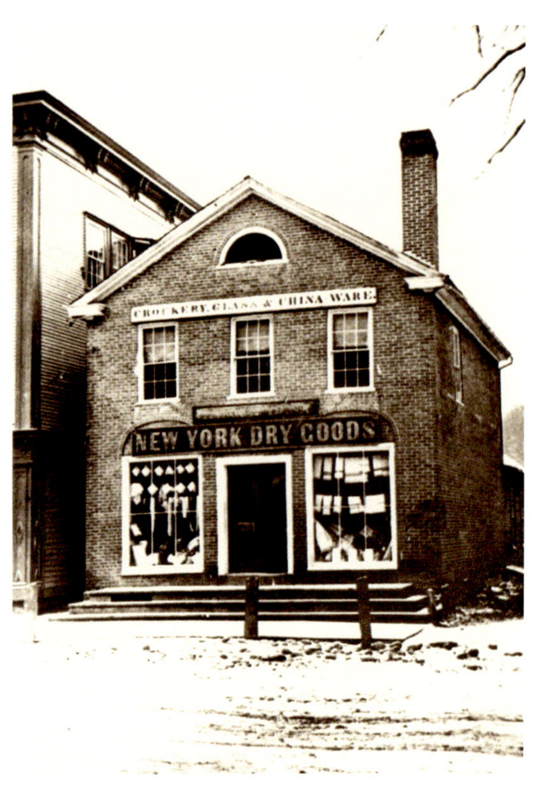

THE DANA NEW YORK DRY GOODS STORE BUILDING: Located to the right of Gillingham's General Store and the Tracy Block, then as now. "Crockery, Glass and China Ware," the sign on the Dana storefront read. Originally built by Charles Dana in 1820, the New York Dry Goods Store operated until 1906. It became the Elm Tree Press in 1907, under Charles' grandsons Edward and Joseph Dana. The Elm Tree Press operated at this location until it relocated in 1972.

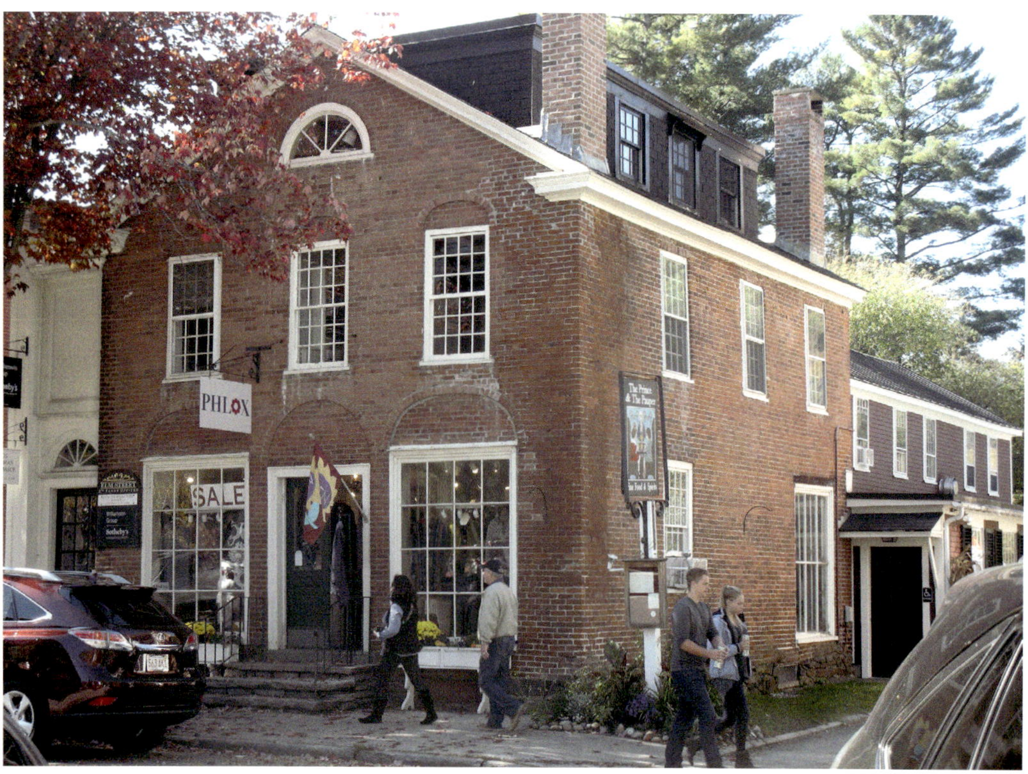

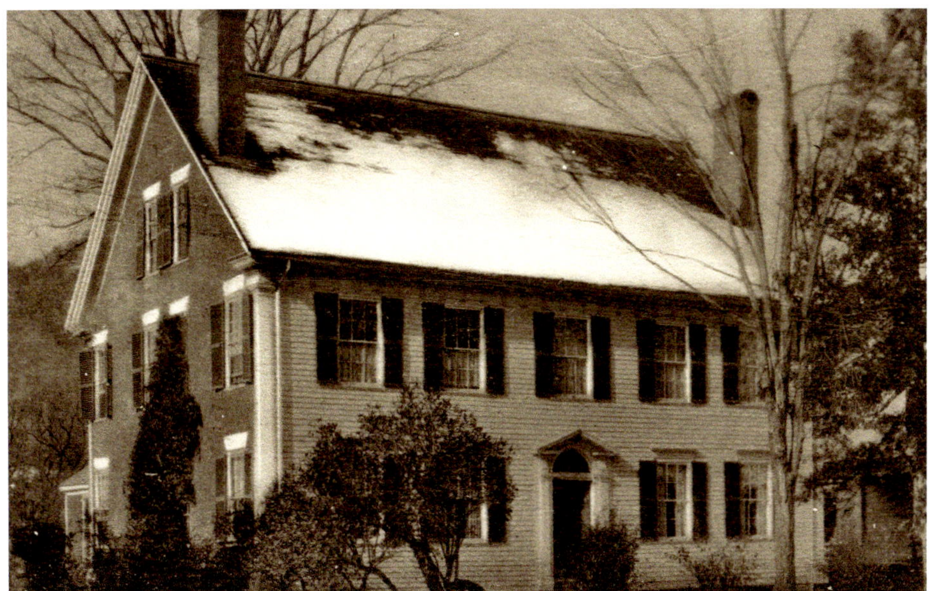

THE DANA HOUSE: Home to the Woodstock Historical Society, completed in 1808. Charles and his wife Mary Gay Swan Dana raised eight children in the home. As their family grew, the home expanded as well. Today this fine building has been preserved and maintained to allow visitors to see how people lived in the 1800s. The large barn behind the home has been converted to display, lecture, and library space. The house is open to the public year round.

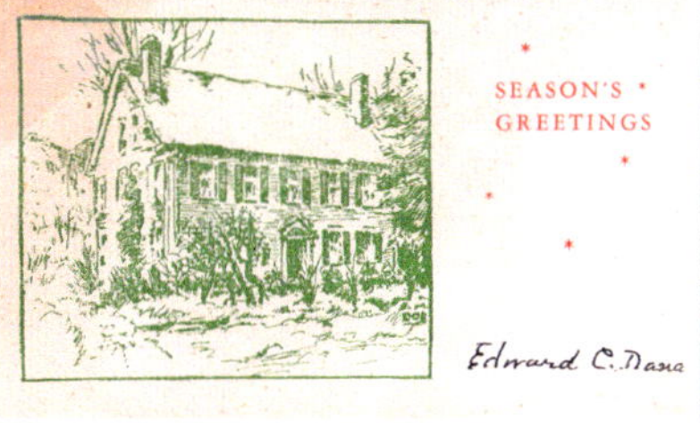

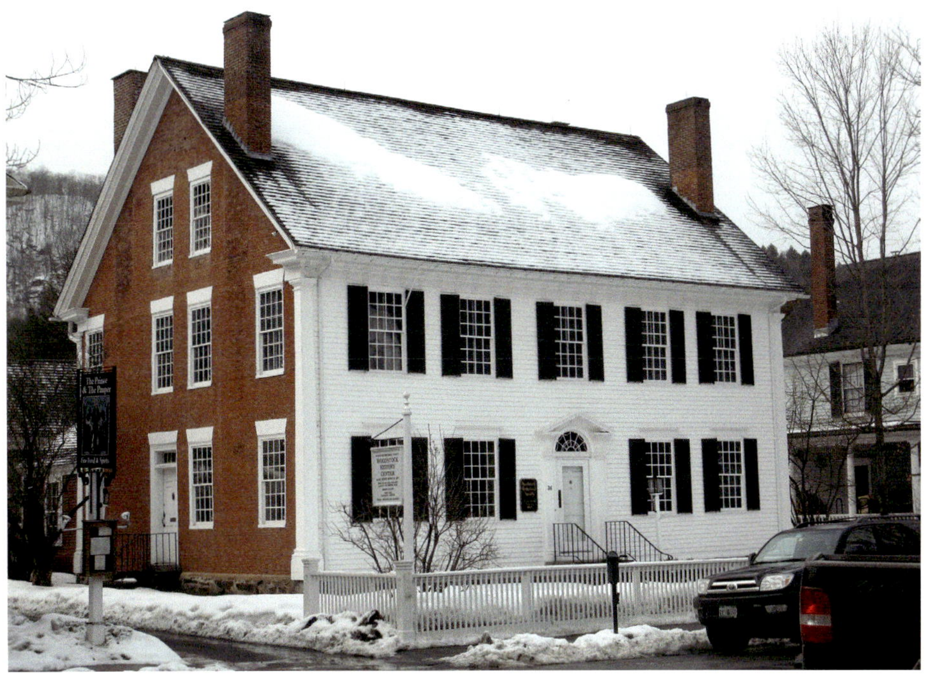

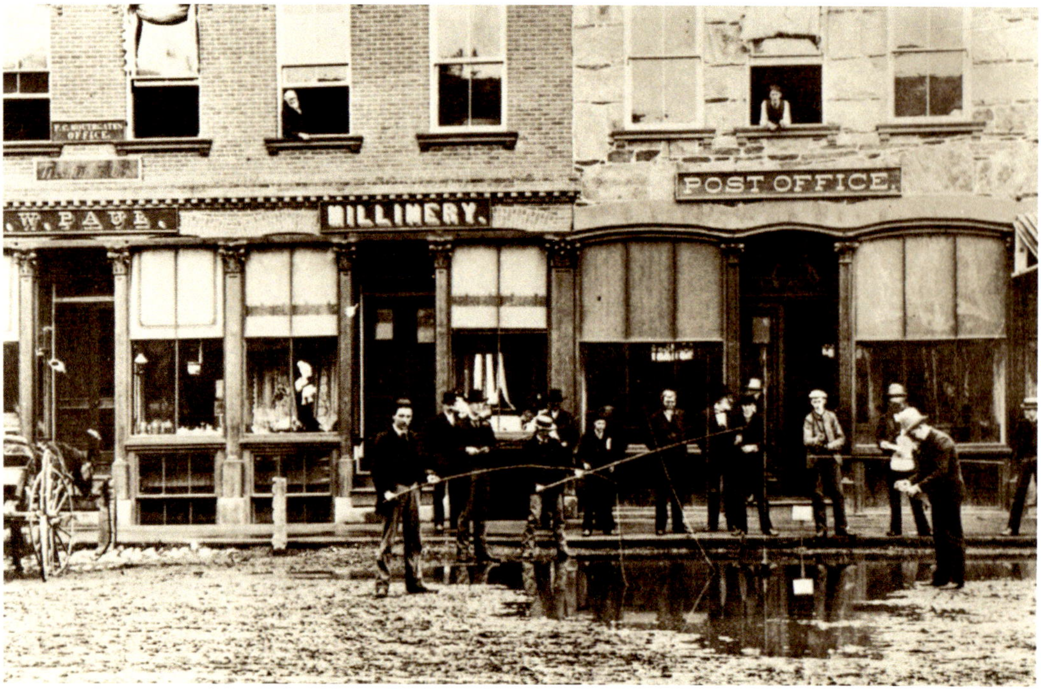

VERY WET SPRING, 1889 ELM STREET: That is the title of this vintage postcard from Woodstock. The Cabot Block in the background above is still there, right across the street from F. H. Gillingham and Son's General Store. This block of stone and brick buildings, was built in 1868 after an 1867 fire destroyed wood-framed Parker's Hotel and several attached businesses at this location. Vermonters have long had a sense of humor about the season often referred to locally as "three months of hard-sledding."

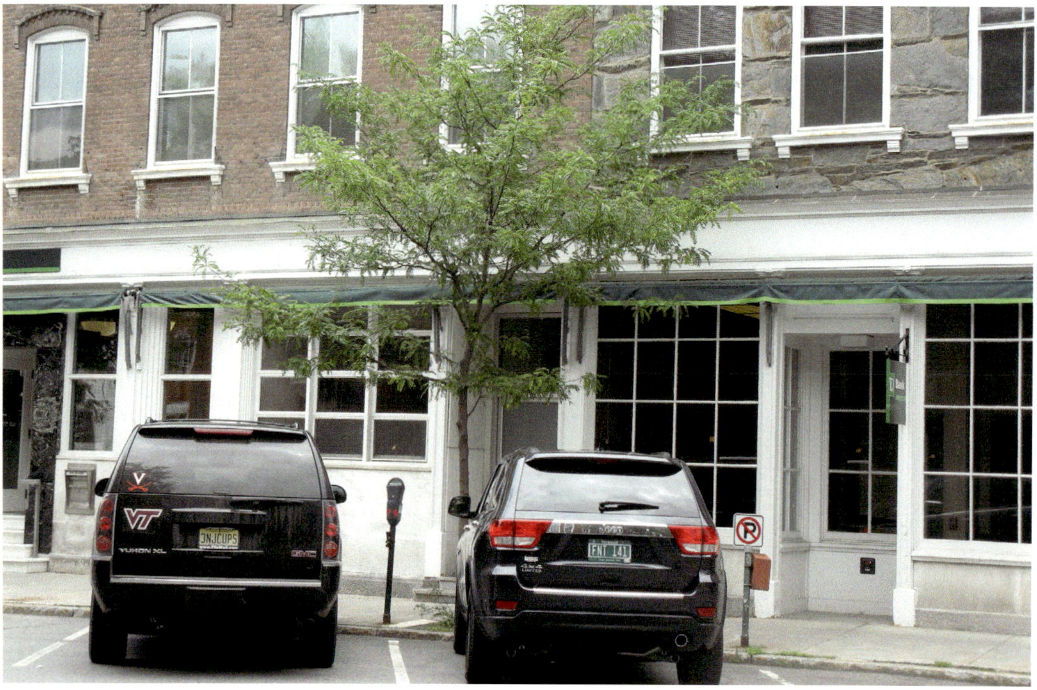

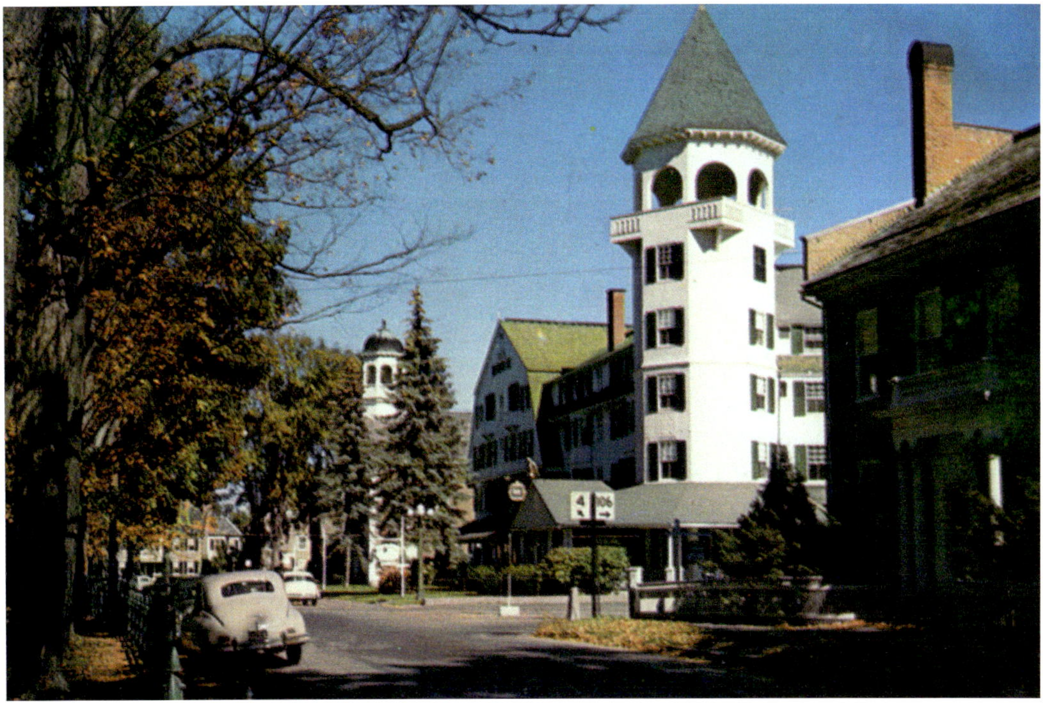

WOODSTOCK INN: It appears again to remind us not only of its historic importance in Woodstock, but also that it is a commercial venue in the center of Woodstock. Notice how close the previous inn building sat to the edge of the street in these images taken over half of a century ago. When the inn was bought, razed and rebuilt by Laurance S. Rockefeller in 1961, it was also moved back considerably from the street.

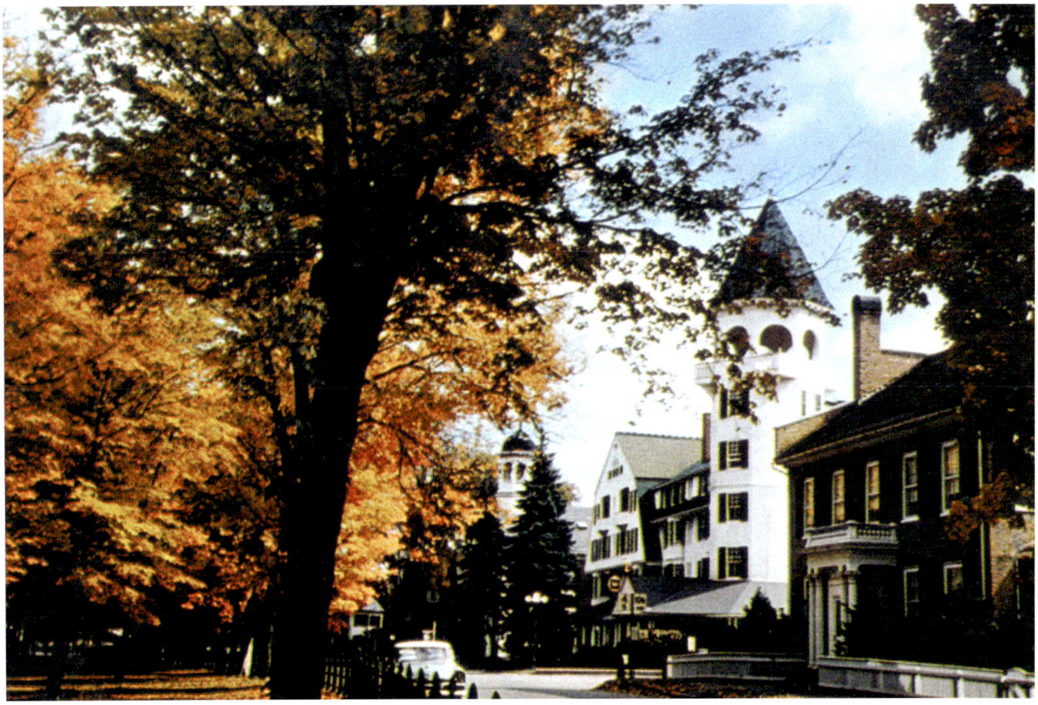

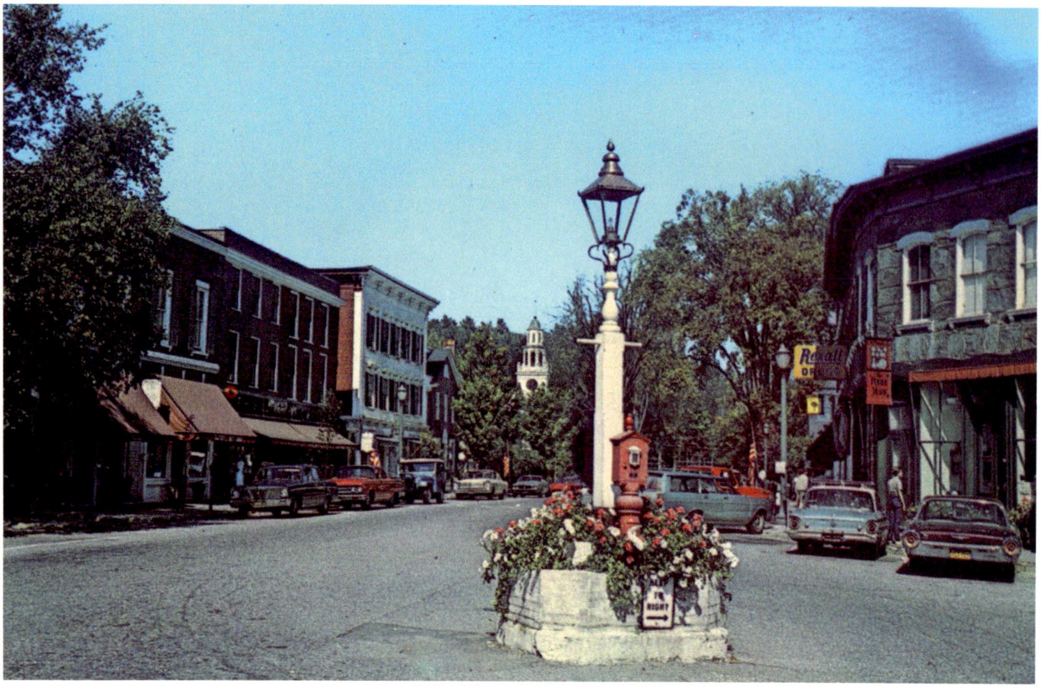

WHERE ELM AND CENTRAL STREETS CONVERGE: At this important intersection, the Cabot Block can be seen on the right-hand side of the photos and Elm Street with its row of commercial buildings stretches out on the left. The photo above dates from the 1960s. This intersection is referred to as The Triangle and the lamp post replaced an earlier monument donated to Woodstock by Frank MacKenzie, see inset. Note the Congregational Church spire in the distance.

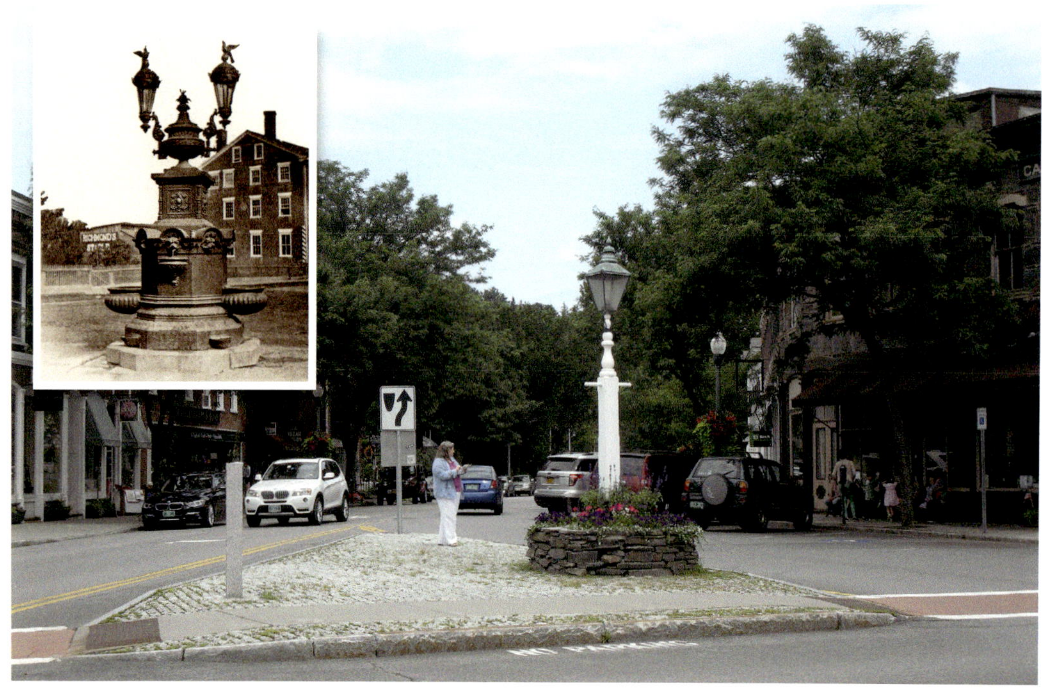

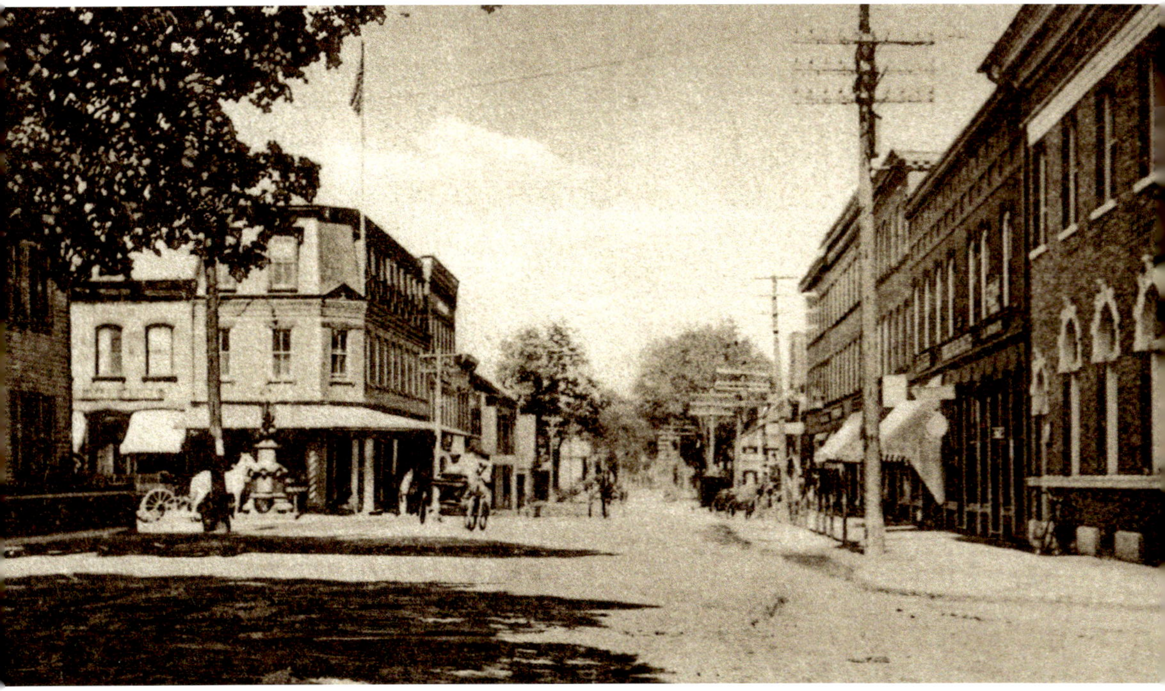

CENTRAL STREET, WOODSTOCK: Edson's Row was a stretch of commercial buildings laid out in 1800 and standing shoulder-to-shoulder from the Churchill Home (now the bank) to the Kedron Brook. These buildings were originally wood-framed and a series of fires destroyed many of them between 1831 and 1860. By 1881 all the buildings in this section of town were rebuilt of stone and brick. Now those buildings, risen from the ashes, are referred to as Phoenix Block.

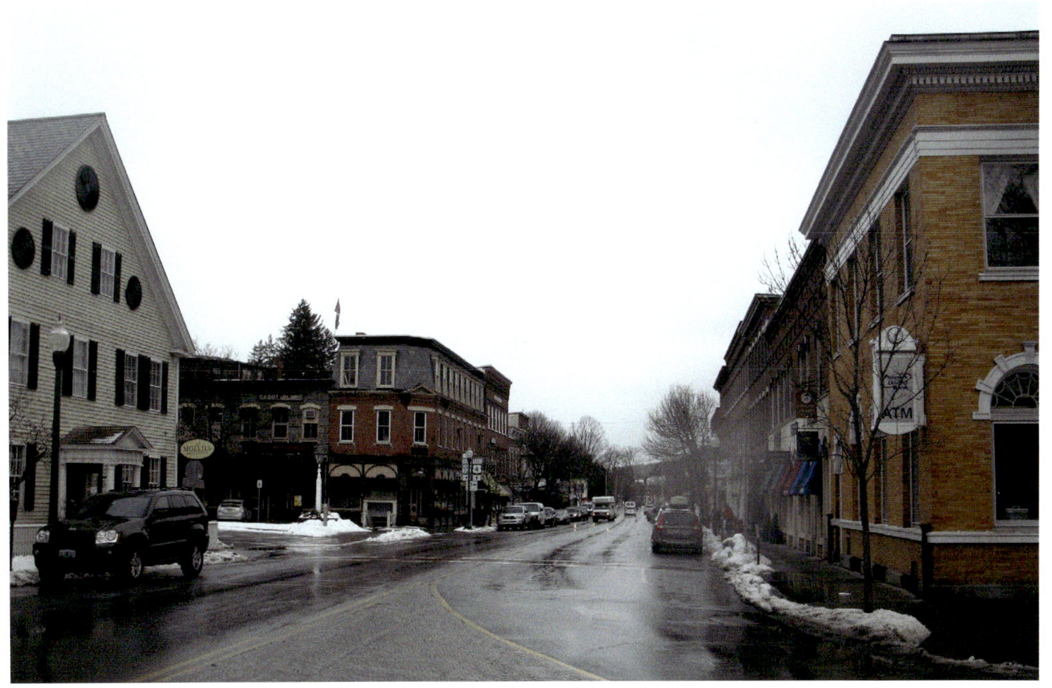

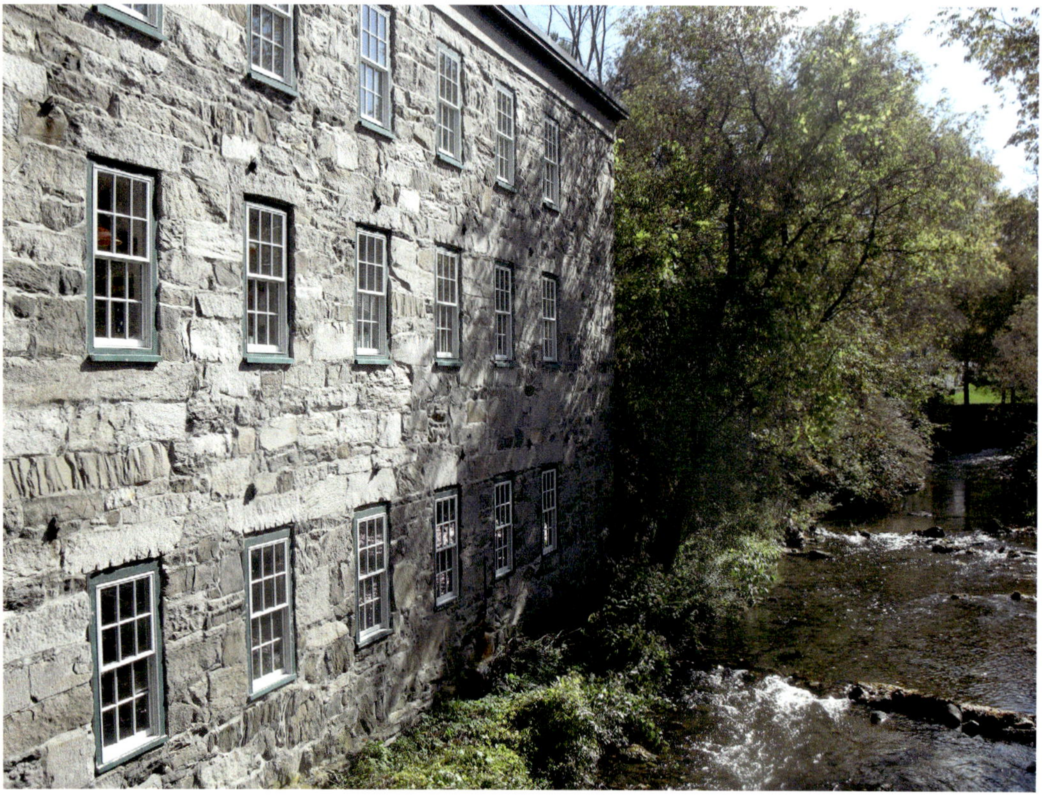

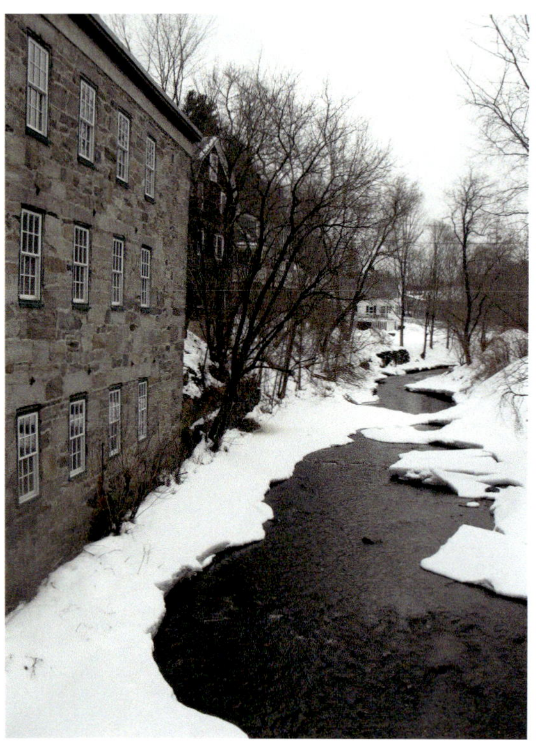

THE LINSEED OIL MILL: It seems to grow from the shore of the Kedron River at this location. This old building on Central Street was built of rough-cut stone in the early 1800s. It's three stories high and was once water-powered by a millwheel in the adjacent Kedron. The linseed oil mill – where flax seed was ground to produce linseed oil – was the first industrial building in Woodstock. This historic building contains a collection of artisan-owned and cooperatively run art galleries in 2016.

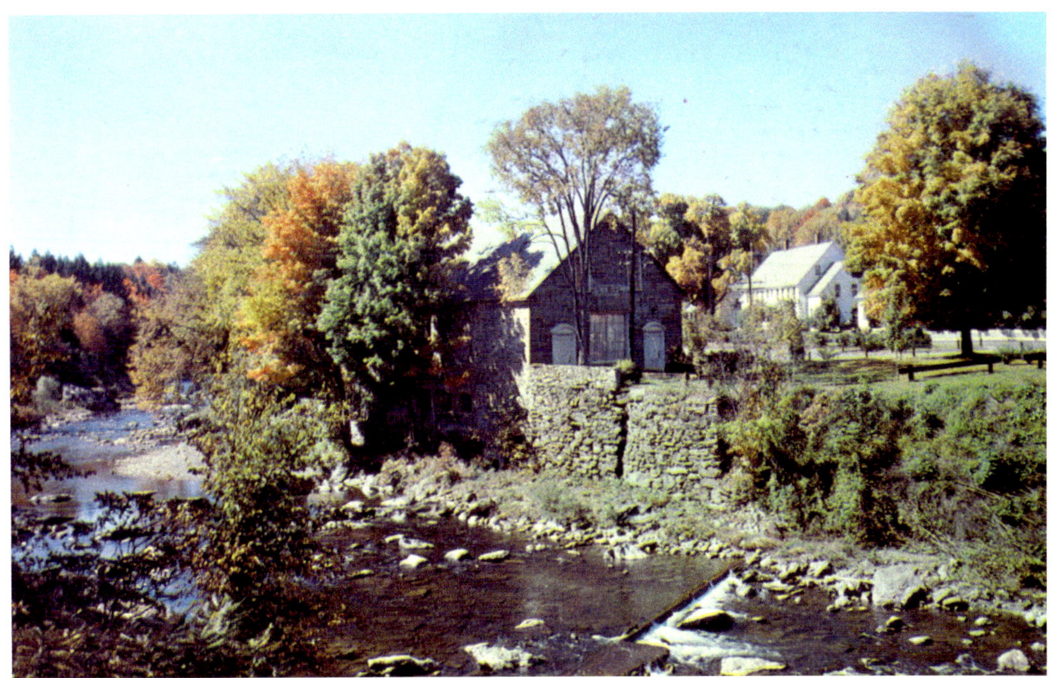

THE WOOLEN MILL: It was acquired and completed by Solomon Woodward in 1847. He built the stone woolhouse seen here in 1866. That foundation is now the Little Theater. The mill closed in 1877, and the buildings converted to saw mill, grist mill, and other manufacturing concerns. In 1943, Mrs. Marianne Faulkner purchased the mill property and donated it to the Woodstock community in memory of her husband, Edward Faulkner. In 1950, with major renovations completed, it became the Woodstock Recreation Center.

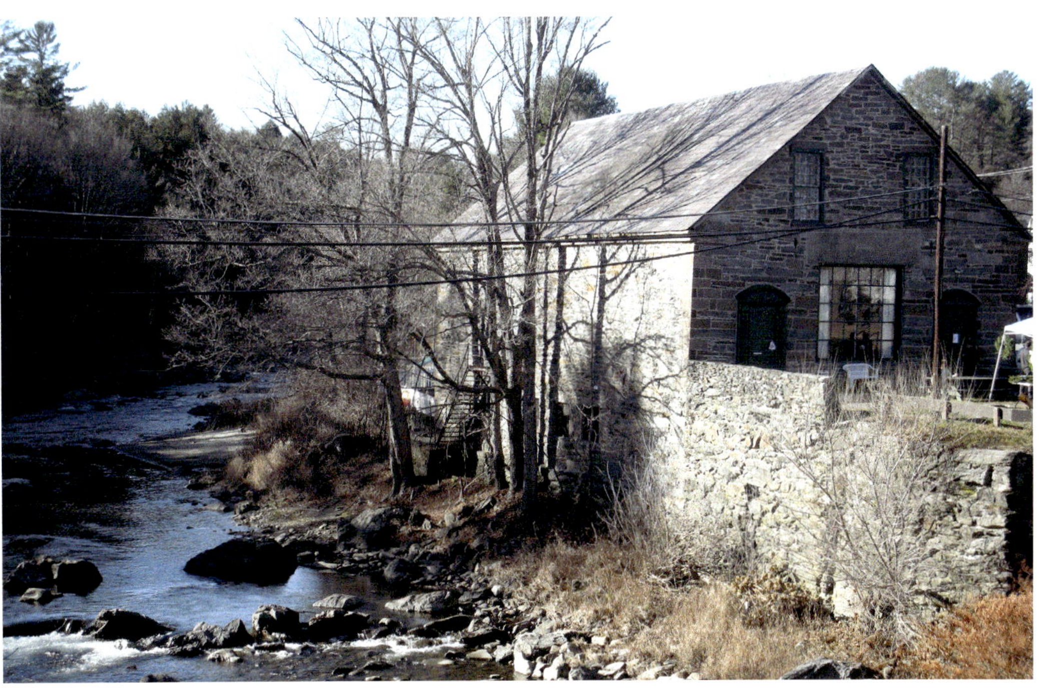

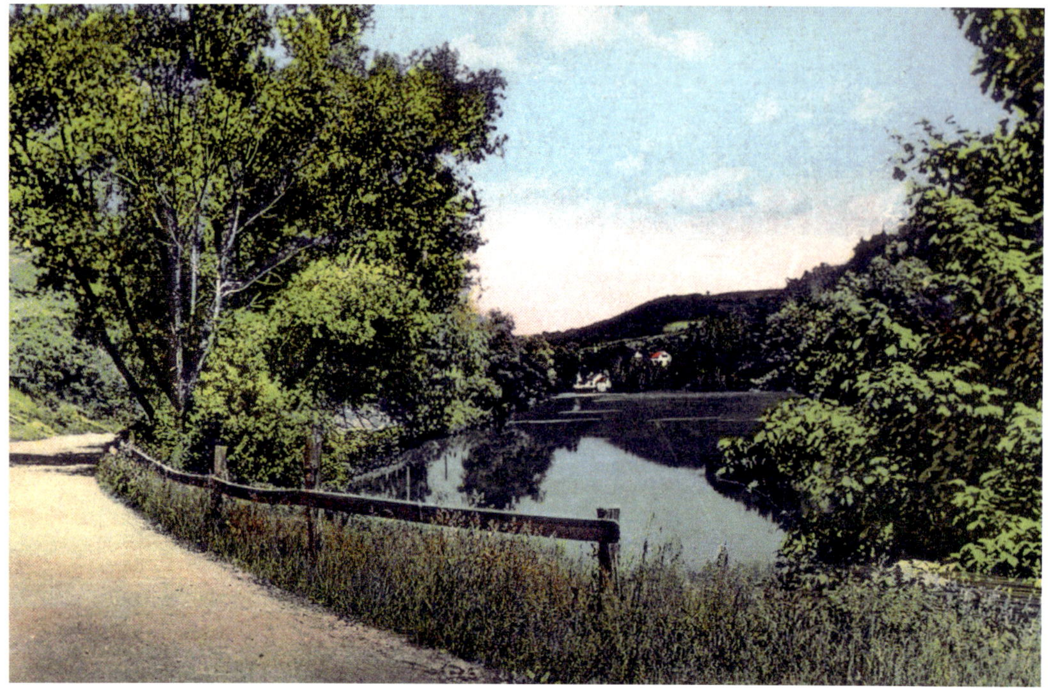

THE MILL POND: Located on the Ottauquechee River in Woodstock and West Woodstock, the mill pond no longer exists, as such. In the 1800s heyday of mills located along the river there, strategic dam placement created the pond. As water entered and exited the pond, a drop in elevation created water power used to operate the machinery of each mill. The dams are gone and the river has assumed its natural course once again.

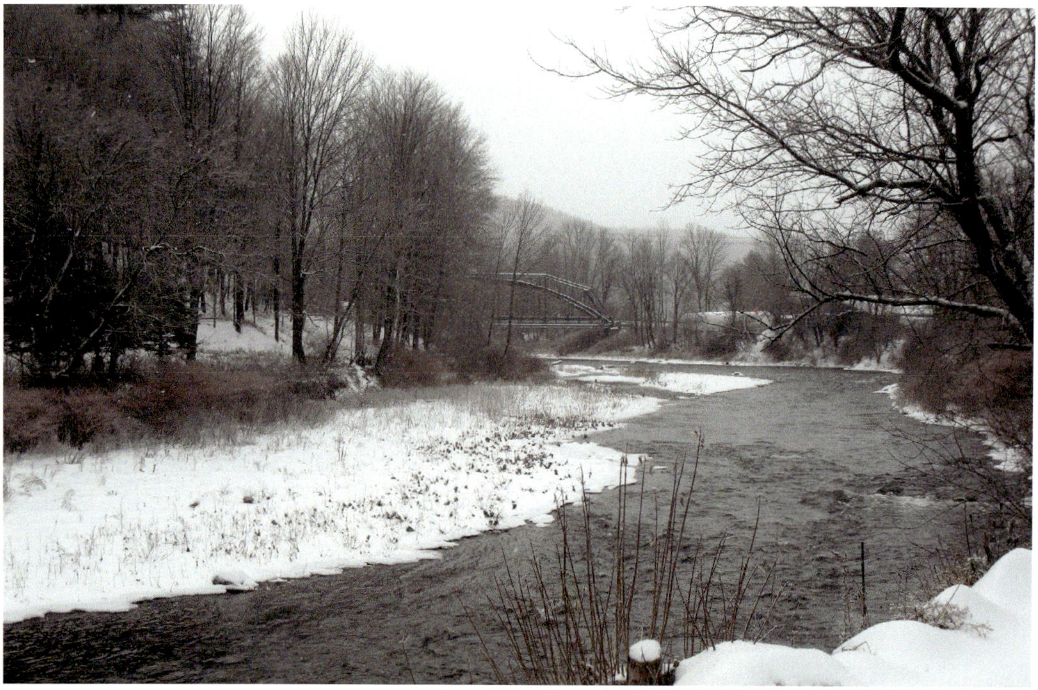

Transporation and Hospitality

These two areas of commerce often go hand-in-hand. People who travel need a place to stay. This early 1900s image shows the Woodstock Inn Stage Coach picking up passengers at the Woodstock Railroad Station to bring them to the inn. Before Woodstock Railway Company built a station in Woodstock in 1893, the stage coach would go to the station in White River Junction, over fifteen miles away,v to pick up and deliver passengers.

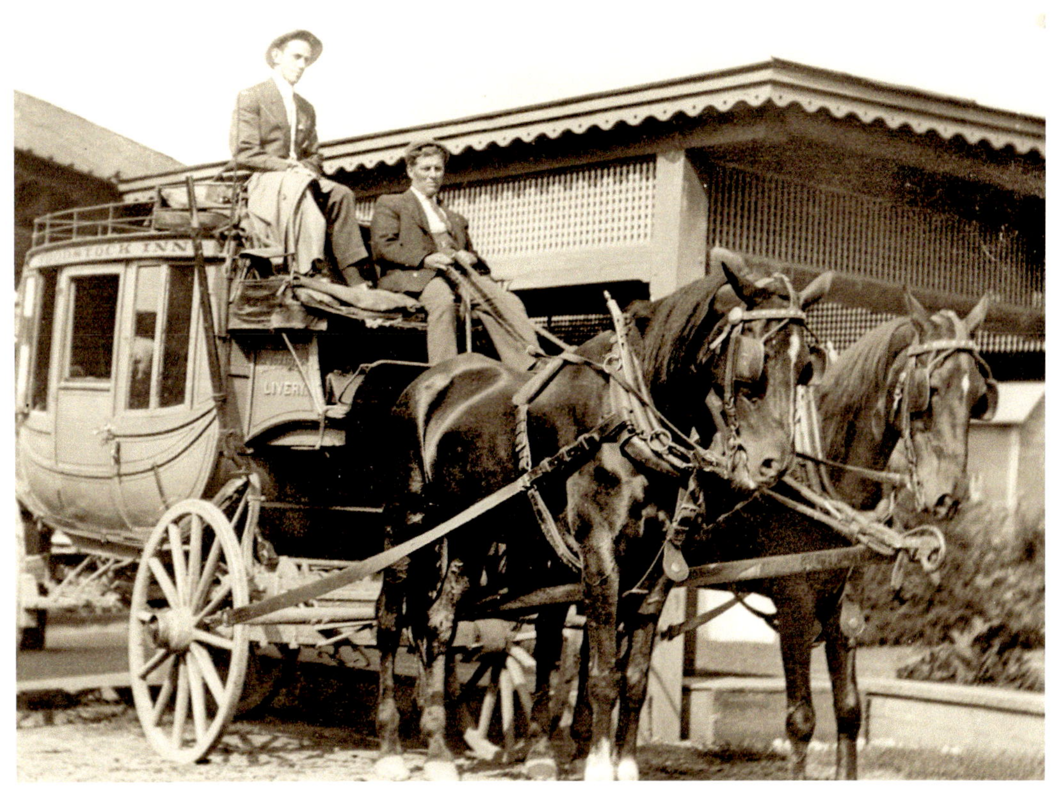

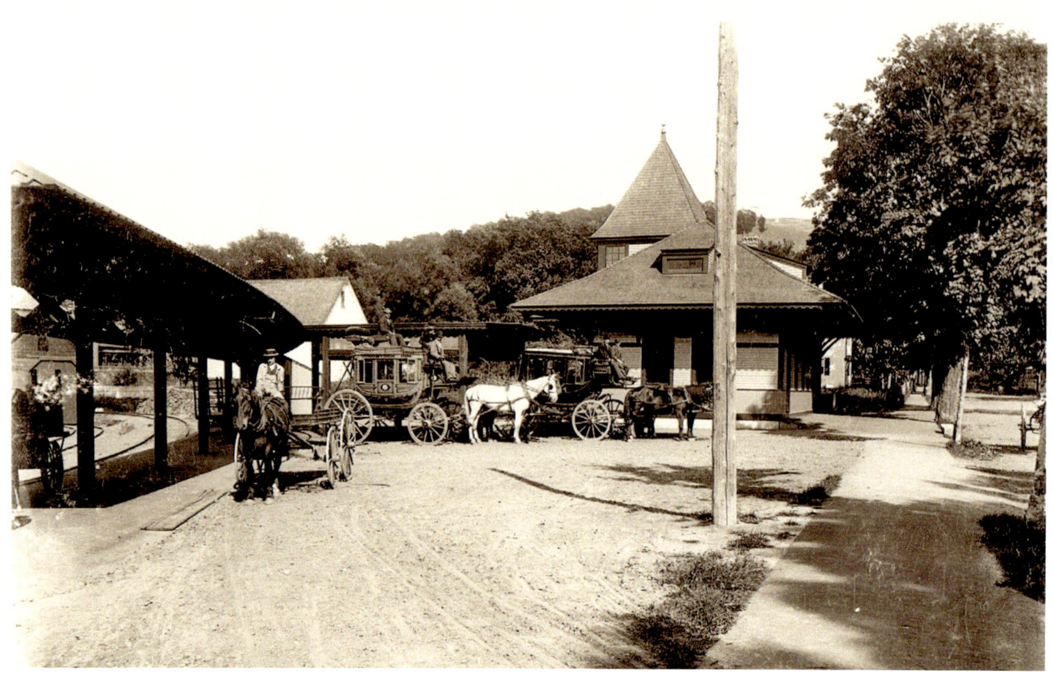

WOODSTOCK RAILROAD STATION ON PLEASANT STREET: Opened in 1893 when the line was extended from White River Junction. A stage coach or a sleigh from the Woodstock Inn met passengers at the station and took them to the inn. Notice the stage coach in this early 1900s image. The last train used the railway in 1933 when the line and station closed. Freight by truck and travel by auto replaced most of the rail business at that time.

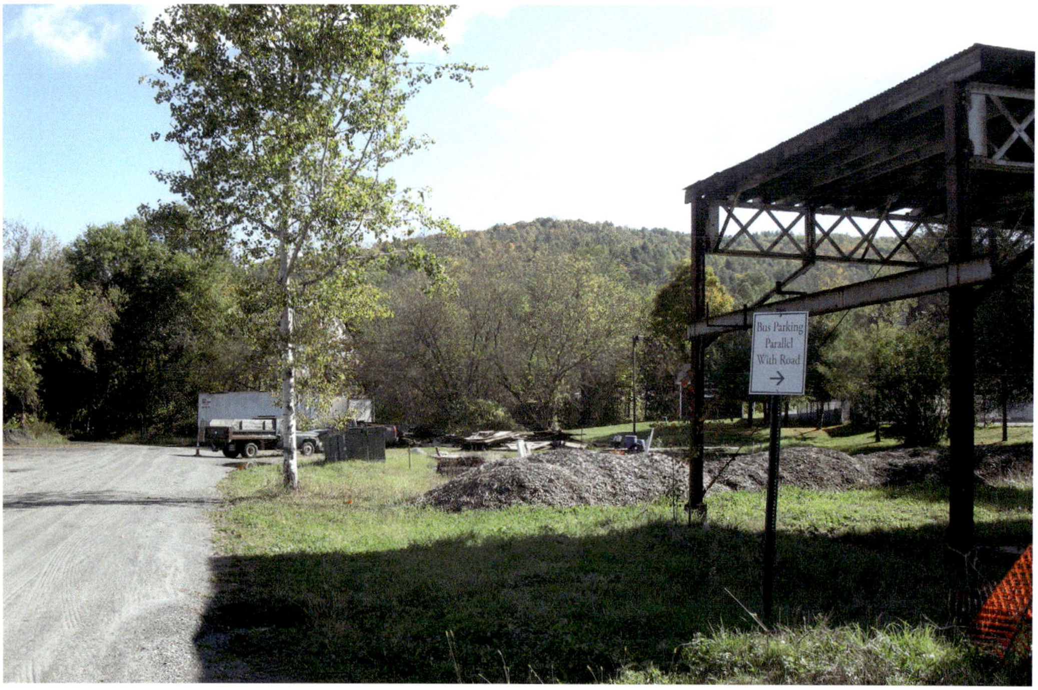

This 1916 Contract: Seen at the right, this contract between the Woodstock Railway Company and F. H. Gillingham's General Store, permitted Gillingham's to lease a piece of property at the rail yard for $10 a year. The leased property was the site of the Gillingham Warehouse. This was a farsighted business move that served the store well. The rail yard, below, contained a turntable, stock yards, freight and passenger station and stationmaster's home as well as warehouses.

This contract made the first day of May 1916 between the Woodstock Railway Company, a corporation under the laws of Vermont having its principal office for business at Woodstock in the county of Windsor andthe State of Vermont, and F. H. Gillingham of Woodstock, in said county and state of Vermont, Witnesseth.

First. That said Railway Company hereby leases to the said Gillingham a piece of land in Woodstock Freight Yard west of the Stock Yard and north of the so-called river track, extending 120 feet on the line of the said river track and about 4 feet distant from track and 24 feet back from said track containing about 2880 square feet. on which said Gillingham has erected a storehouse.

Second. Said Gillingham agrees to pay said Railway Company ten (10) dollars per year rental for the above, payable in advance on or before May first of each year.

Third. This contract cancels the contract dated July 1st 1897.

Fourth. Either party to this contract may cancel same by giving to the other party six months notice in writing and if said Railway Company at any time wishes to have said storehouse removed from said premises said Gillingham shall cause same to be removed within six months after having bee notified in writing to do so.

Signed -

F H Gillingham

Woodstock, Vt.

May 1st, 1916.

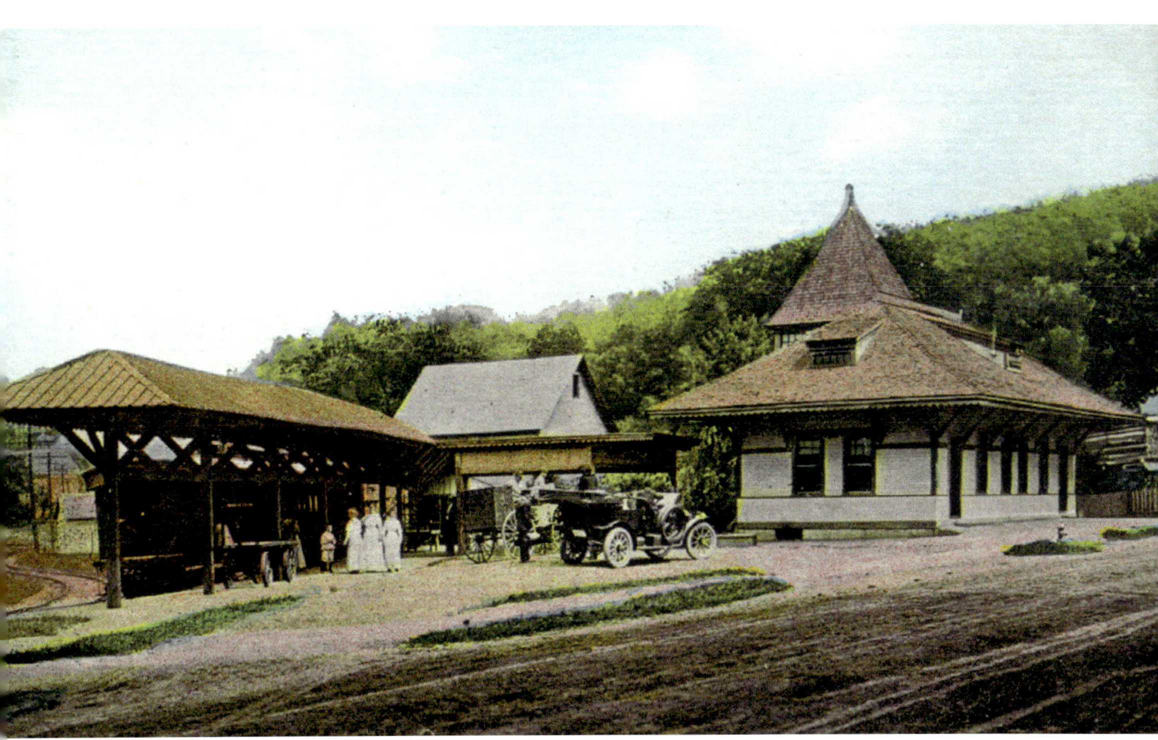

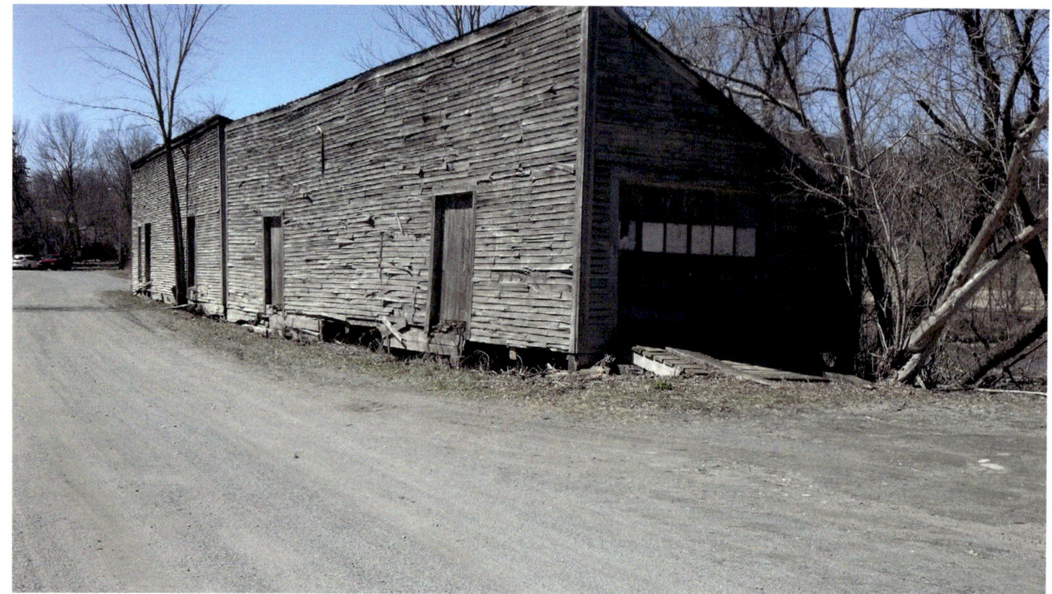

GILLINGHAM'S WAREHOUSE: This stood at the Woodstock Railroad Station for over one hundred years. F. H. built it in the early 1900s; see page 43. When Gillingham's ordered bulk goods delivered by train, they were stored here until needed. The warehouse was razed in 2013, eighty years after the closing of the railyard. This station warehouse was just one of many resourceful and successful business practices that assured Gillingham's a competitive edge in the local market, and its survival until today.

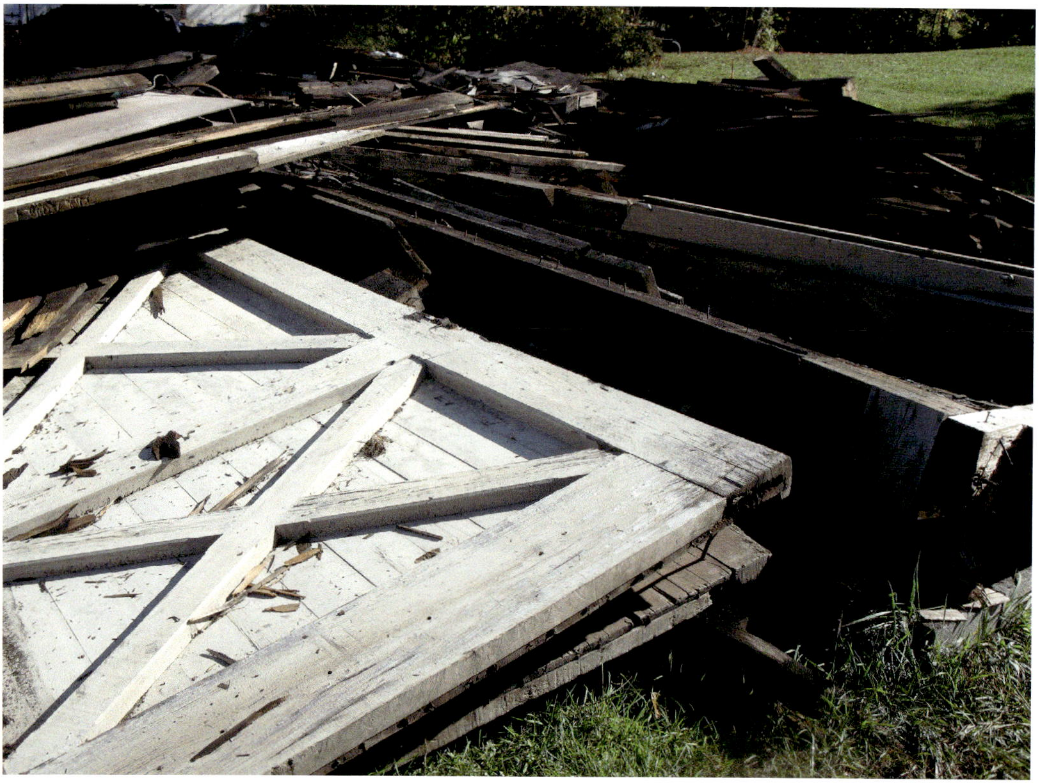

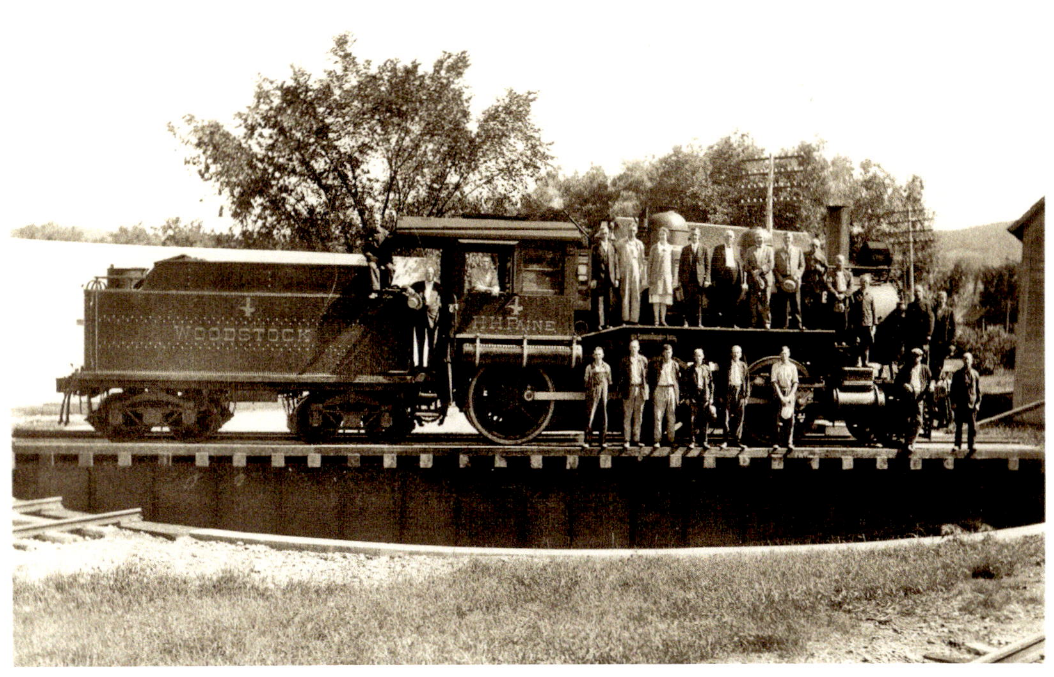

THE TURNTABLE AT WOODSTOCK RAILROAD STATION: Shown above with the H. H. Paine Train, named for engineer Harry Paine, atop. The turntable remains peek through the snow, below, at the former railyard site. Turntables were usually located within roundhouses but when they were outdoors, uncovered, as in the Woodstock Railroad yard, they often had a covered rail shed nearby where repairs and maintenance could be performed. This turntable was located at the terminus for the Woodstock rail line.

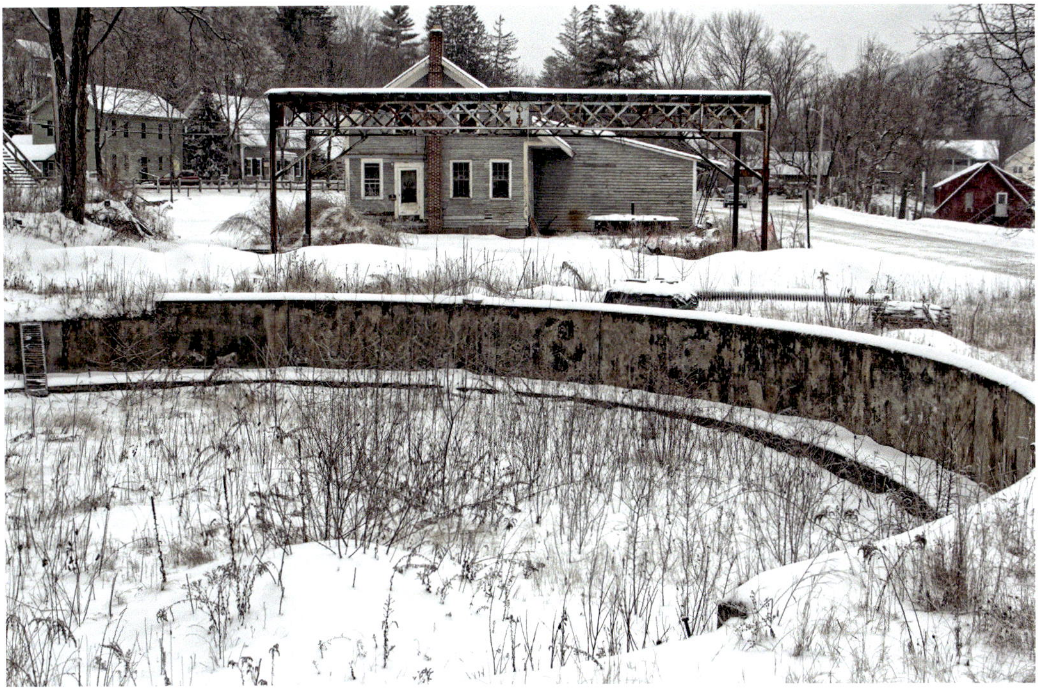

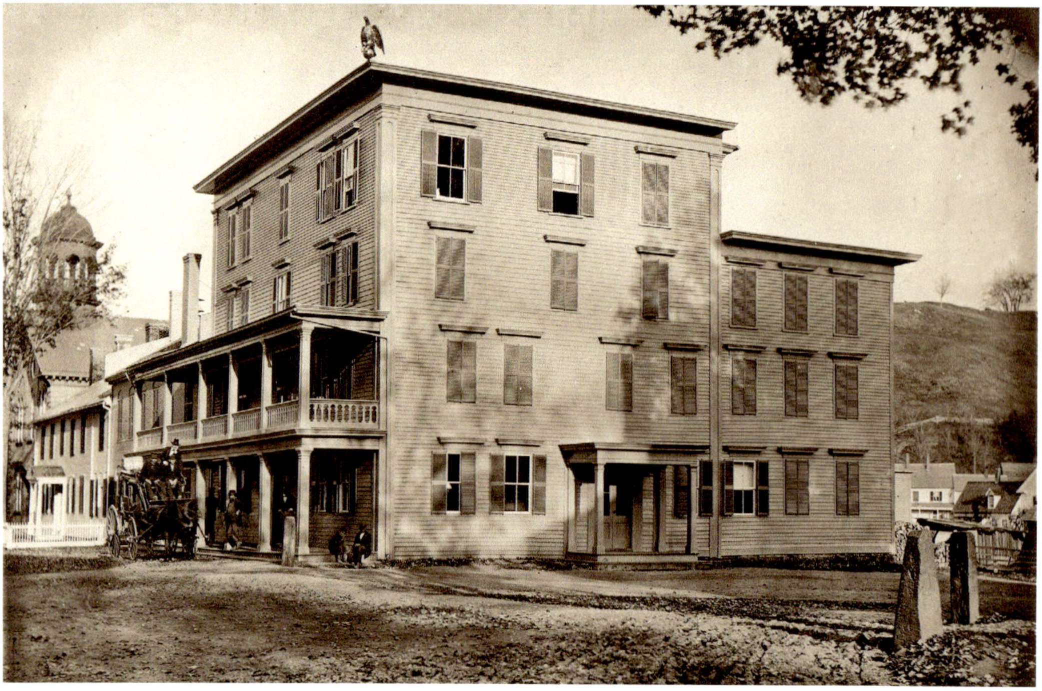

EAGLE HOTEL: Built in 1867 and removed when the original Woodstock Inn was built on the site in 1892, it replaced a series of lodgings for travelers dating from the 1700s. In 1793 Captain Israel Richardson built Richardson's Tavern. In 1830 it was renamed the Eagle Hotel. In 1840 it became the Church Hotel; and in 1869 it reverted to the Eagle Hotel. The Eagle, long a symbol of hospitality in Woodstock, still adorns the current Woodstock Inn.

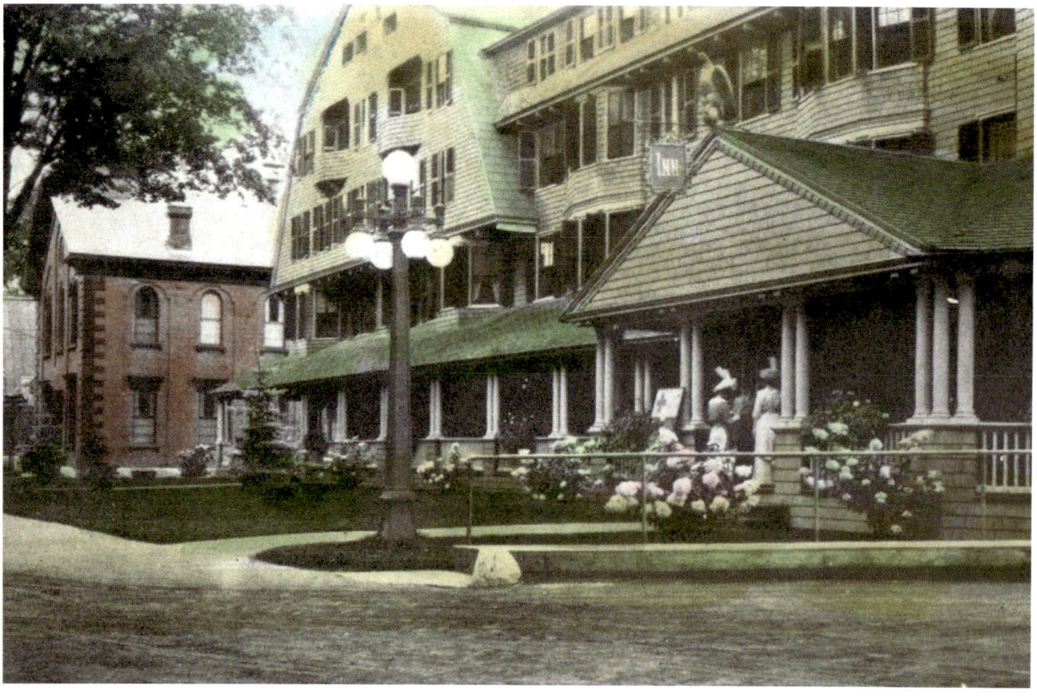

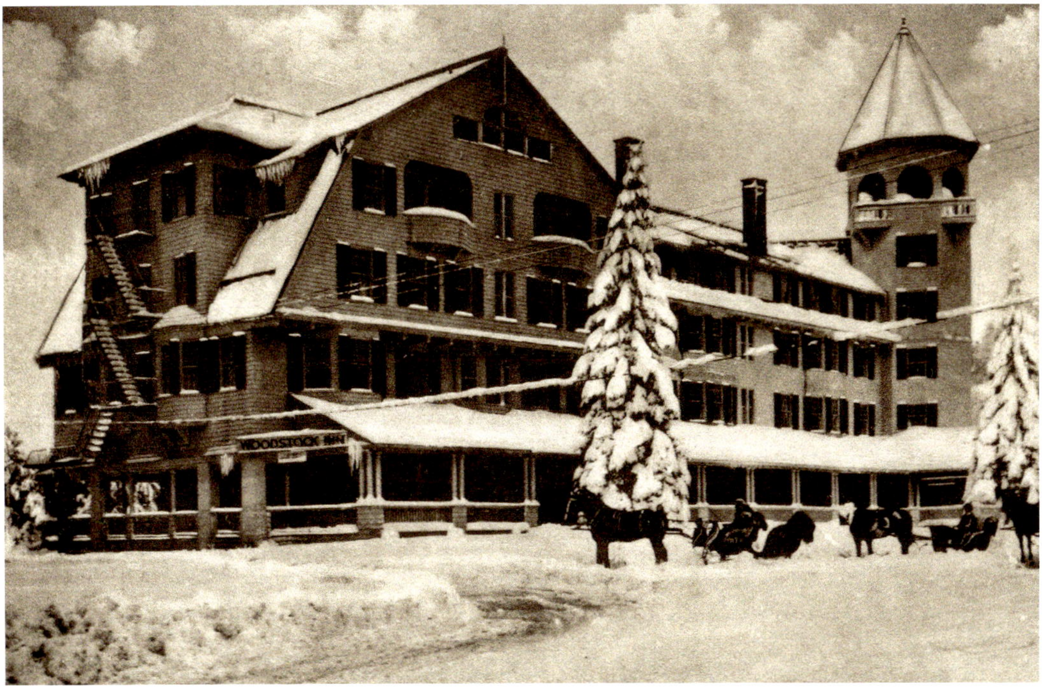

WOODSTOCK INN IN WINTER: The inn has been a destination for generations of travelers for over a century. Early on, Woodstock realized that the abundant natural resources there attracted many visitors. The inn capitalized on this lifestyle by offering snowshoeing, tobogganing, skiing, skating, and sleighing parties. Inside, many rooms had fireplaces and the meals in winter catered to visitors who spent time outside and wanted hearty fare.

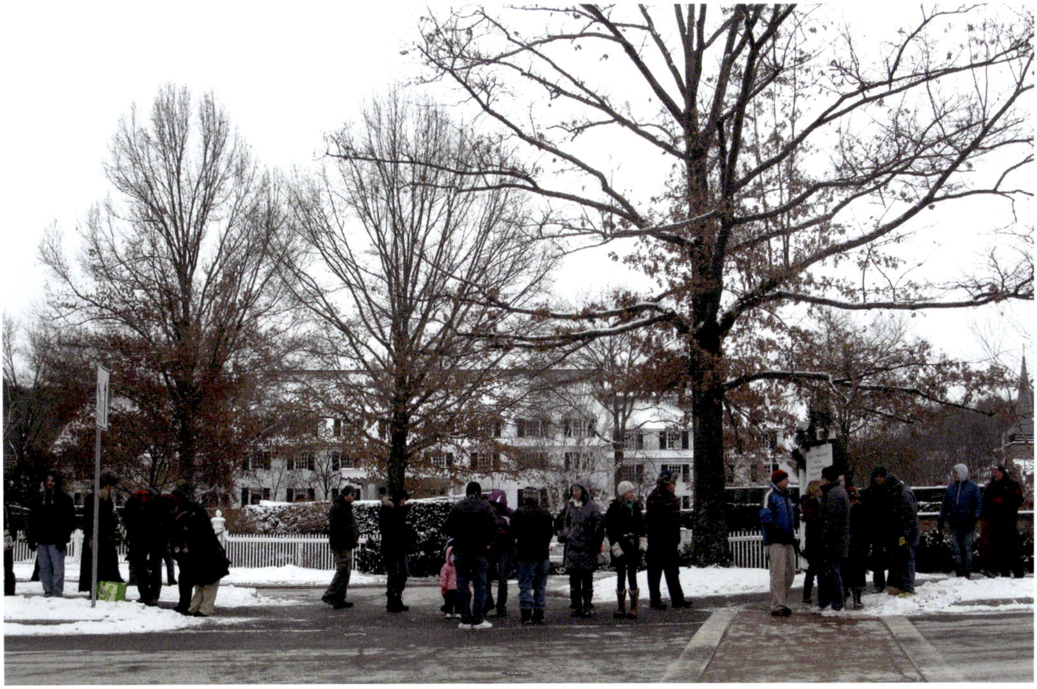

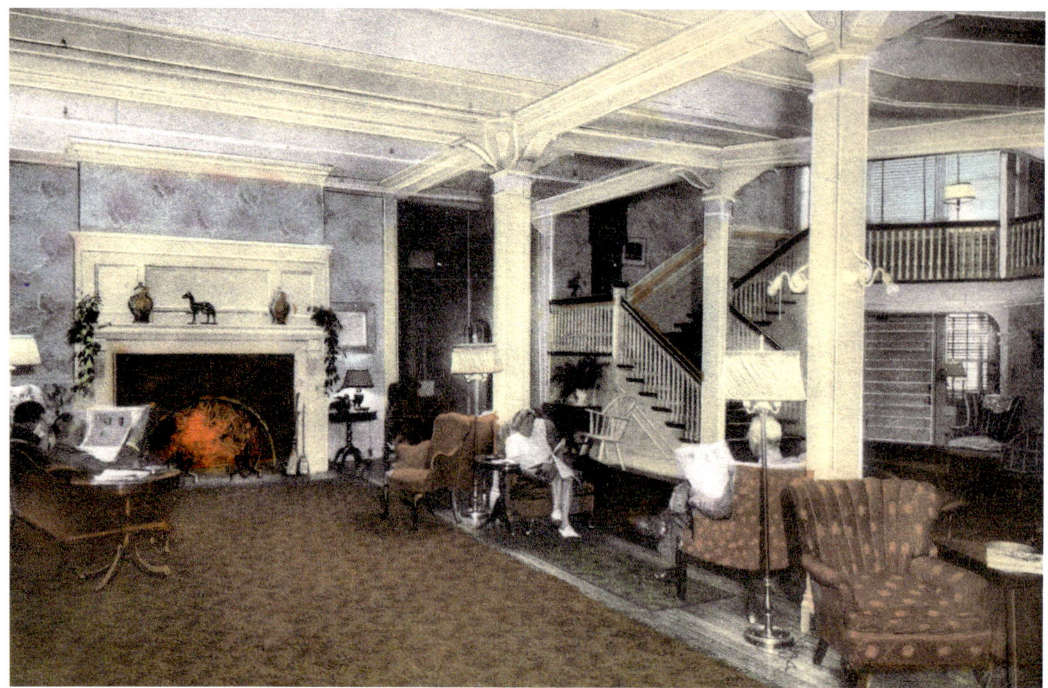

WOODSTOCK INN LOBBY: Its enormous fireplace is undoubtedly the heart of the inn. In the lobby of the original Woodstock Inn above, built in 1892, the fireplace figured prominently. The current Woodstock Inn continues the tradition with a massive hearth and fireplace lit at the hint of crispness in the air. It roars to life with gigantic logs, ready to warm the toes of cold-weather skiers and travelers. Creative seasonal displays grace this elegant space as well.

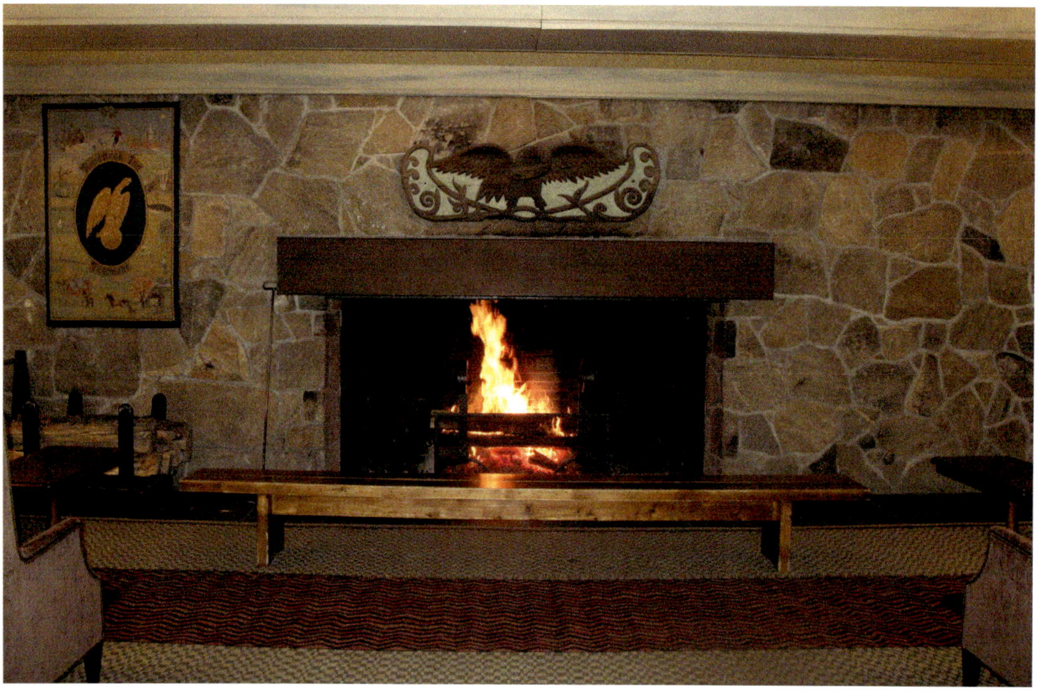

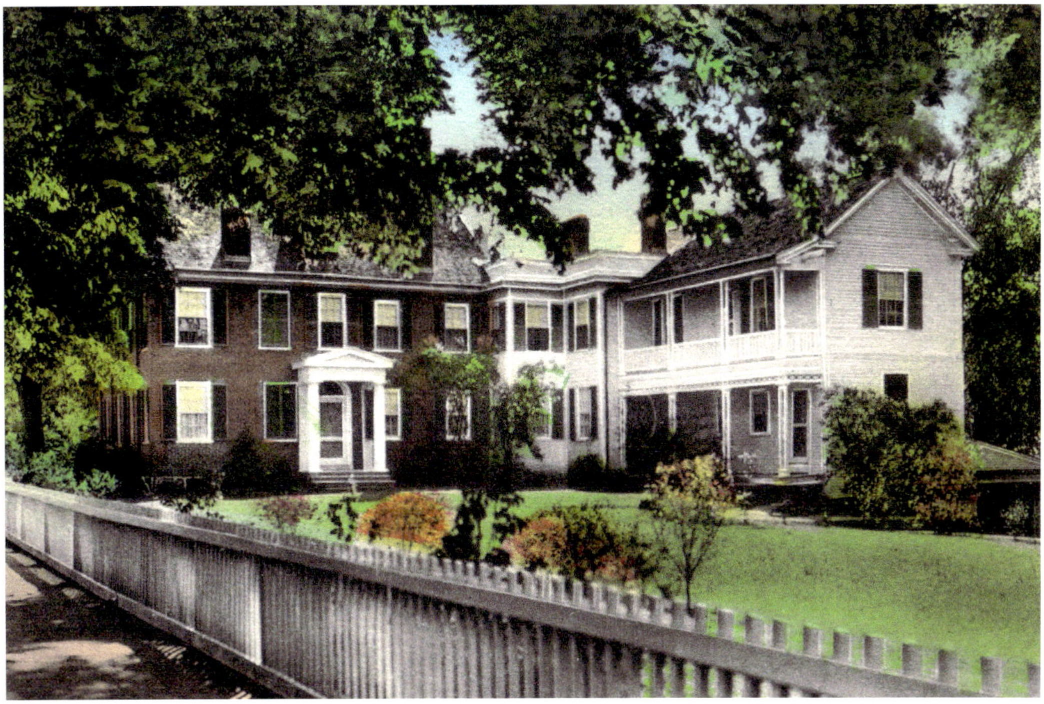

ELMWOOD INN: Also called The Lauren and the Blue Horse Inn, it was built in 1831 by Joel Eaton. The house has seen many incarnations. It is rumored to have been a stop on the Underground Railroad and local lore has it that General Lafayette slept here. The east wing was added in the 1860s and used as a recovery home for Civil War veterans. The inn became a private residence in the early twenty-first century.

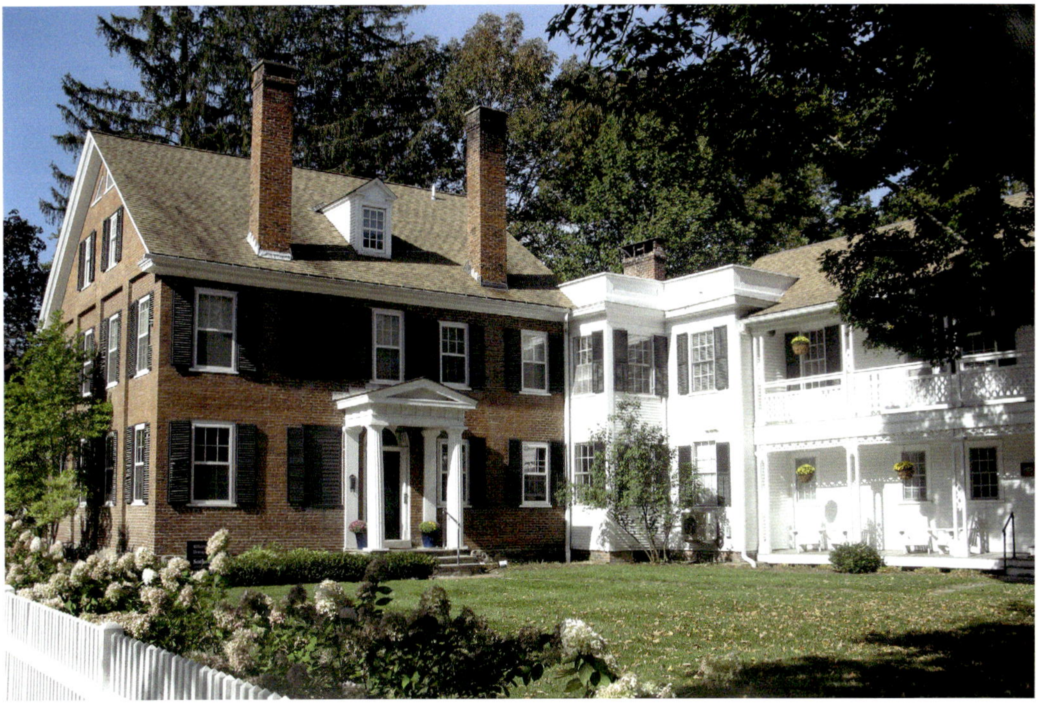

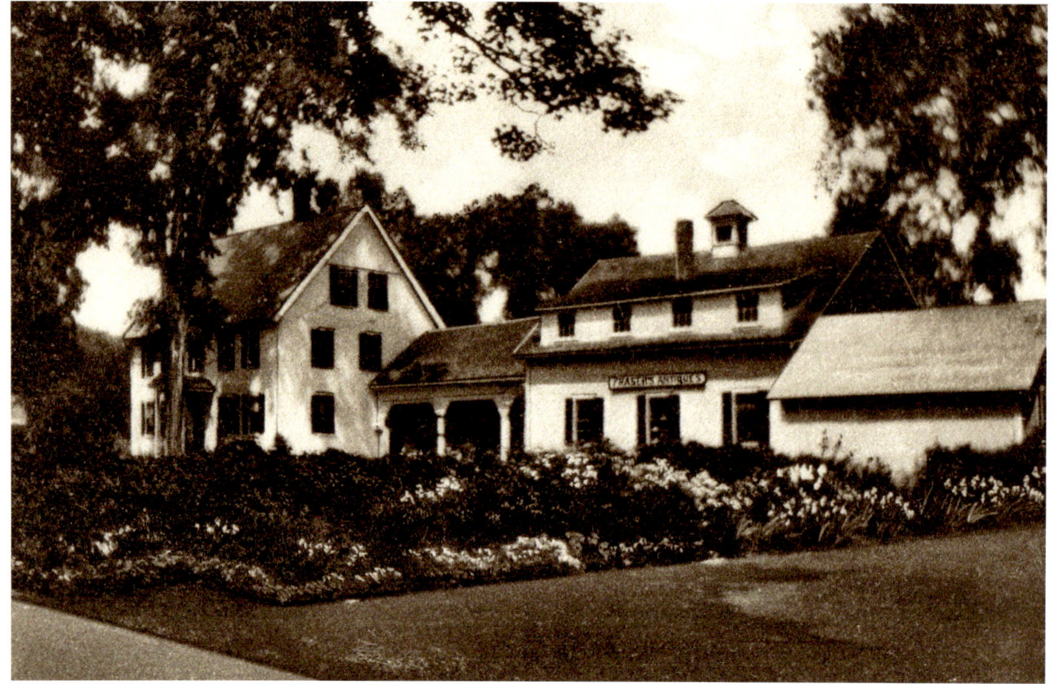

FRASER TOURIST HOME AND ANTIQUES SHOP: Located in an old Vermont farmhouse, above, the shop earned its living on Pleasant Street for many years. The Fraser family lived at and operated the inn here in the 1930s, close to the Woodstock Railroad. The Frasers also had an antiques business in one of the outbuildings of the old farm. It is hard to imagine this classic farmhouse in the current setting, below, where the modern motel has taken its place.

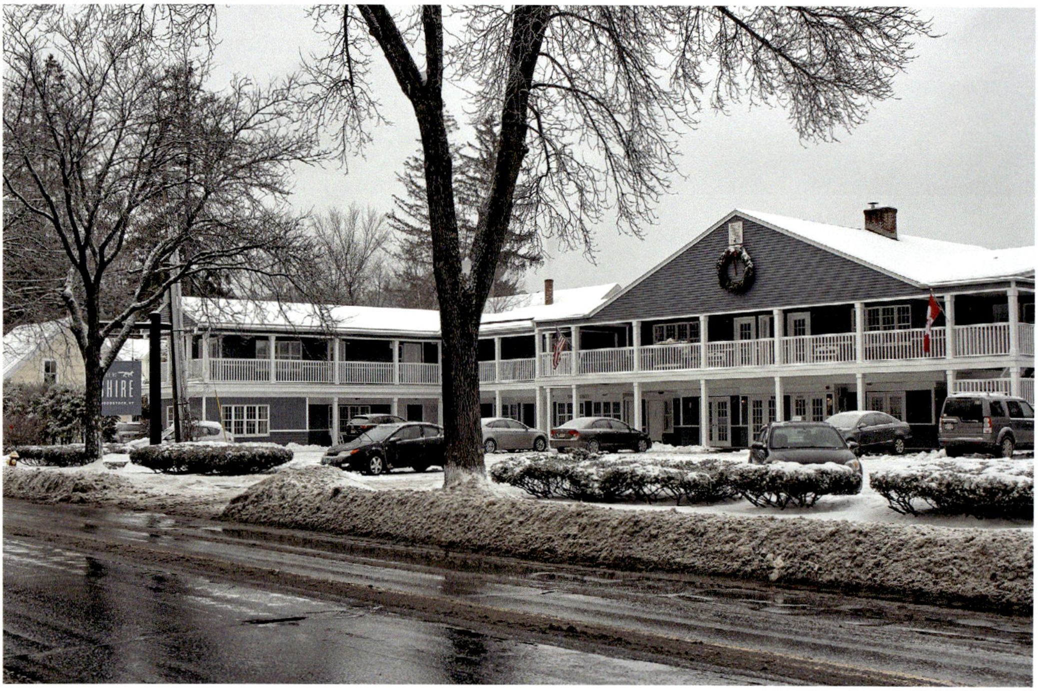

Residences and Residents of Note

In the 1800s, residents George P. Marsh and Frederick H. Billings embraced, wrote about, and employed environmental conservation on their extensive properties in Woodstock. In that time, they were visionaries. George Marsh was politically influential on local, national and international fronts, but his heart never left Woodstock. Frederick Billings was president of the Northern Pacific Railroad and was instrumental in saving the industry when it was struggling in the 1870s. He was also crucial to the creation of the Woodstock rail line. In the 1900s, Laurance S. Rockefeller continued their work and made those contributions self-sustaining into perpetuity. This is an incredibly simplistic summary, but extensive books have been written about the significant works of these farsighted men. I just reference and honor their long-range influence here.

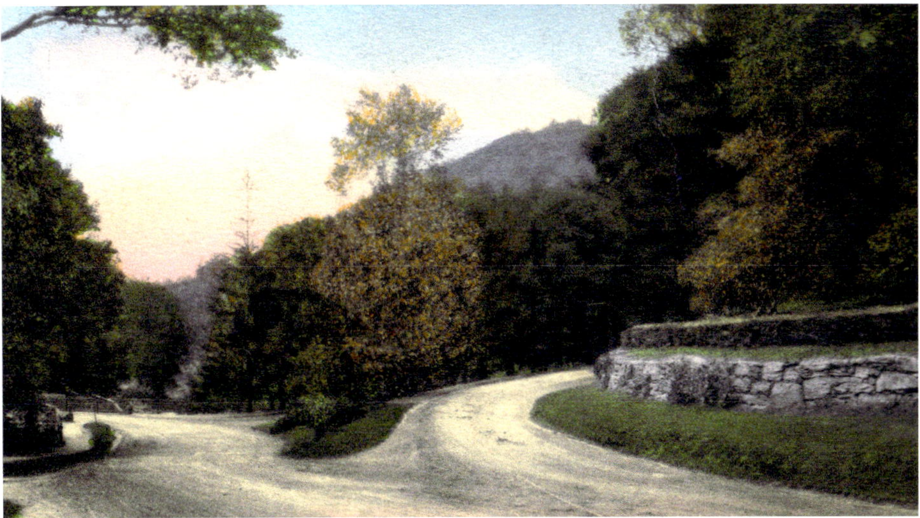

Intersection of Elm and River Street: This is where you turn right after crossing the Elm Street Bridge to visit the Billings Farm & Museum or the Marsh-Billings-Rockefeller Mansion and National Historical Park. Mount Tom rises steeply on the left and contains numerous hiking trails. The park pays tribute to three significant Woodstock conservationists, mentioned above. The farm demonstrates 17th century farming in Vermont and continues a legacy of high quality dairy production and responsible agricultural practices. The park and farm are open to the public.

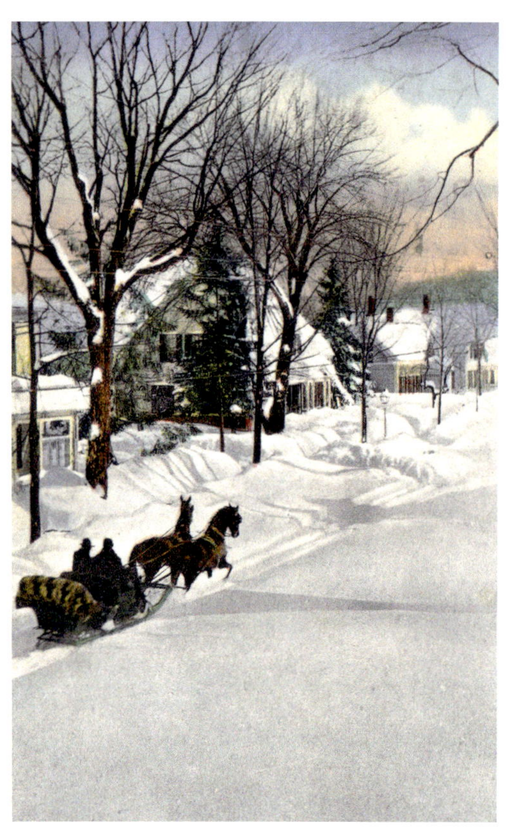

"PLEASANT STREET VIEW 1913": That's the title of this old postcard image at left. It was taken over 100 years ago. Although progress has changed the main mode of winter travel, it has not changed the magic of a snowy winter's day in Woodstock. Houses, lots and landscaping can change a lot in 100 years, but many of these homes on Pleasant Street have weathered time with grace, as the image below can attest.

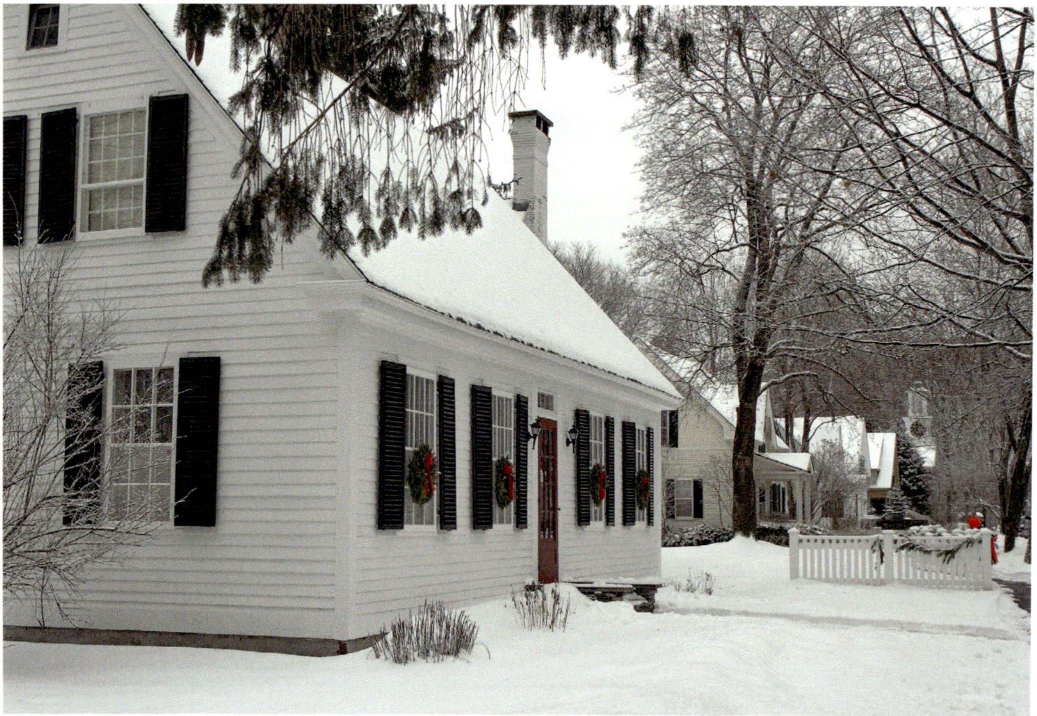

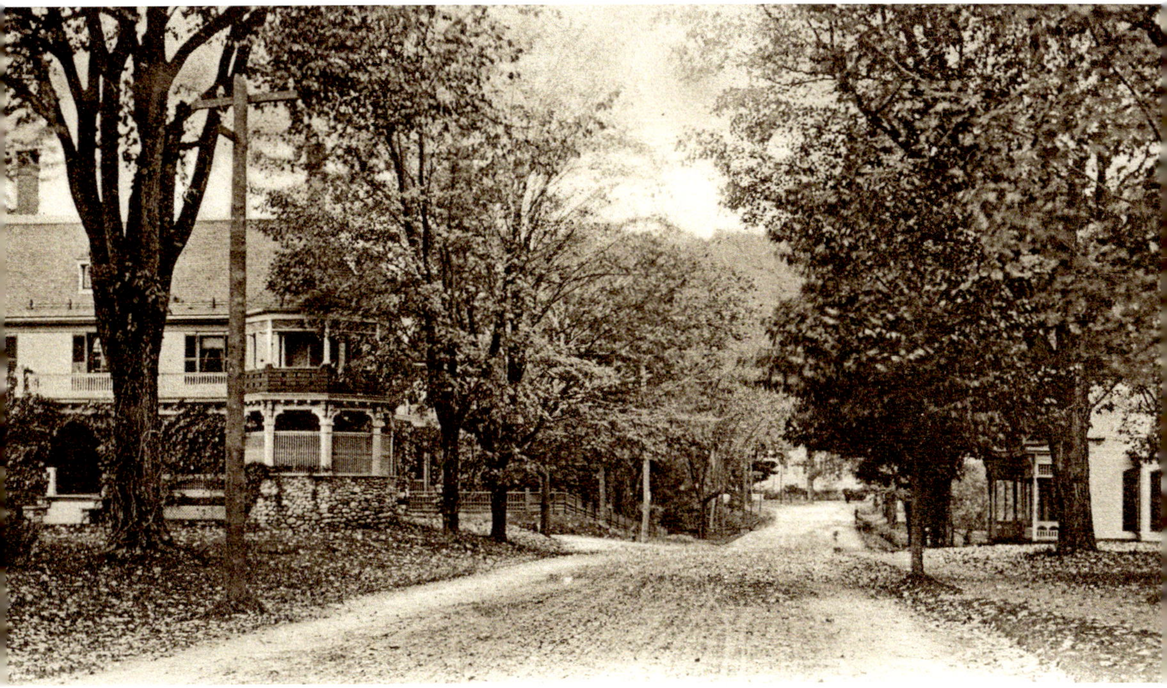

WHERE BOND AND PLEASANT STREETS MEET: The image above shows two stately homes in an era of elegance. Pleasant Street was established in 1807 and extends from Elm Street across from the Congregational Church to the eastern edge of Woodstock where it meets Hartland Hill. The view above is looking up Bond Street from Pleasant Street toward Central Street, and below, we are looking down Bond Street toward Pleasant Street.

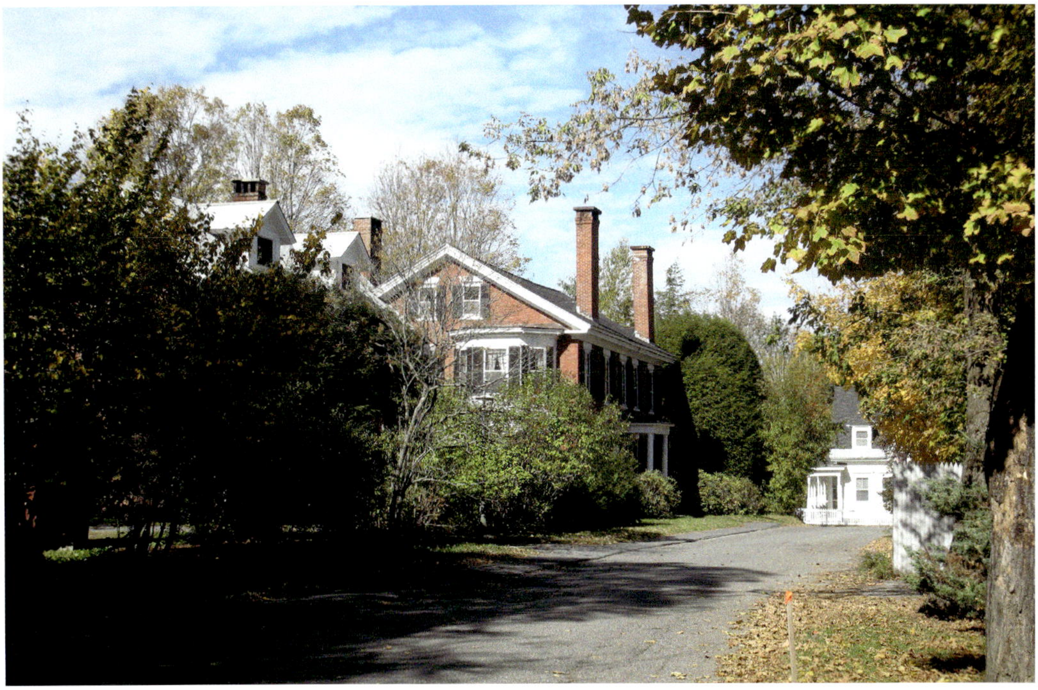

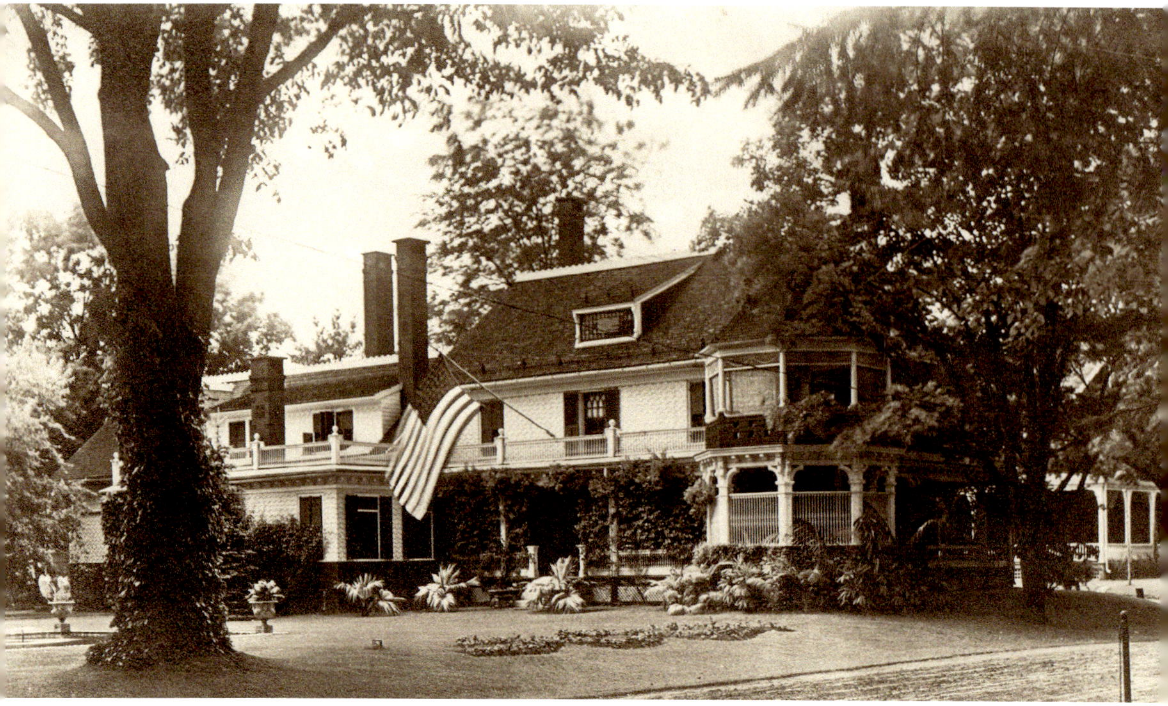

3 BOND STREET: A graceful brick and wood-framed Federal style home built in 1836, with later additions. It was the home of Ole Billings and family. Frank MacKenzie, one time Bridgewater Woolen Mill owner, also lived there. The turreted porch was removed long ago. The clapboard addition to the right was added at some point after the original brick structure was built.

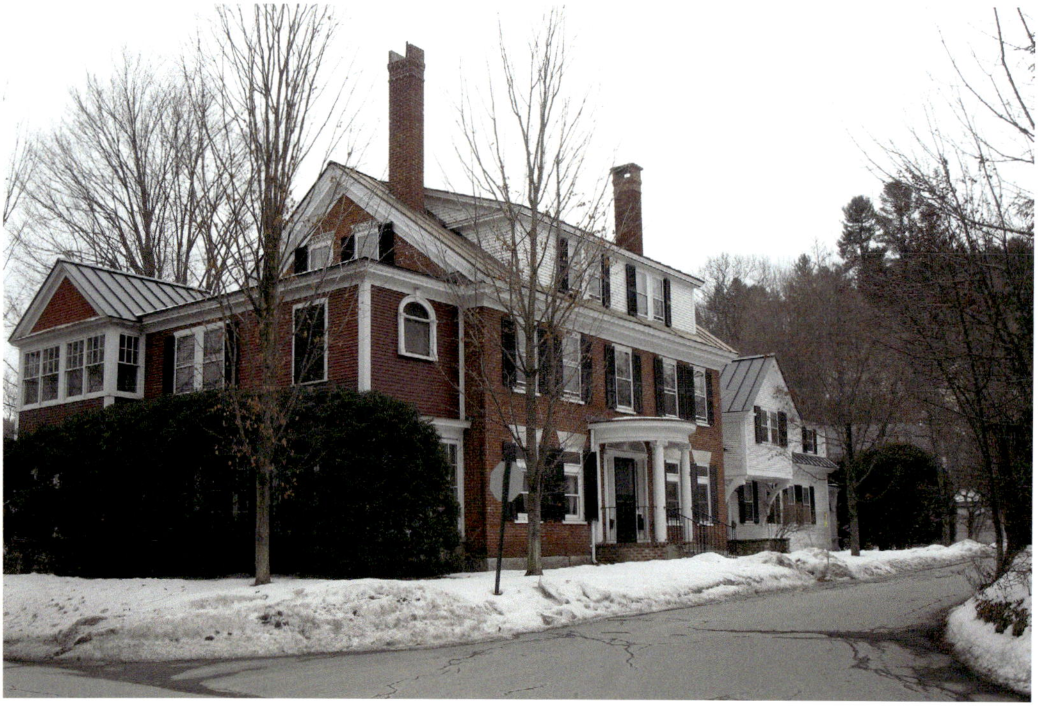

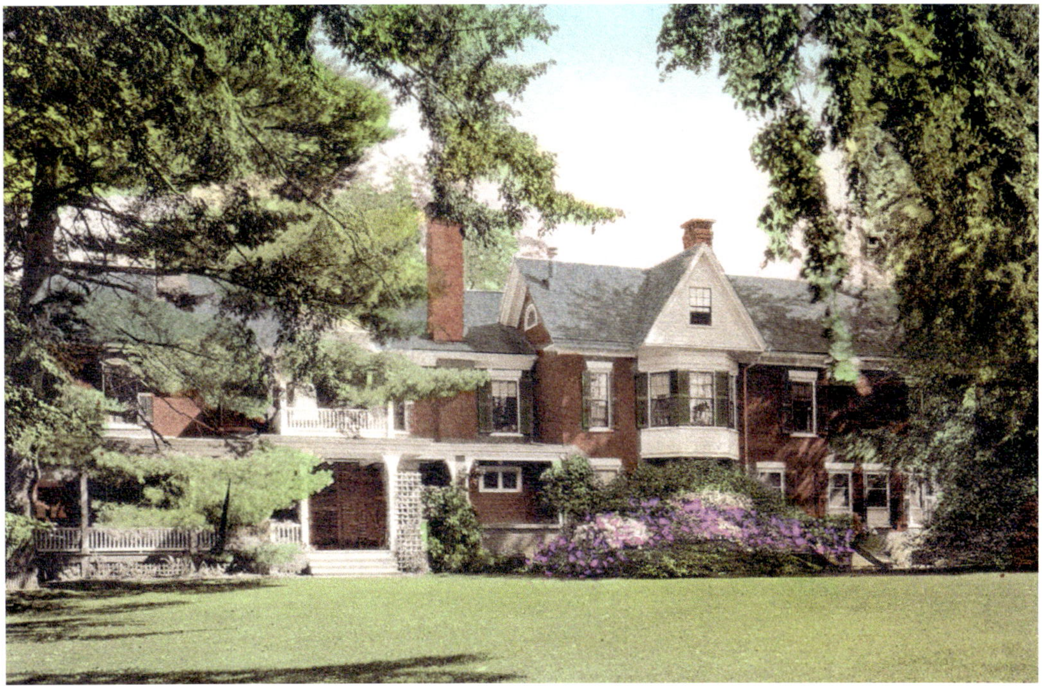

4 BOND STREET: Built in 1808, this home has been in the Billings family for generations. It is a fine Federal style brick home with a later wood-framed addition and a wonderful wraparound porch. It was first owned by Franklin Noble Billings, then Governor Franklin S. Billings. After that it became the home of Franklin S. Billings Jr., Speaker of the House of Representatives, Chief Justice of Vermont Supreme Court, Federal District Judge, and family.

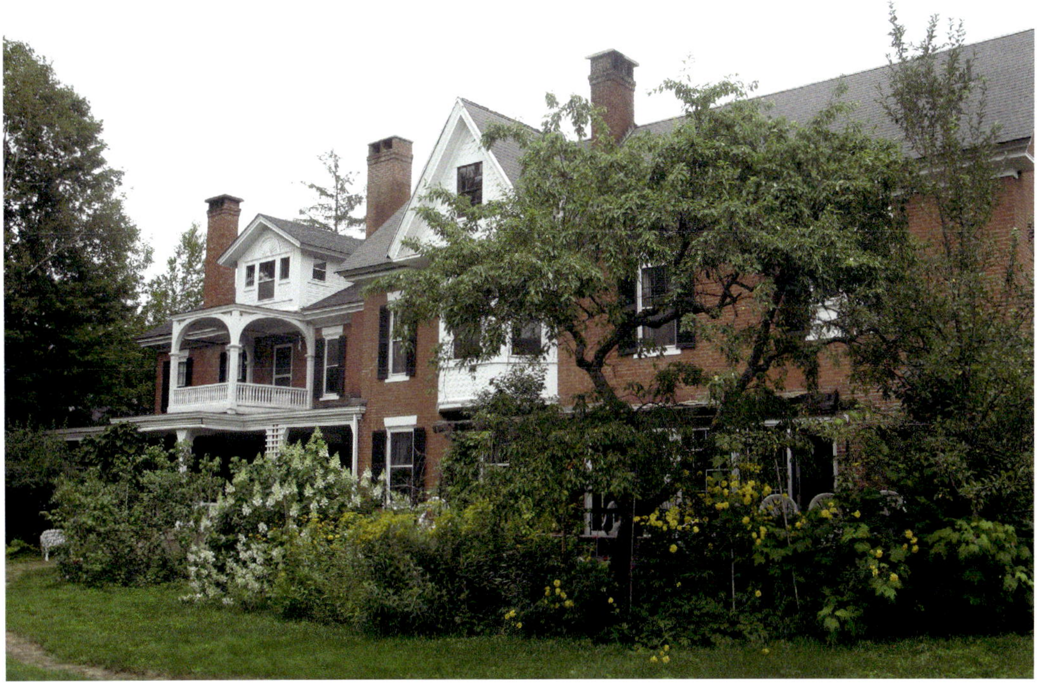

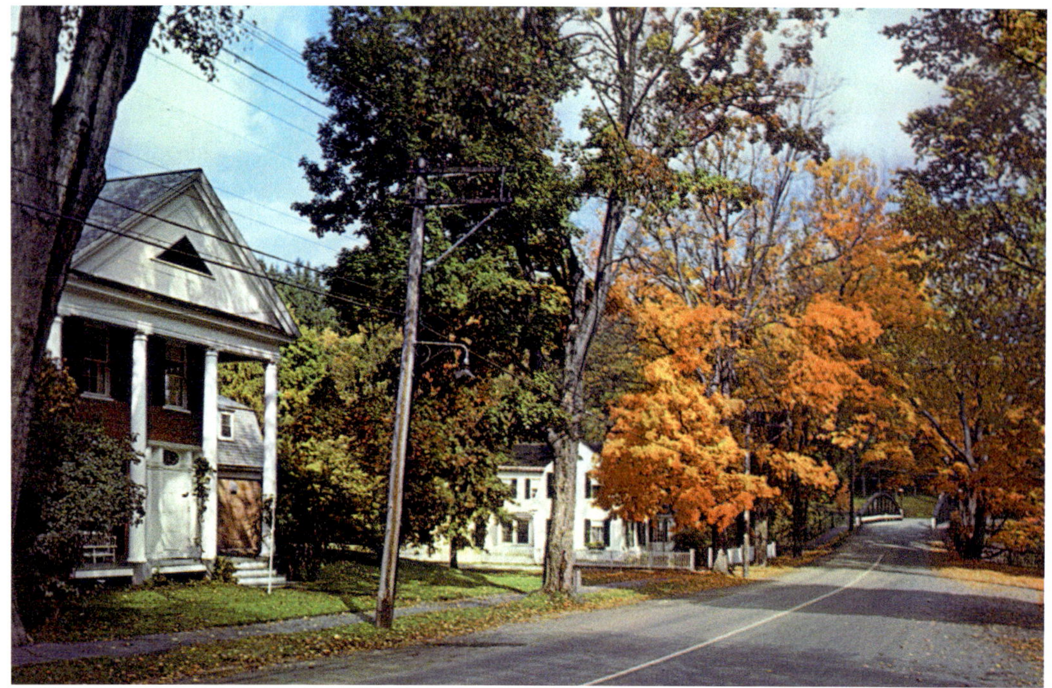

HOUSES ON ELM STREET: Elm Street has many beautiful homes built in the 1800s, still well-maintained. The Alwyn house above and below, a brick house with columns, was built in 1829. It's said that each column was carved from a single tree. A nearby wood-frame mansion with a distinctive rail around the top was built in 1809. Vermont's 34th Governor (1872-1874) Julius Converse, bought an 1821 mansion on Elm Street in 1856.

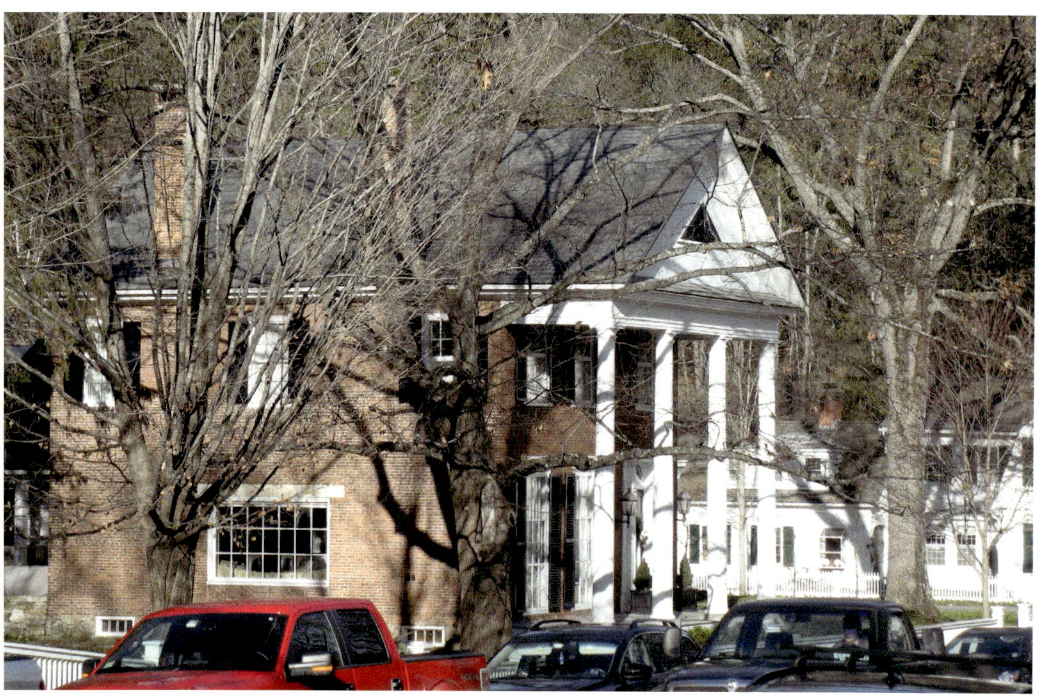

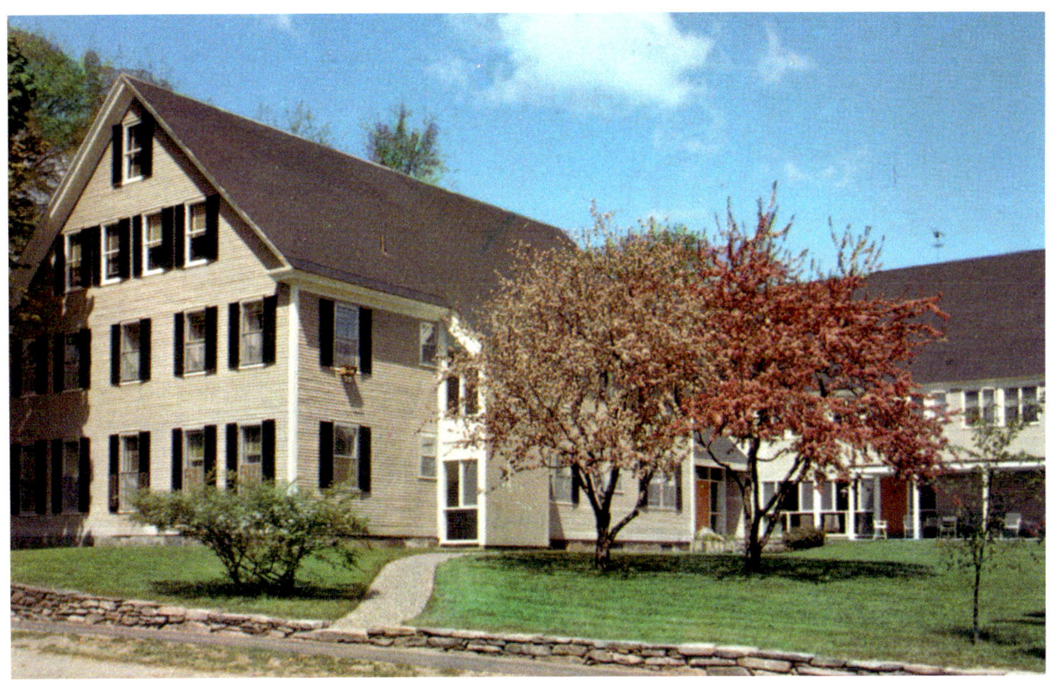

THE HOMESTEAD: This was originally housing for the Woodward Woolen Mill workers employed across the street. This property was donated to the town of Woodstock by Mrs. Edward D. Faulkner after her husband's death in 1929. The former mill housing shelters many of Woodstock's retired residents as an assisted living community, providing services for residents with intermediate needs. Besides the Homestead, Mrs. Faulkner provided funds and property for the Woodstock Recreation Center, Faulkner Park, and trails on Mt. Tom.

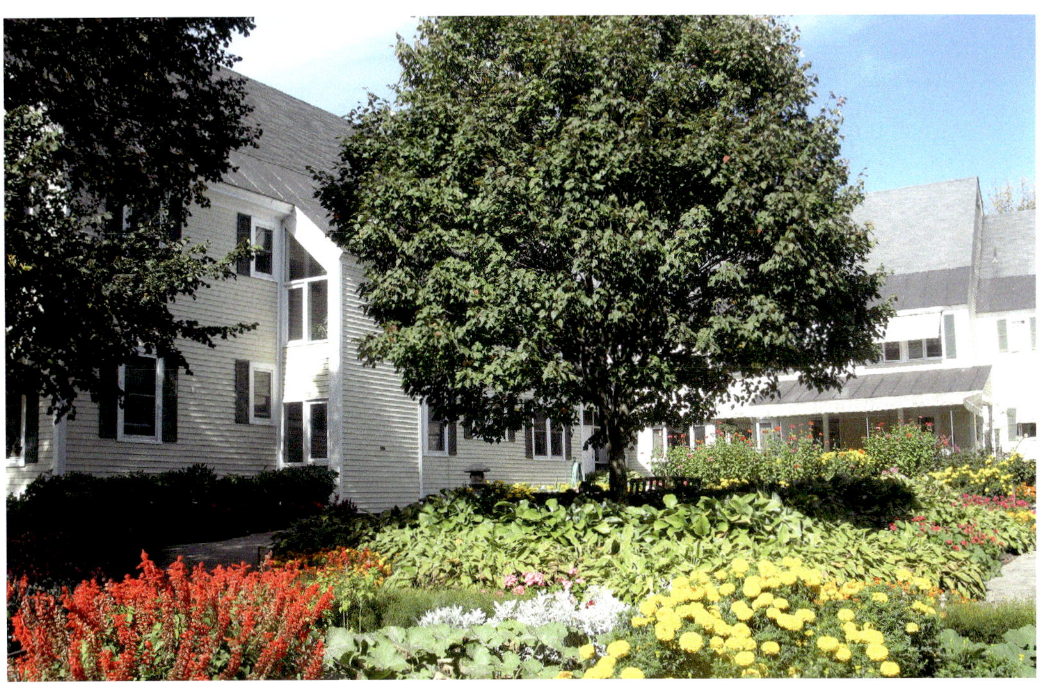

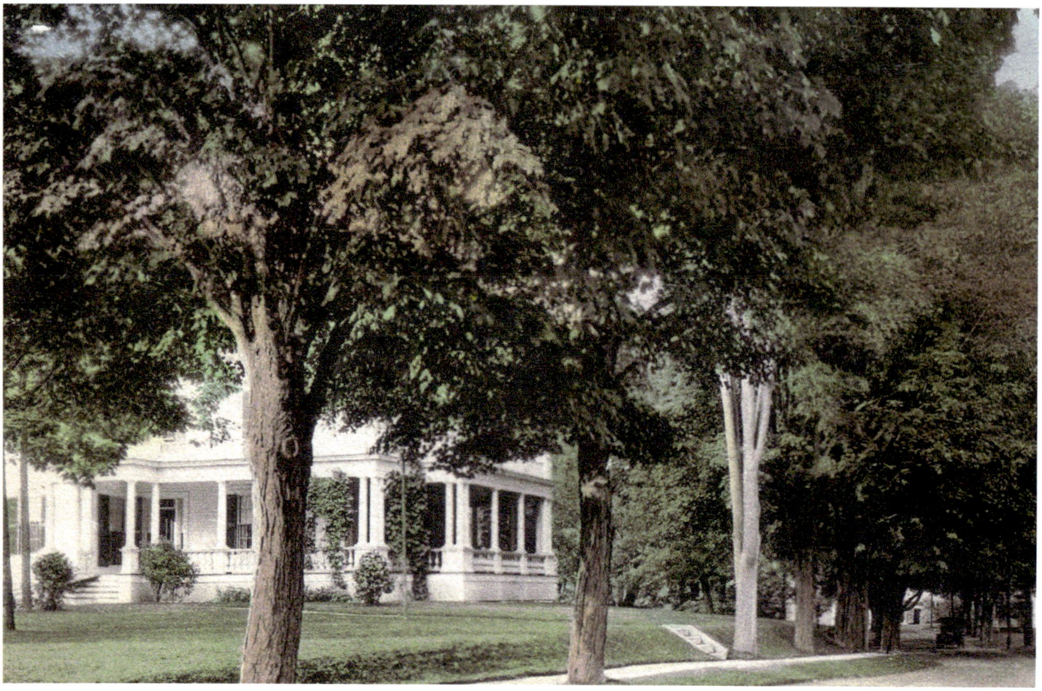

MOUNTAIN AVENUE: Located between North Park and River Streets, Mountain Avenue, formerly Union Street, is home to Middle Bridge. To me, walking along Mountain Avenue, in many ways, feels like strolling back through time. When I enter Middle Bridge from busy North Park Street and emerge out the other side, it is as if suddenly, everything has slowed down. The genteel homes and tree-lined streets there are inviting and picturesque.

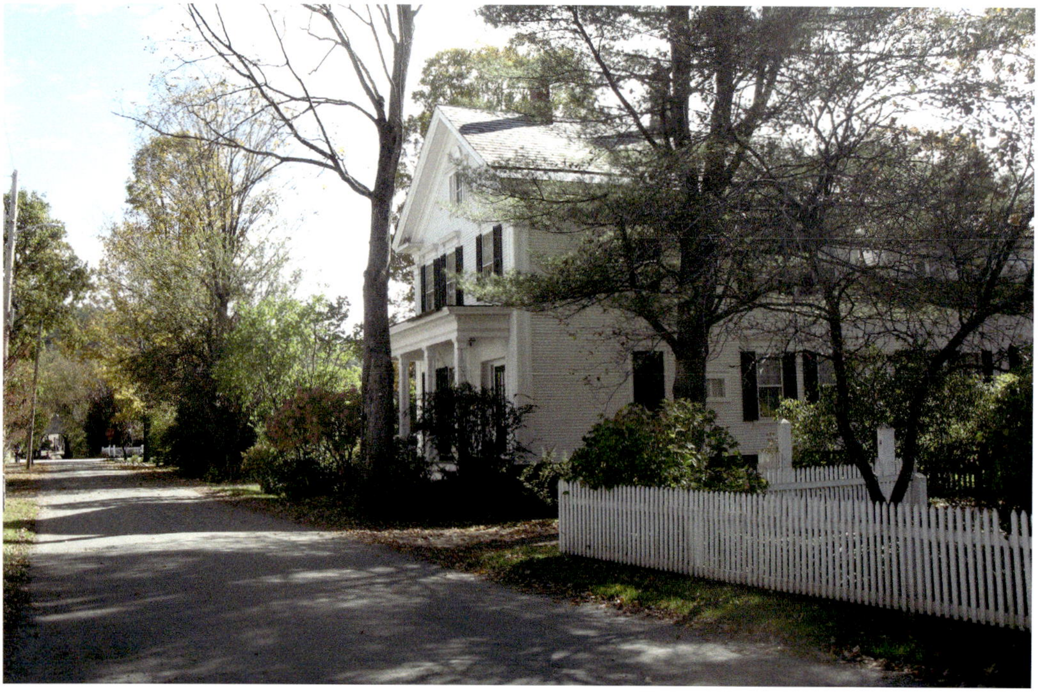

Faith

Churches surround The Green like comforting compass points: the Congregational to the north, the Christian to the east, the Catholic to the south and the Episcopalian to the west. Three current churches detailed below, and the former Christian Church, boast bells cast in the Paul Revere foundry in Boston, Massachusetts. The dates those bells were installed and their weights are as follows: The Congregational Church bell, 1818, and 711 pounds; the Episcopal Church bell, 1827, and 695 pounds; and the Christian Church bell, shown below, 1828, and 872 pounds. No equivalent data is available for the Paul Revere bell at the North Chapel, Unitarian Universalist Church. The Woodstock Inn also possesses two Paul Revere bells, bringing the Woodstock total of Paul Revere Bells to six!

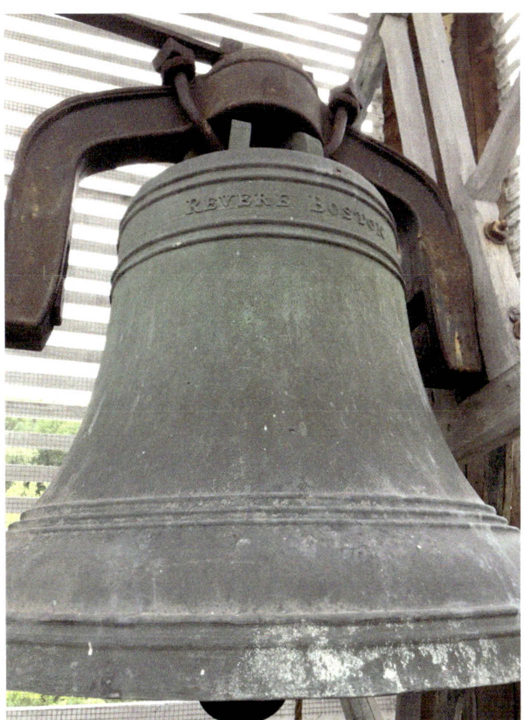

CHRISTIAN CHURCH: Built of brick on Pleasant Street in 1827. It remained an active church in Woodstock until the membership fell too low to maintain the church. At that time, the church was deeded to the Masons of Woodstock, becoming Masonic Lodge #31 in 1949.

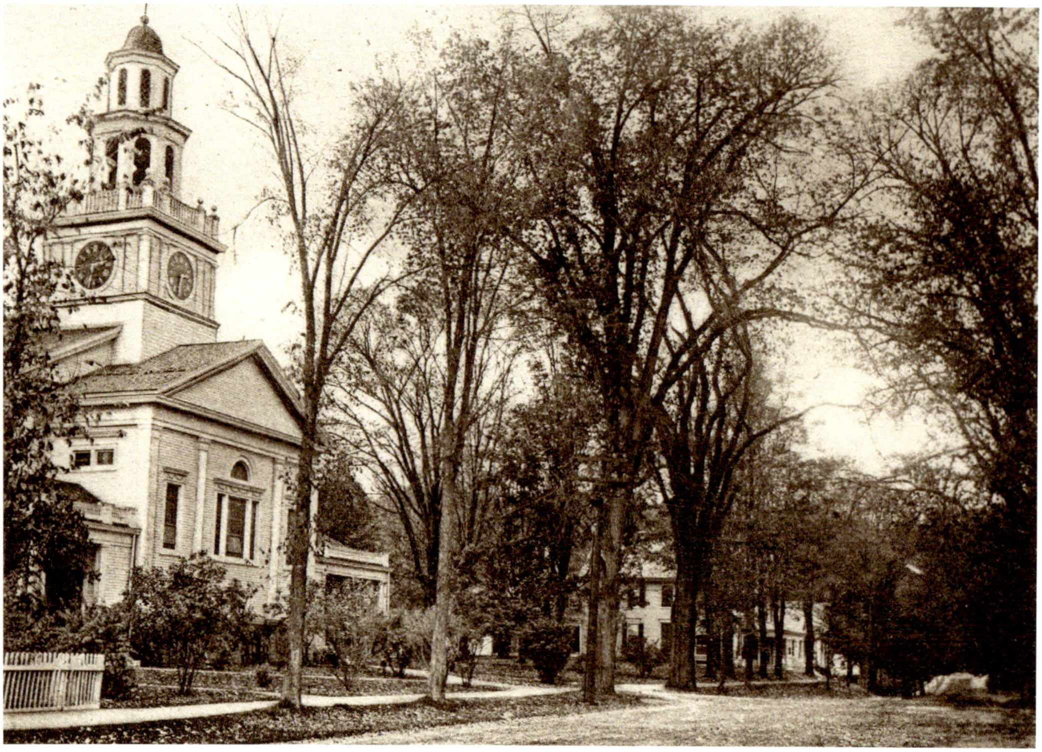

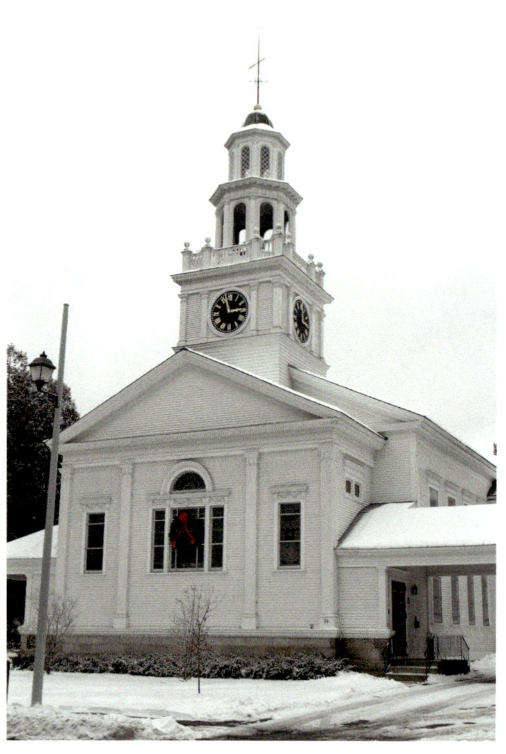

CONGREGATIONAL CHURCH: Also known as the White Meeting House, it was built in 1807. The white-clapboarded, wood-framed Romanesque style building nestles under the protective shoulder of Mount Tom. In the 1880s it was remodeled and the Billings chapel was added. In 1950 it was remodeled again. This church supported abolitionist beliefs long before the Civil War. The church sits prominently in the center of Elm Street and the head of Pleasant Street. The Paul Revere bell is displayed on the covered porch.

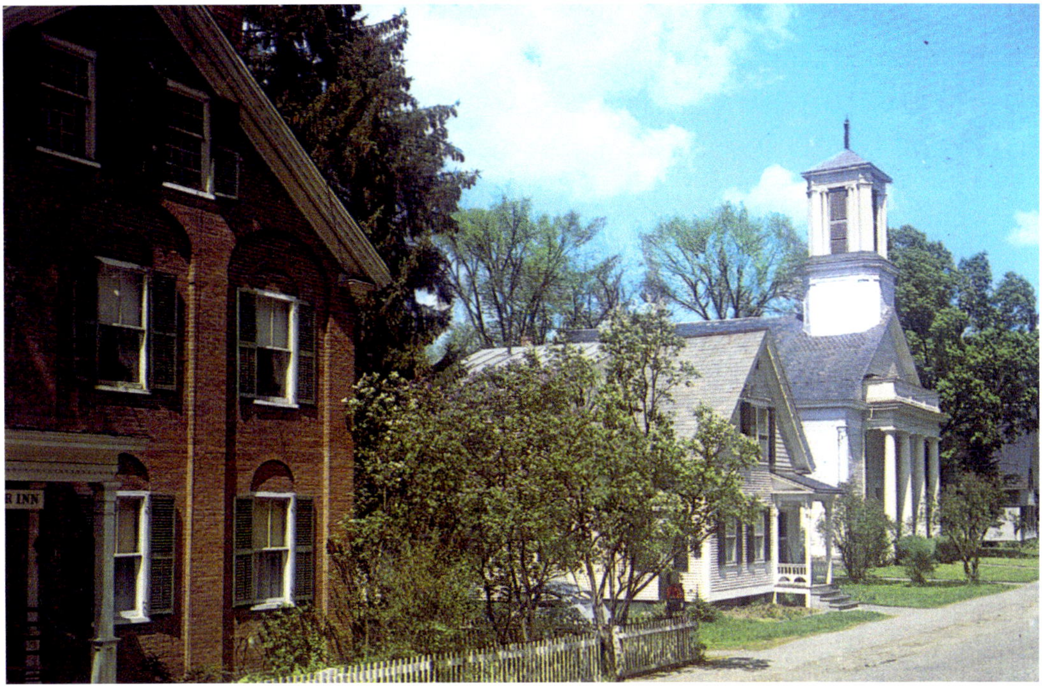

UNITARIAN UNIVERSALIST CHURCH: Also called the North Chapel, it was organized in Woodstock in 1786. At that time, many members of the Baptist and Congregational Church began to attend Unitarian Universalist services. By 1834, Unitarian Universalist members dwindled to near zero. New energy, however, saved the congregation in 1835 and the current North Chapel church was built. This church contains the largest of the Paul Revere bells in Woodstock.

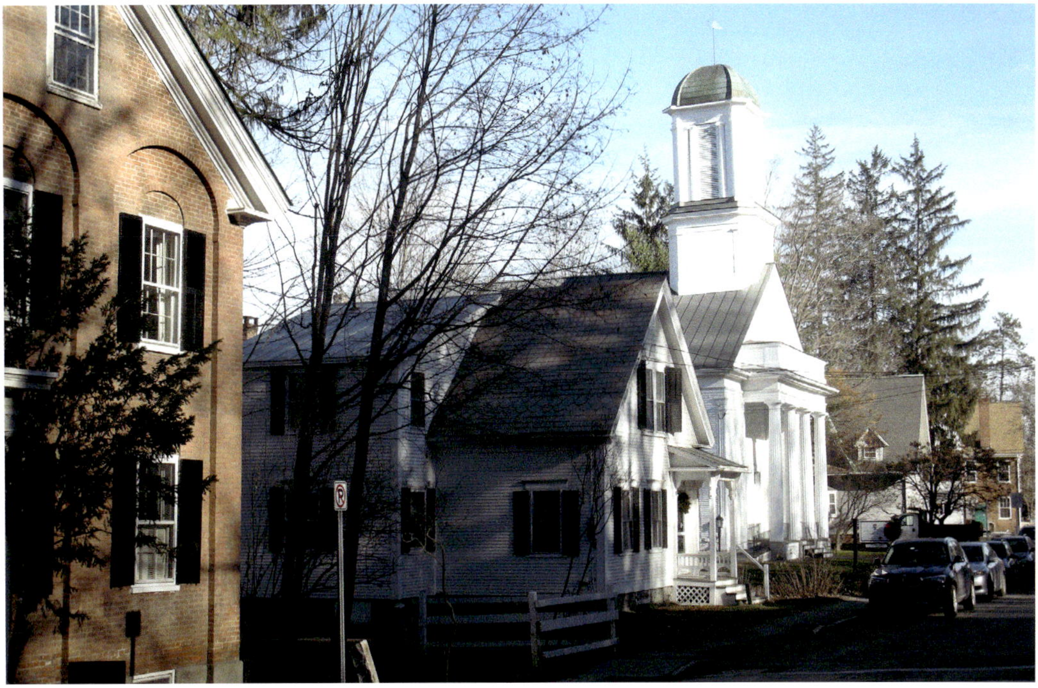

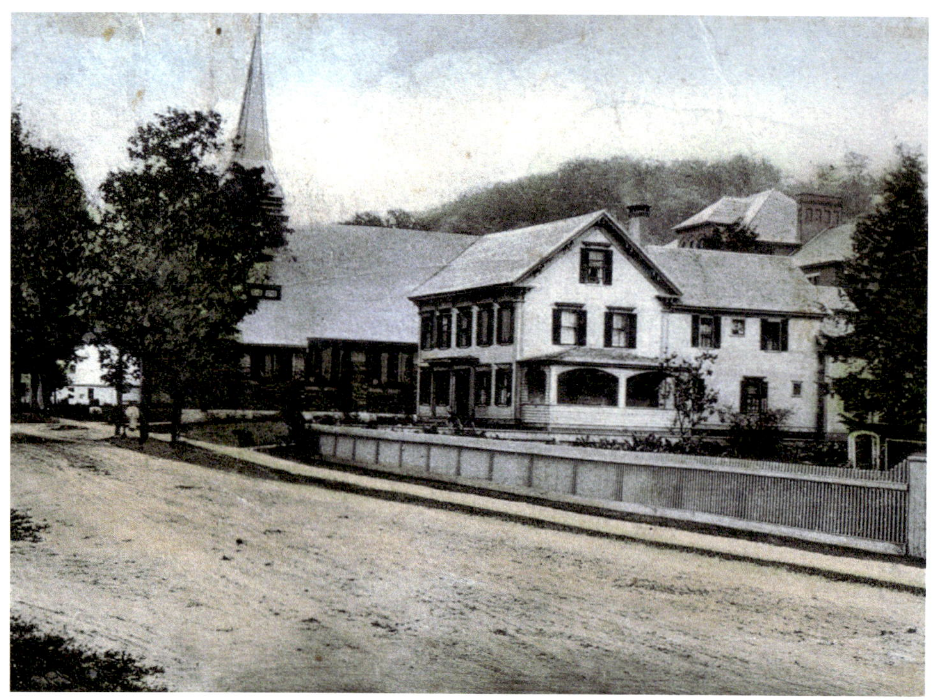

CATHOLIC CHURCH AND PARISH HOUSE: Located on South Street, the first Catholic Our Lady of the Snows Church in Woodstock was built of wood in 1895. It was destroyed by fire in 1903. The entire community rallied and by the next year, 1904, a new church had been built at the same site of enduring stone. The stone church remains, as well as the original Parrish House located next to it.

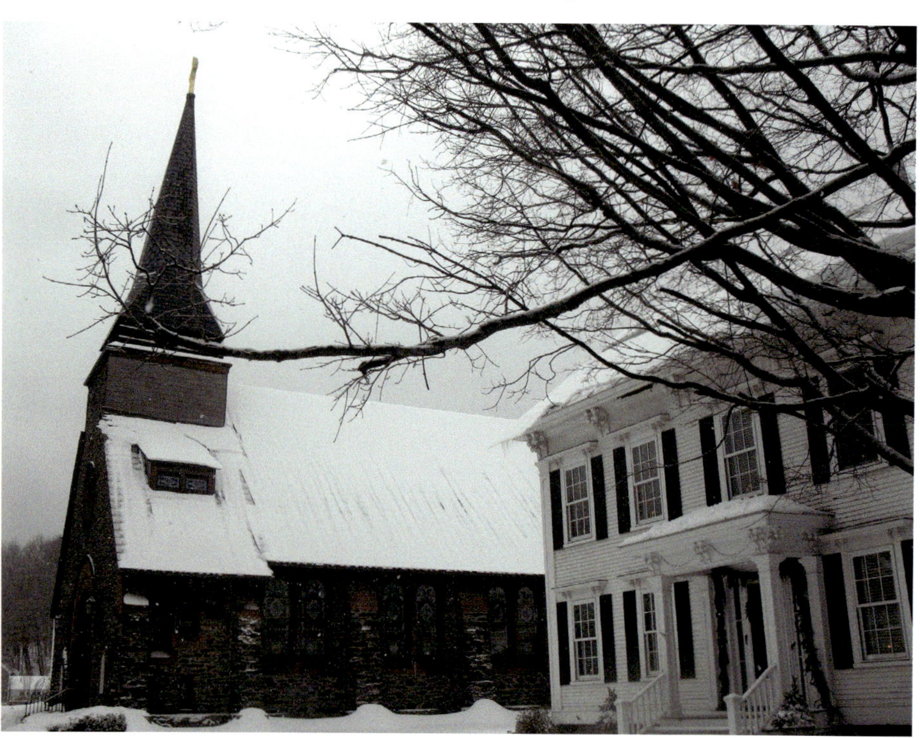

Recreation and Natural Resources

Due to the extreme generosity of several Woodstock residents, Woodstock has a great variety of recreation options. Woodstock is blessed with abundant natural resources. Mount Tom and Mount Peg have been the source of hiking trails for numerous years. Sledding, skiing, and sleigh rides compliment Woodstock's winter history. In the summer, Woodstock has golf, swimming, biking, ball games, fishing, and boating. In 1895 Henry H. Vail donated property to Woodstock's citizens, now called Vail Field, where ball games are common. Marianne Faulkner donated the remains of a woolen mill for the town's recreation department and the Marsh-Billings-Rockefeller Mansion grounds, now a National Park, offers miles of trails.

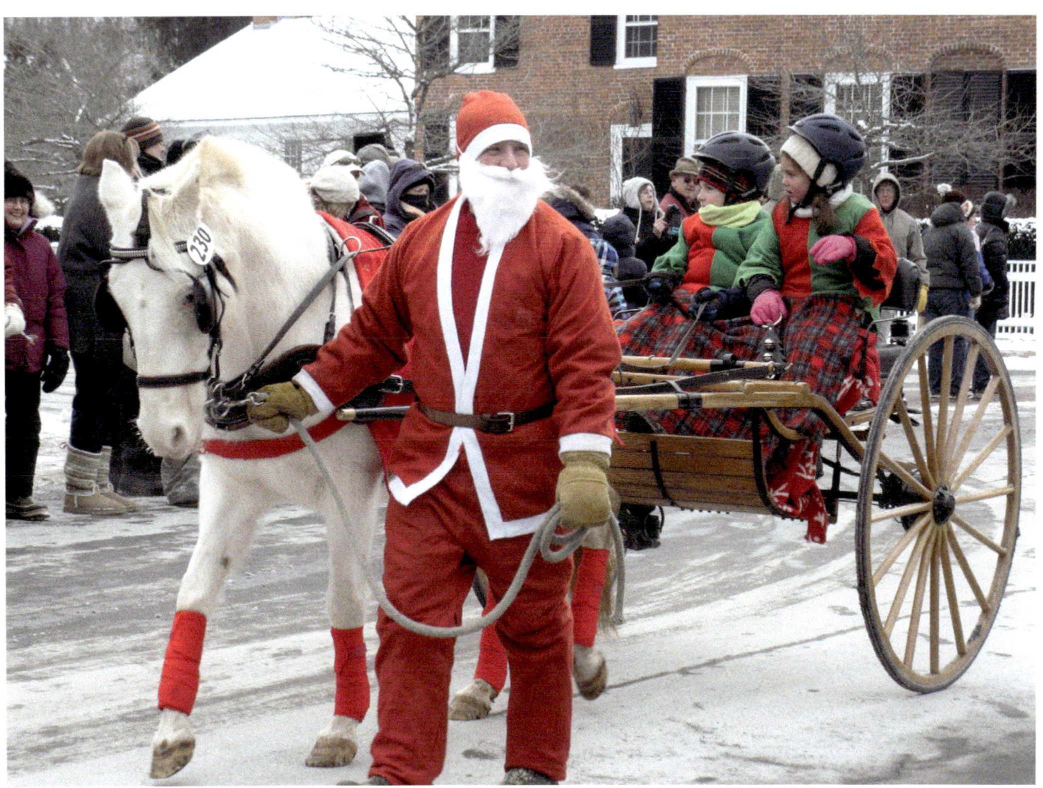

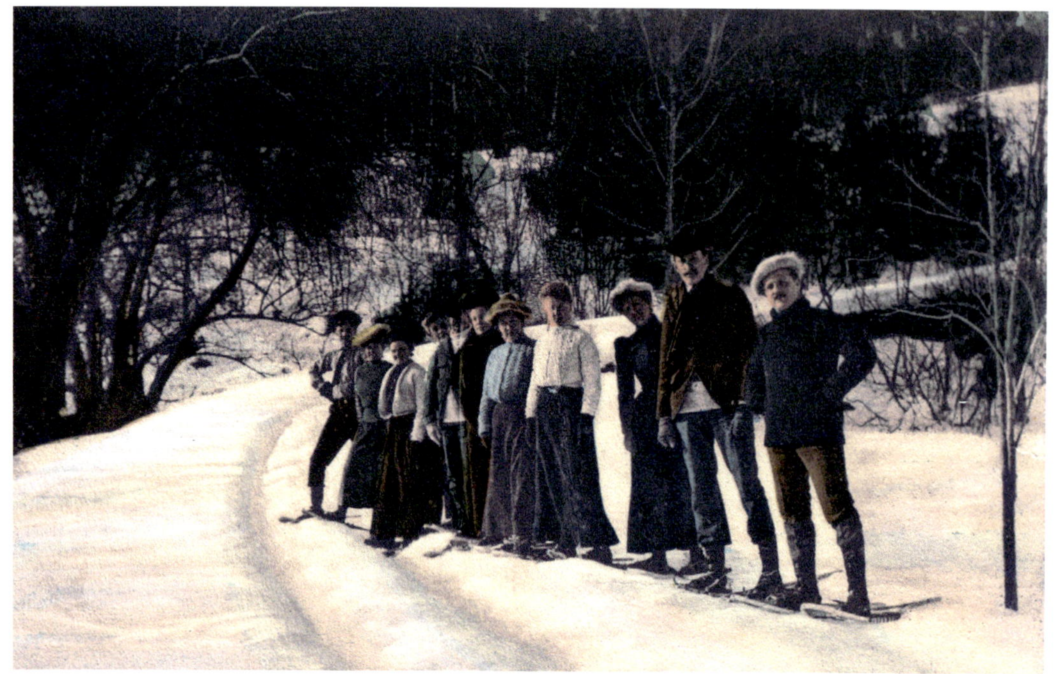

WINTER RECREATION IN WOODSTOCK: It's just part of the lifestyle here in that season. Northland skis were sold and repaired at Gillingham's and Woodstock claims the first ski tow in the United States. The Woodstock Inn sponsored sleighing, tobogganing, snowshoeing as above, and skating parties. Their stables held several horses for the coaches and sleighs. Sleigh rides are still offered locally and the village hosts an annual Wassail Weekend every December, with indoor and outdoor activities including a parade, as below.

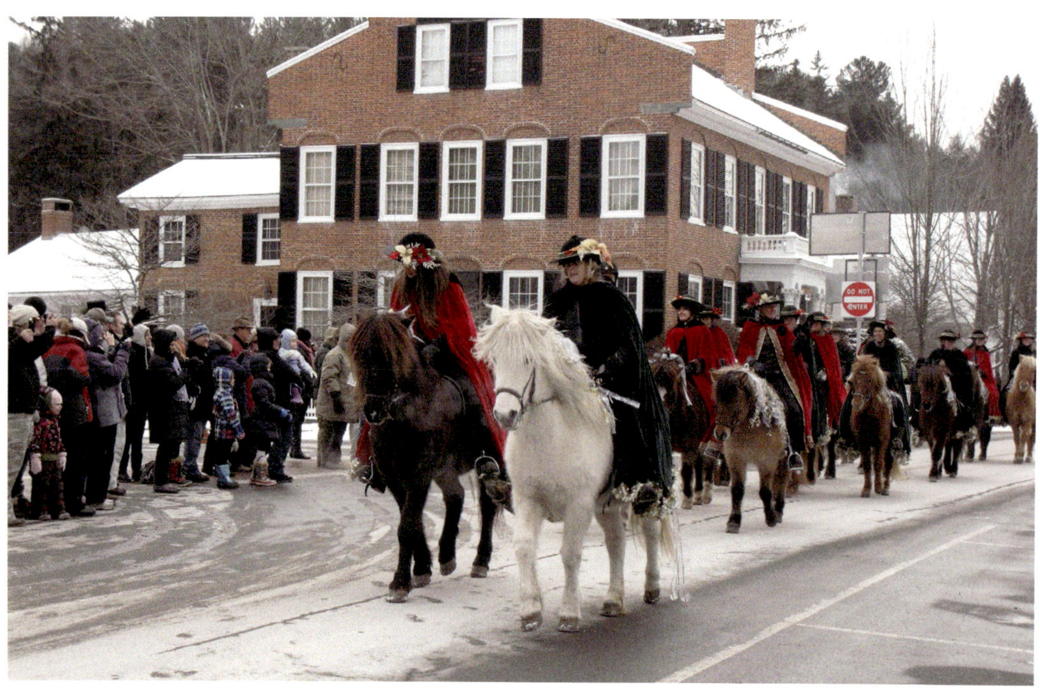

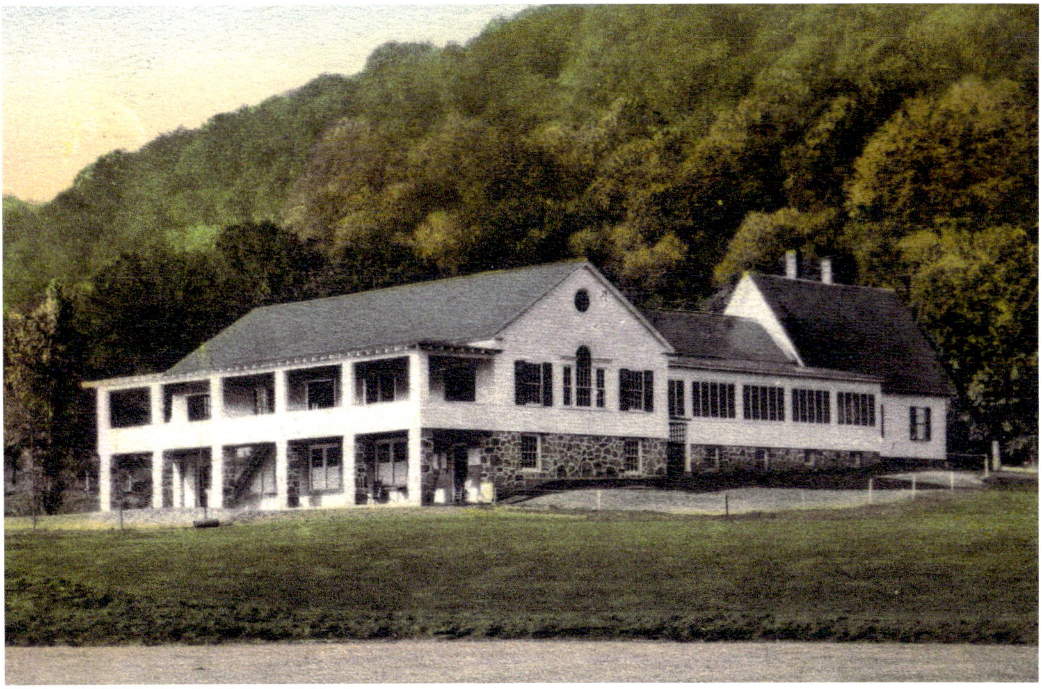

WOODSTOCK COUNTRY CLUB AND CLUB HOUSE: These are part of the Woodstock Inn property and are located just a couple of minutes from the inn, on the road to South Woodstock. There was a nice 9-hole course for years, the first golf link opened in 1896, and then Laurance S. Rockefeller purchased the club in 1961. Rockefeller hired Trent Jones to design an 18-hole course which remains very popular and challenging to this day.

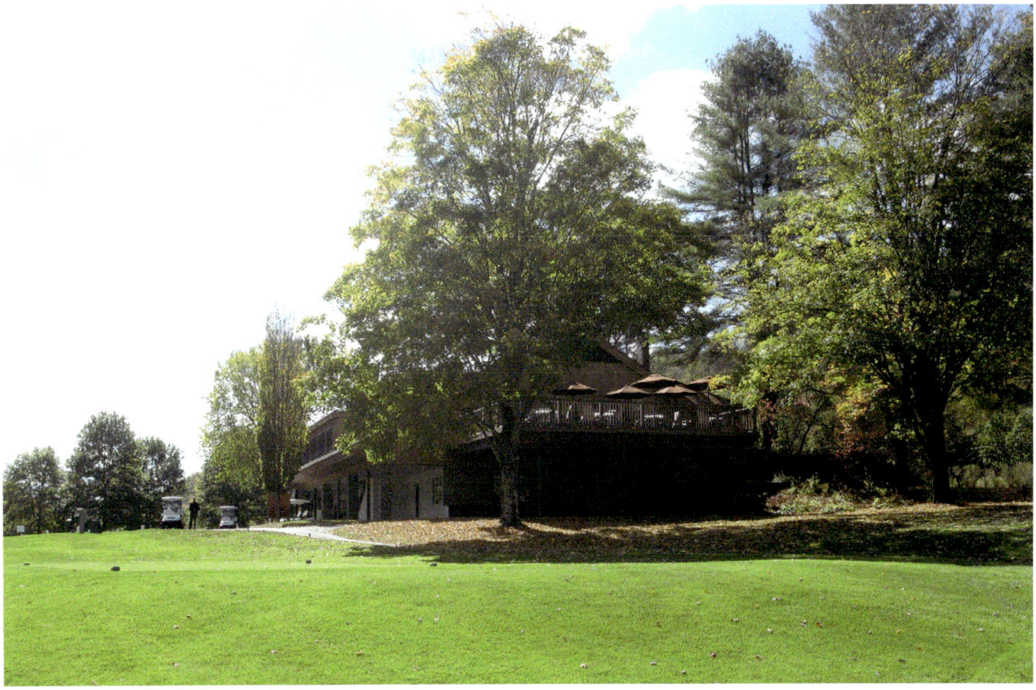

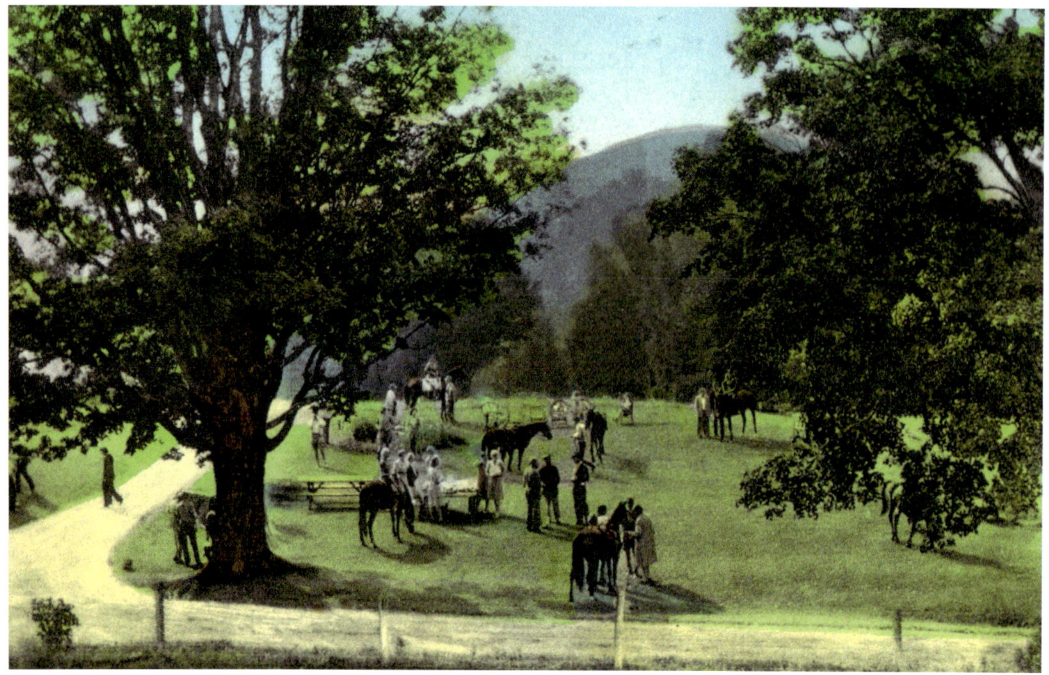

MOUNT TOM AT 1,340 FEET AND MOUNT PEG AT 1,080 FEET: These mountains are visually prominent from most of Woodstock. Charles Marsh and later Frederick Billings, worked to reforest the mountains and create several miles of footpaths and carriage roads around their sides. Pastures at the base of Mount Tom above, were popular picnic spots where visitors and locals alike spent leisure time. The Pogue, below, is a pond on Mount Tom that has featured in local lore and a movie as well. Mysteriously, no one seems to know for sure, how Mt. Tom and Mt. Peg were given their names.

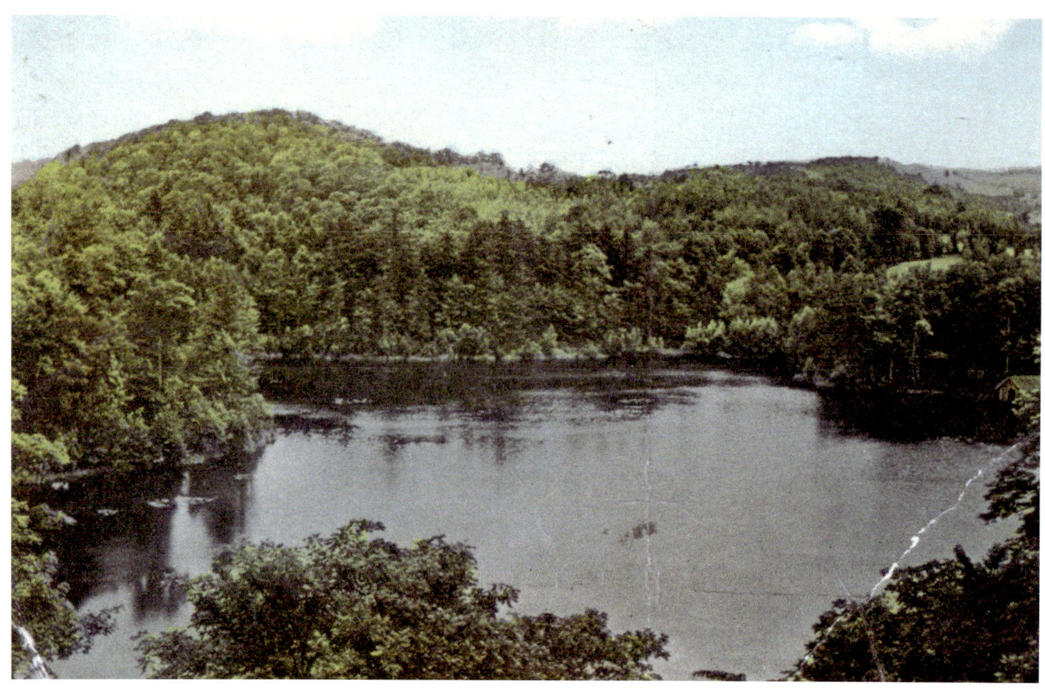

Waterways and Bridges

Woodstock is divided, or joined, depending upon your perspective, by the Ottauquechee River. A community thus situated, must employ bridges or some other connection, to work as a cohesive whole. Woodstock has turned this situation to her advantage with a series of bridges, both elegant and practical, crisscrossing her banks. The views of, and from, the waterways and bridges in this region, can be breathtaking.

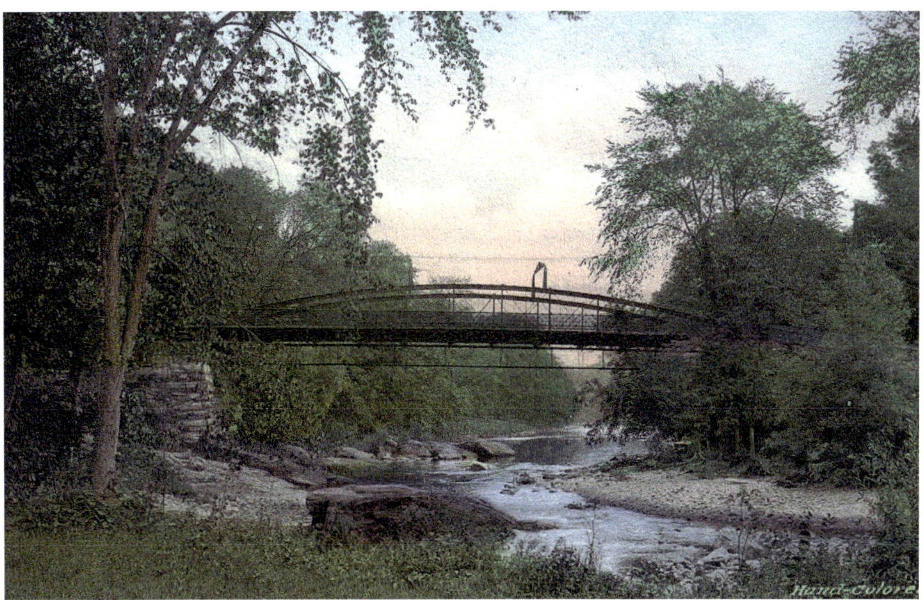

Elm Street Bridge: This bridge, pictured above, as seen from down river, is a real survivor. Originally, it was a covered wooden bridge. That was replaced in 1870 with one of cast and wrought iron using a Parker pony truss design. It crosses the Ottauquechee River at Elm Street. This bridge was rehabilitated in 1900 and 1980 due to safety concerns. It endures in the same location, sturdy and safe.

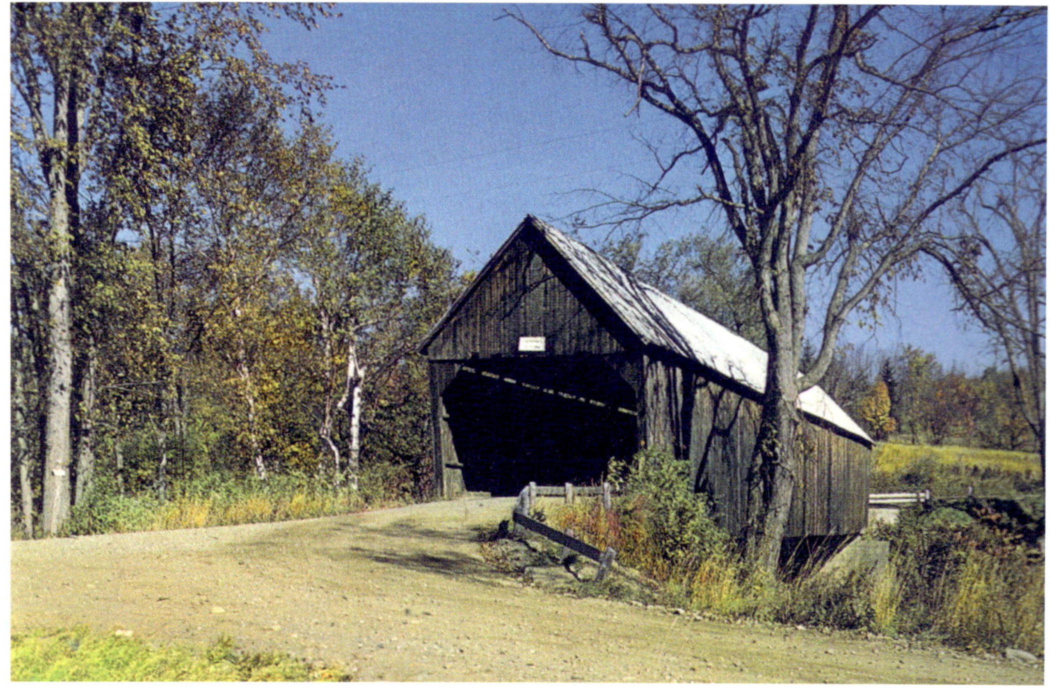

LINCOLN COVERED BRIDGE: Located off Route 4, near Lincoln Corners in West Woodstock. The bridge was built of wood in 1877, featuring a unique Pratt truss-arch system and spans 136 feet. It was renovated in 1947 and again after sustaining serious damage during tropical storm Irene in 2011. West Woodstock is a hamlet of Woodstock Village, where the local Union Junior and Senior High Schools, as well as *The Vermont Standard* newspaper, and some agriculturally-related businesses are located.

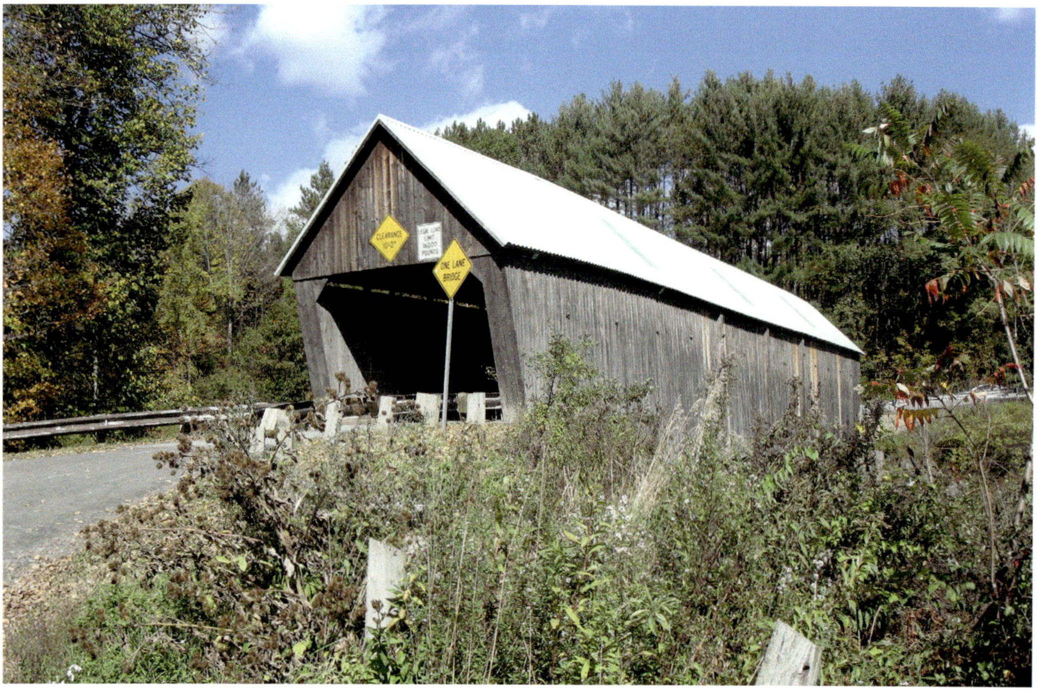

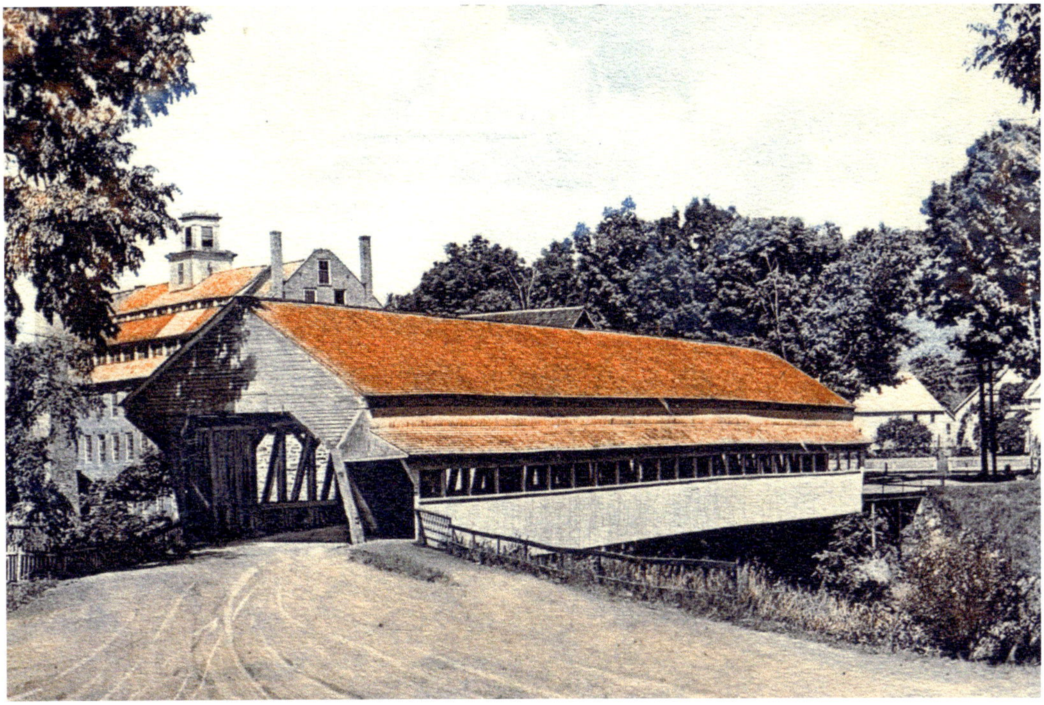

UPPER BRIDGE: Originally built as a wooden covered bridge, as seen above, it's been replaced with steel construction, below. Note the covered walkway built into the wooden design, much as the current Middle Bridge employs today. In the vintage image, the woolen mill is clearly seen in the background. The remains of that mill have been transformed as the Woodstock Recreation Center and Little Theatre.

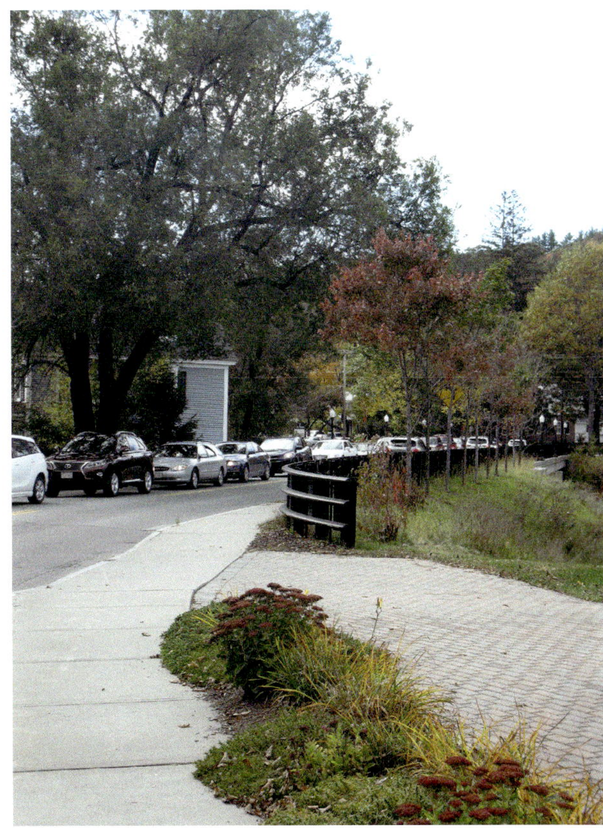

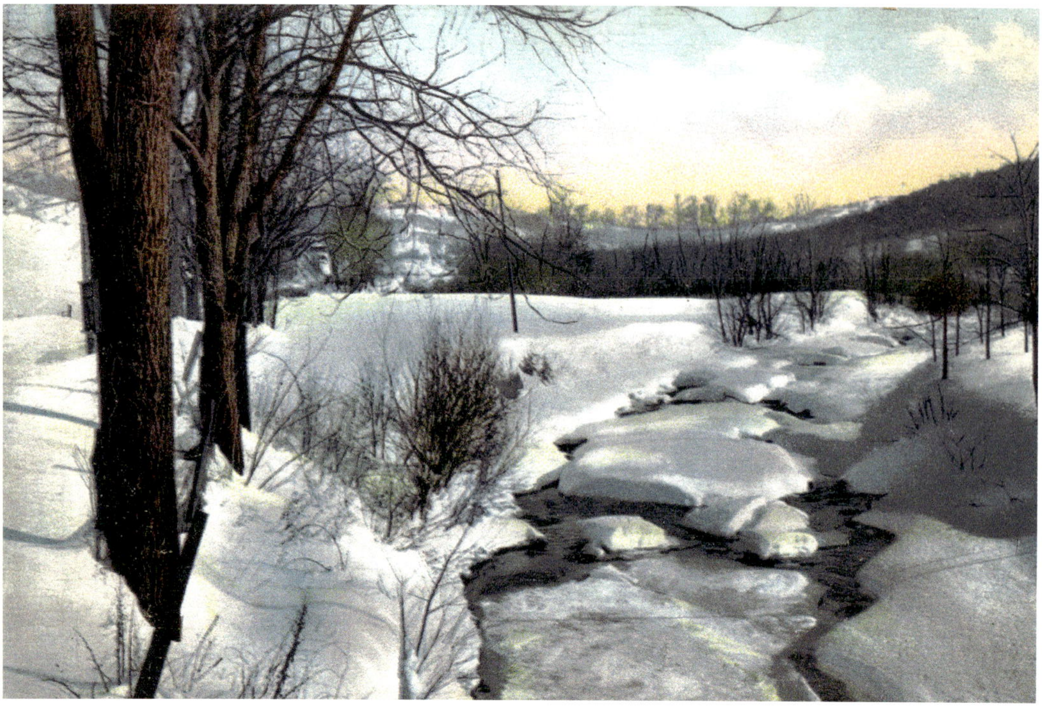

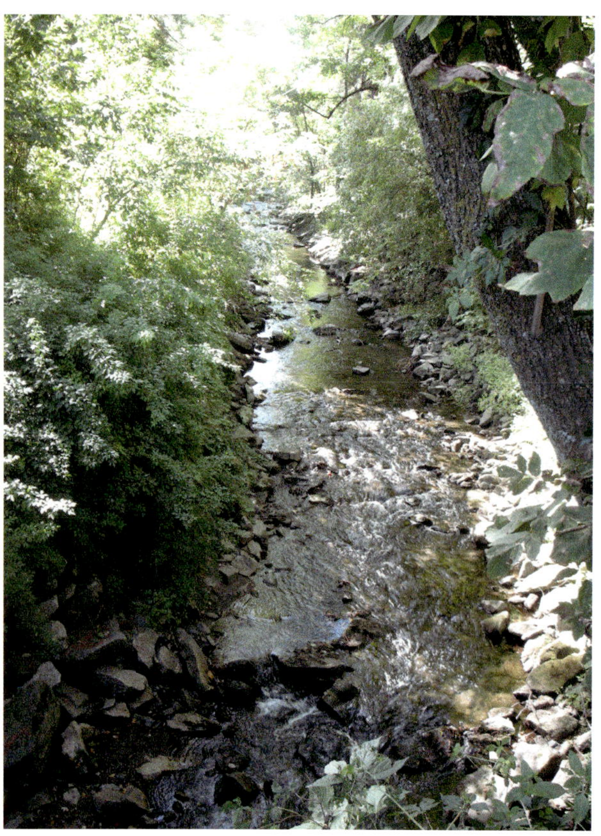

KEDRON BROOK: The Kendron flows through Woodstock where it was once a major source of water power for several mills along its course. One such is the Linseed Oil Mill where the canal can be seen from the bridge beside the former stone mill building on Central Street. The Kedron, seen above and below in different seasons, is nine miles long. The brook's source lies in Reading Gulf where it flows north through South Woodstock, then to Woodstock where it merges with the Ottauquechee River near Billings Farm.

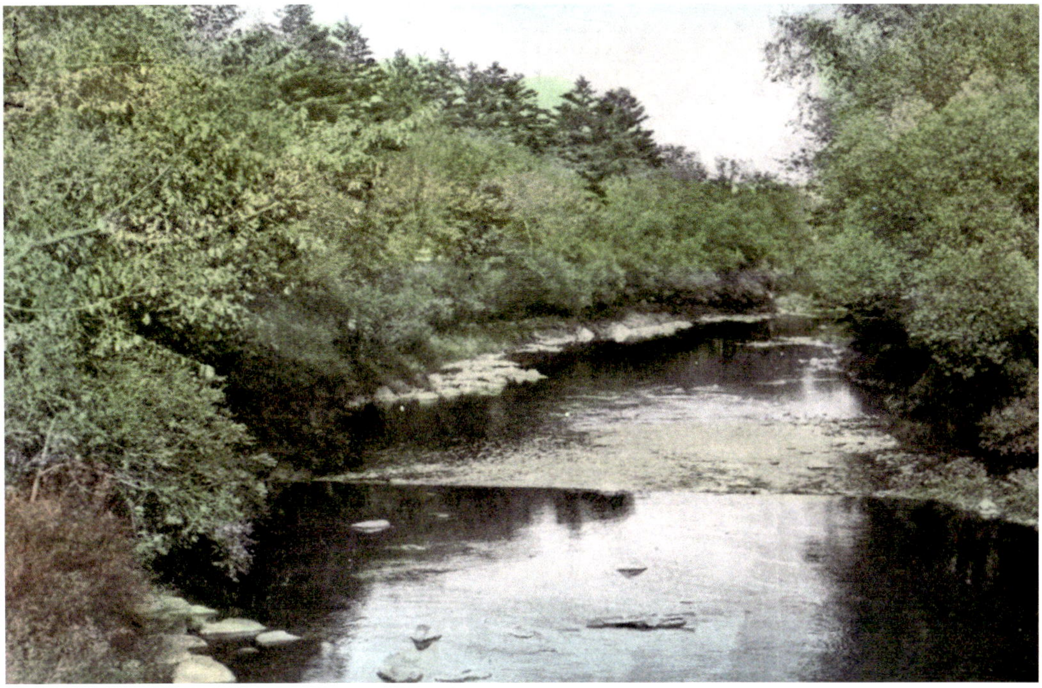

Ottauquechee River: It is a tributary of the Connecticut River and totals forty-one miles long. Its headwaters are in the town of Killington, Vermont, northwest of Woodstock. It flows through Bridgewater, Woodstock and Quechee, joining the Connecticut River in Hartland, Vermont. Tropical Storm Irene in 2011, wrought considerable damage to the Ottauquechee River and the townships along its banks. Efforts to re-establish and rebuild the river banks and properties along them will continue for several years.

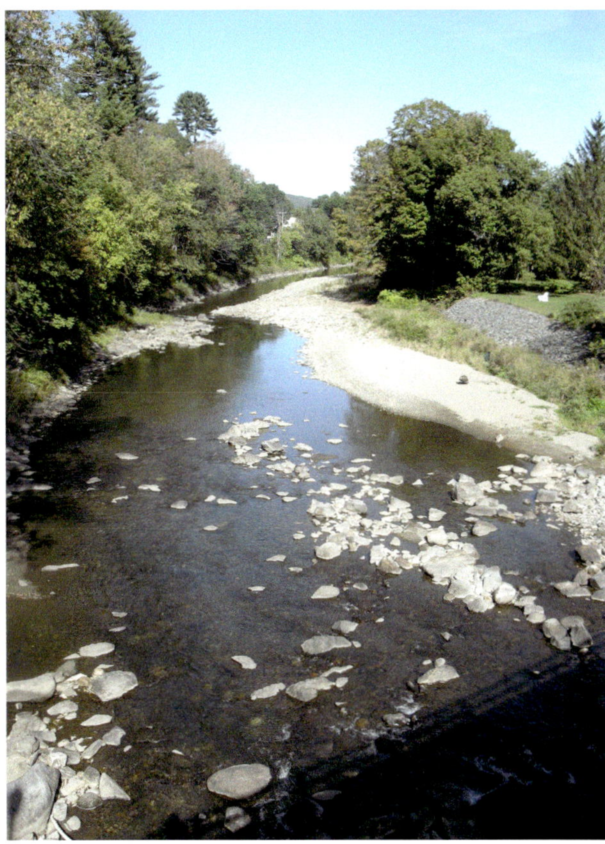

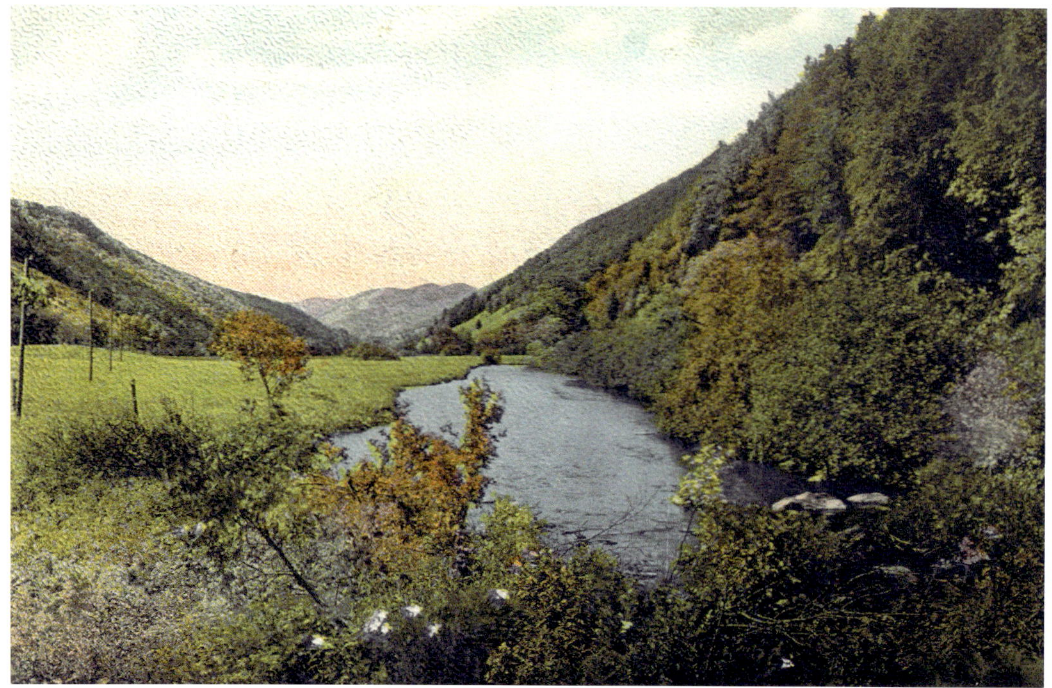

Ottauquechee Valley in Windsor County: This vale cradles the Ottauquechee River. In Woodstock, Mount Tom and Mount Peg act as stoic guardians of the village in the valley. The roads along the river's course afford some of the most alluring scenery in the northeast. In the past, towns within this valley sprang up to take advantage of the water power and the fertile valley soil along the banks of the Ottauquechee River.

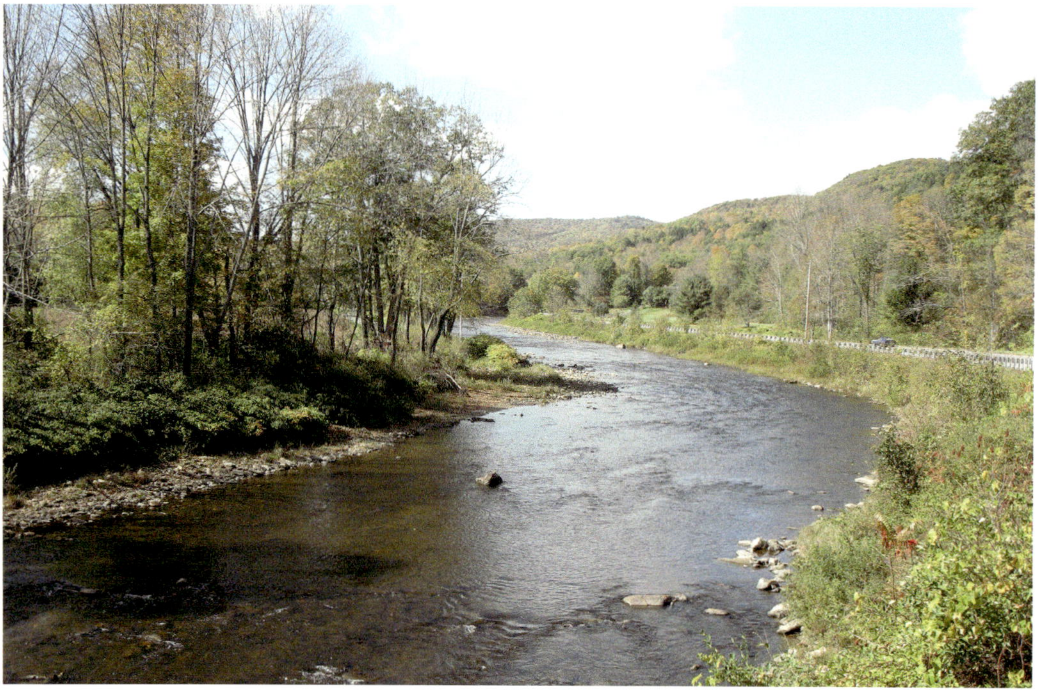

MUNICIPAL

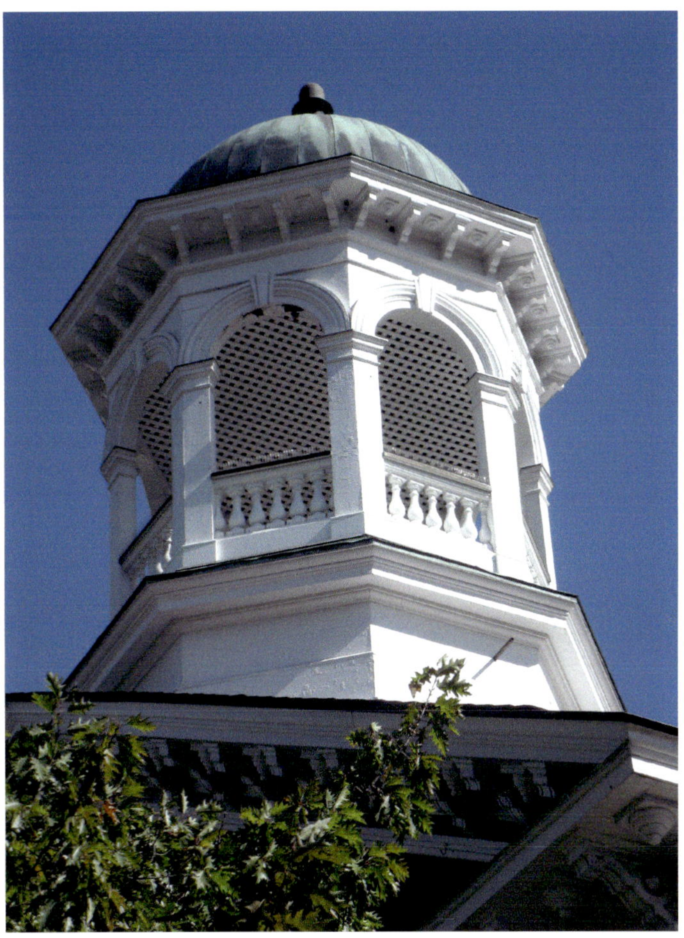

WOODSTOCK: Both the shire town of Windsor County, Vermont, and the village the town encompasses, are named Woodstock. The technicalities between the town and village are not apparent to the casual visitor and to avoid undo confusion, I will just refer to the region as Woodstock. As such, it holds some Windsor County facilities such as the court house and the former county jail. Some of the municipal buildings, such as the town hall and library, fall into other sections of this book and a few more are collected here. Above is the cupola of the Windsor County Court House, located "on" The Green.

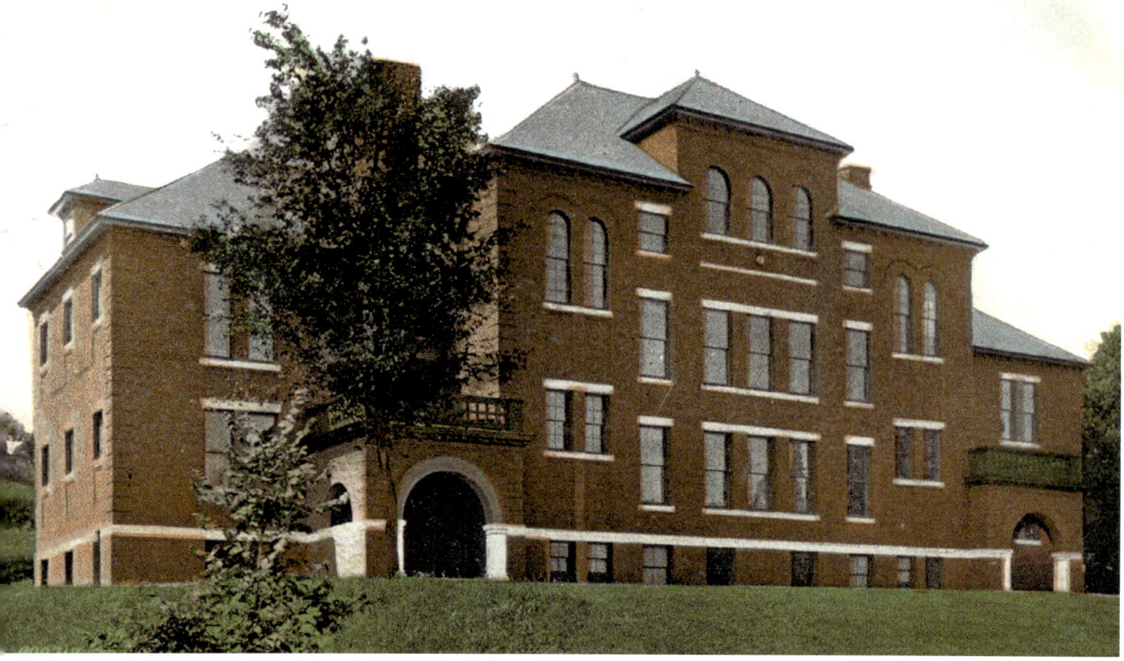

WOODSTOCK HIGH SCHOOL: The school, seen above on a postcard postmarked 1907, was located on School Street, near the current Woodstock Elementary School. The first public school in the community was located "on" The Green in 1812. For years, in the early days of the settlement, education was available at a variety of homes, barns, sheds and wherever room and a teacher could be found. The present Windsor Central Supervisory Union Senior High School was built in West Woodstock in 1956.

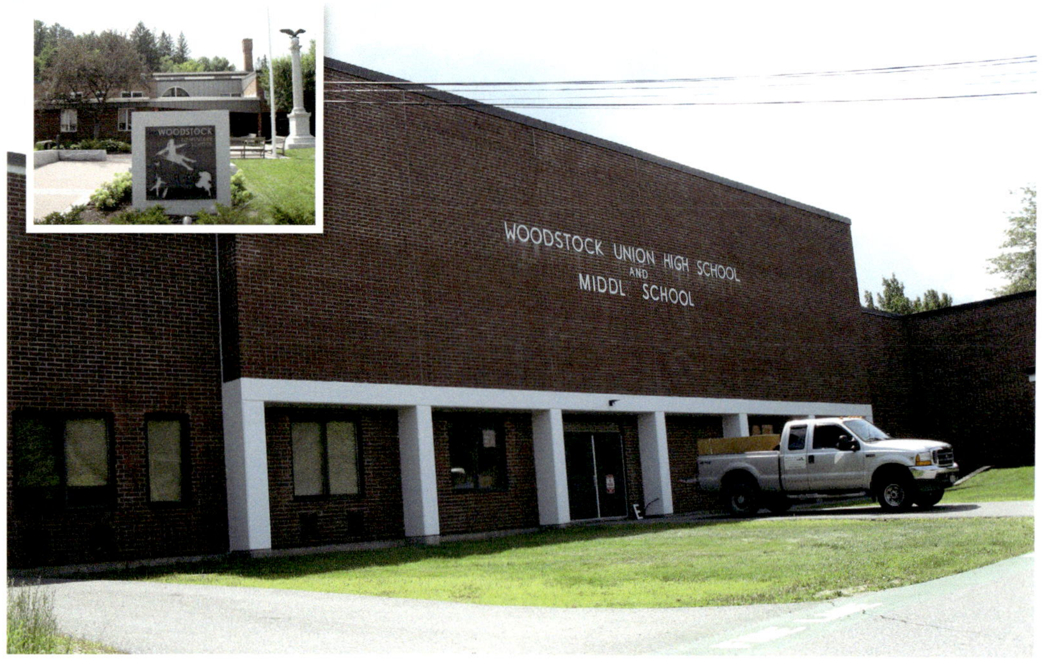

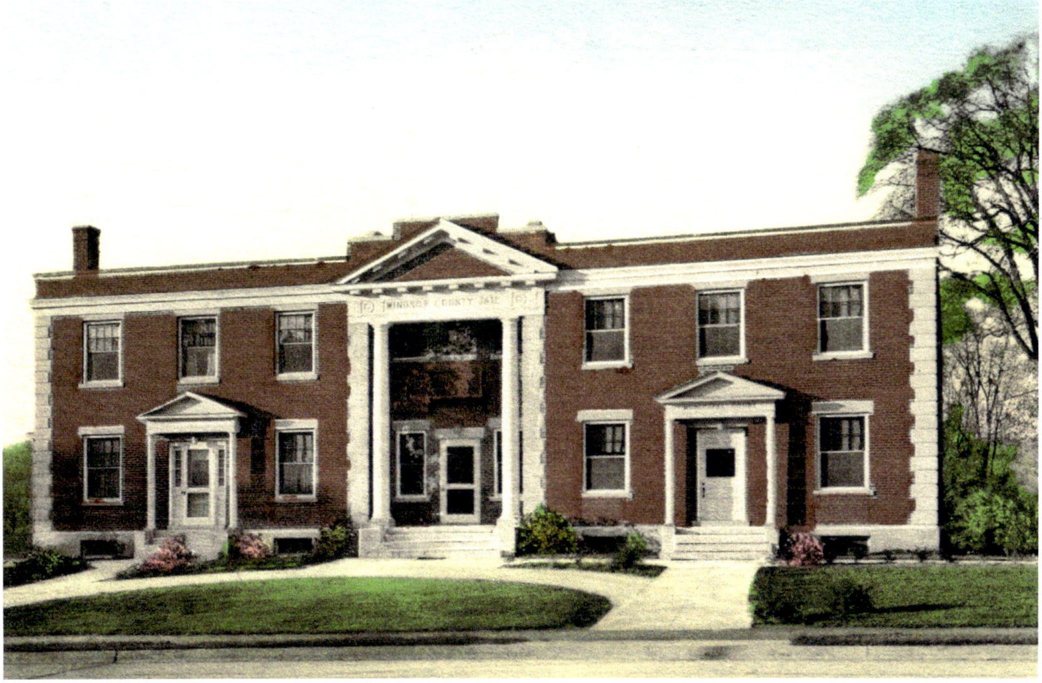

WINDSOR COUNTY JAIL: This jail was built in Woodstock in 1937. There were county and town jails in other Woodstock locations previously. This facility housed inmates until the county jail was moved to the town of Springfield in 2002. The county sheriff and his family lived on site in this building until 1969. This building continues to house the Windsor County Sheriff's Office, the Windsor County Treasurer, the Windsor County Clerk, a television station and two Assistant Windsor County Judges' Offices.

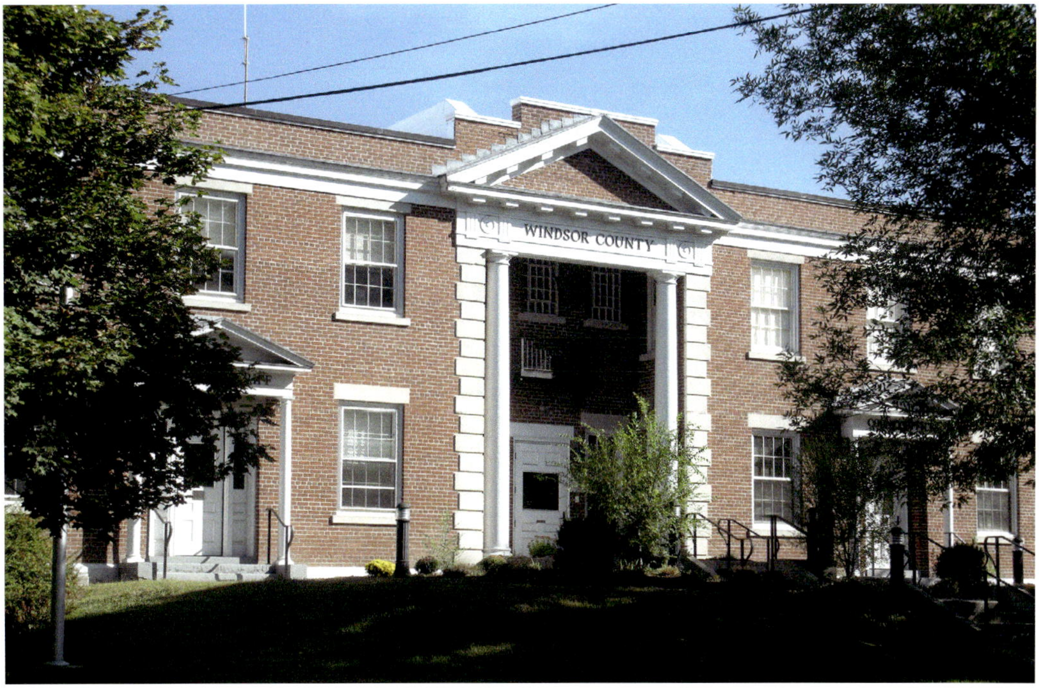

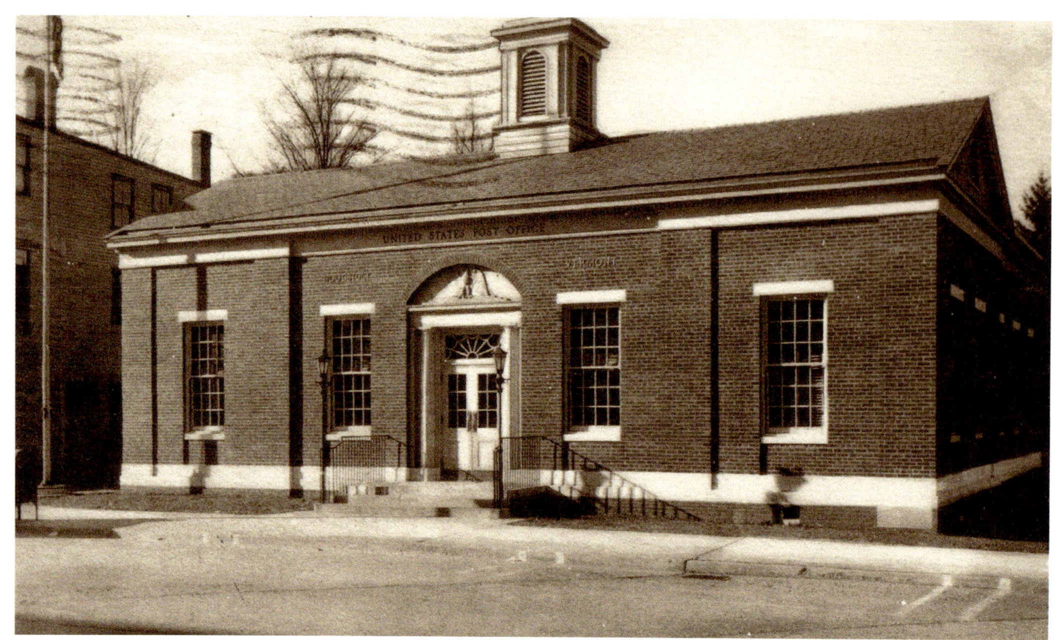

CURRENT WOODSTOCK POST OFFICE: This building on Central Street was a jail before renovations and conversions in 1937. The firing range in the basement and bars on some windows remain a testimony to the past. The Woodstock Post Office was located previously at several other downtown locations. The US Postal Service released a commemorative stamp in 1938 honoring the new Woodstock Vermont Post Office; see the inset. The image above is from a postcard postmarked 1945.

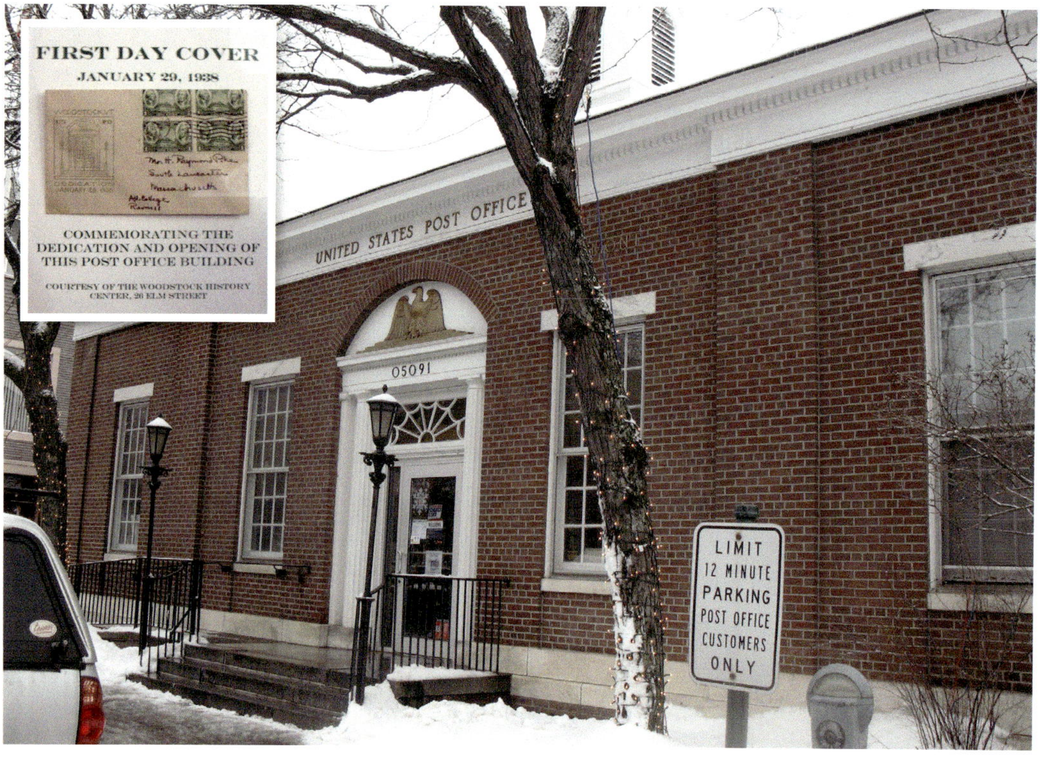

Other Nearby Communities

Bridgewater, Vermont

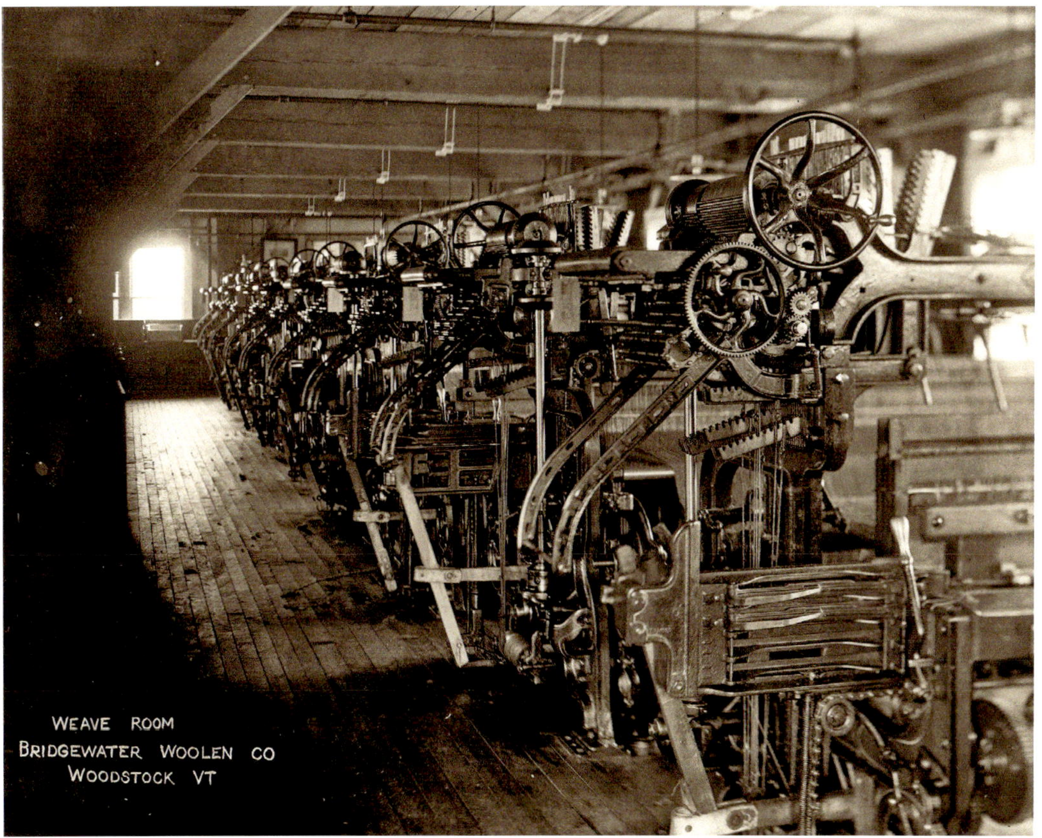

BRIDGEWATER: A town eight miles west of Woodstock along Route 4. It contains several hamlets: West Bridgewater, Bridgewater Village, Bridgewater Corners, and Bridgewater Center. This former woolen mill community contains bed and breakfast inns, the revitalized Bridgewater Mill markets and shops, and a lot of Ottauquechee River frontage. This combination makes Bridgewater an appealing community with a historic past.

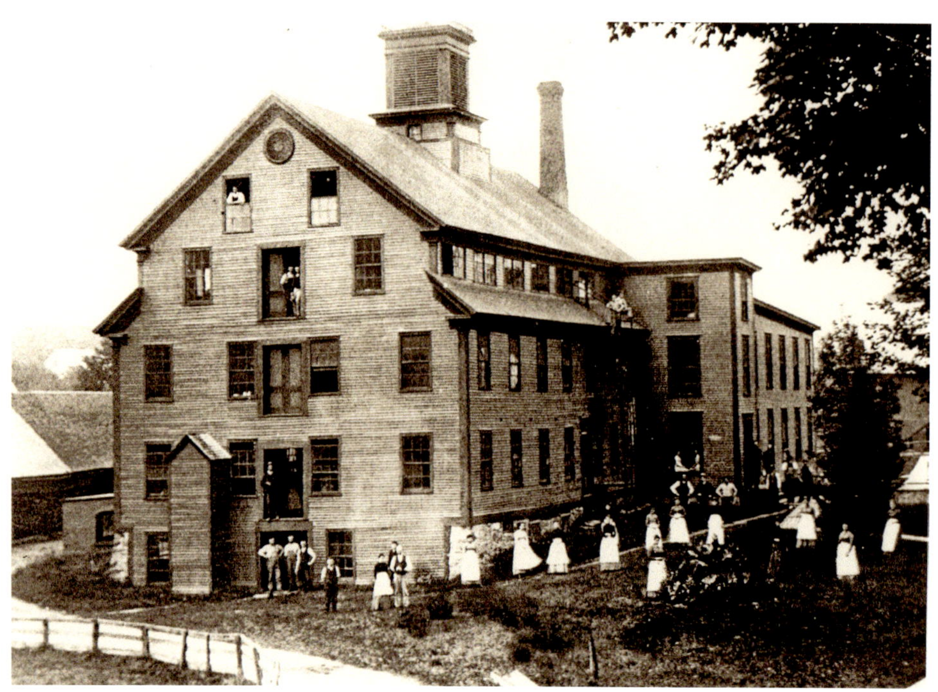

BRIDGEWATER WOOLEN MILL: Built in 1852, it was the center of community life for many decades in Bridgewater. The original water wheel was eventually replaced by a coal-to-steam plant. Flooding caused the mill to close in 1973. Due to the foresight and imagination of some key people The Bridgewater Mill, as it's known today, thrives once more. The local post office, a weaving studio, thrift shop, goldsmith, master furniture craftsman, Italian restaurant and other businesses make the Bridgewater Mill an interesting destination.

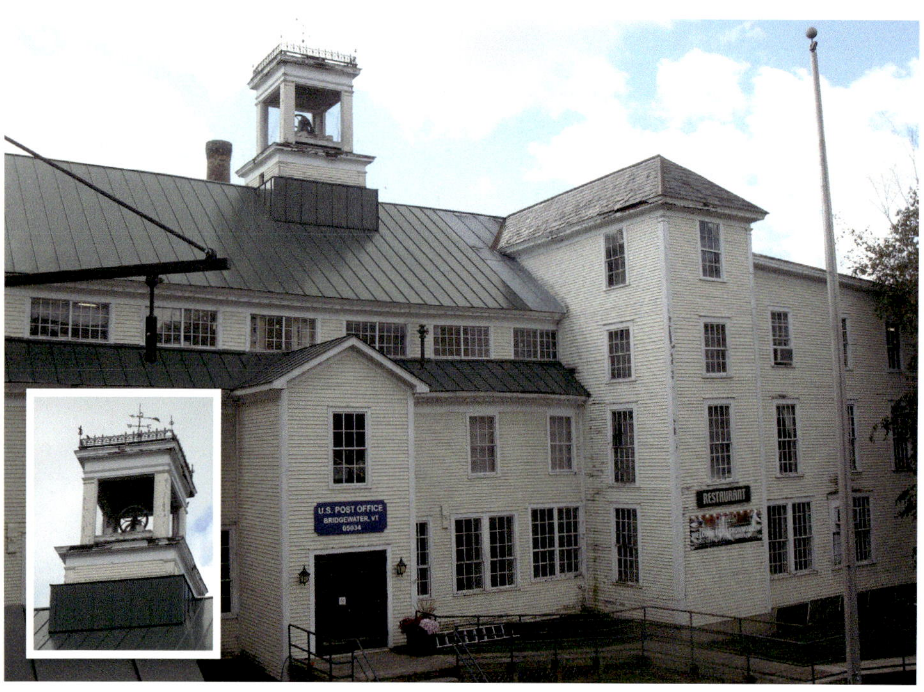

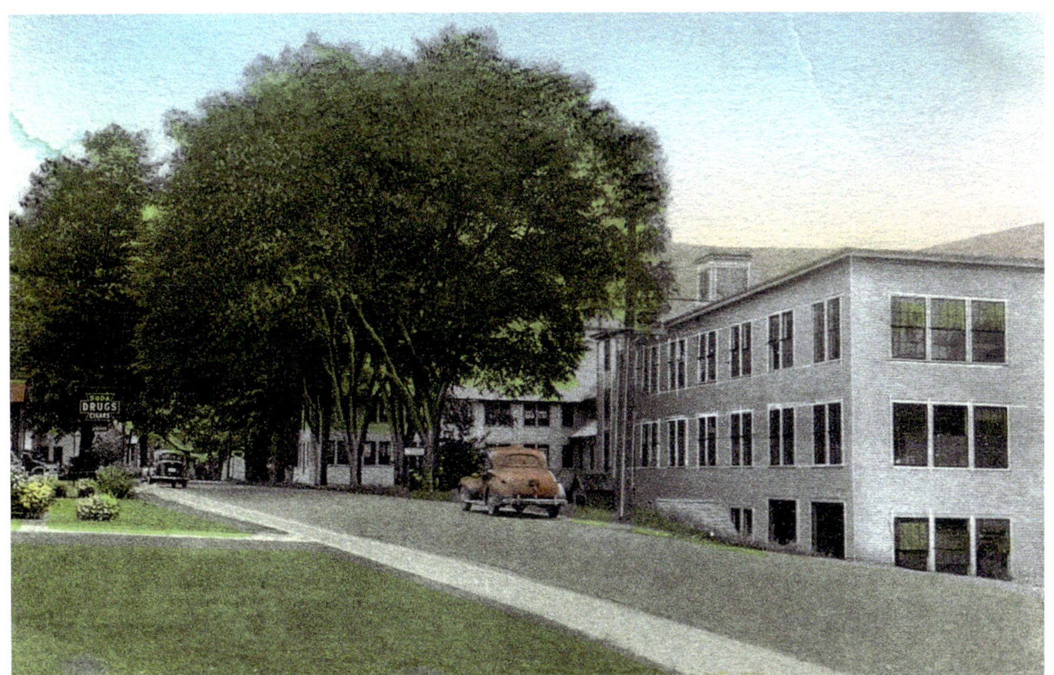

BRIDGEWATER WOOLEN MILL: The mill produced uniforms and blankets during both World Wars. The fire station was built close as many mill workers were also firefighters. Historic Bridgewater Mill is one of the oldest surviving commercial buildings in the state. It was listed on the National Registry of Historic Buildings in 1976. This mill was owned by Frank MacKenzie in its prime, then known as the MacKenzie Woolen Mill. It was also known as the Bridgewater Woolen Company. Some of the original mill housing nearby has been converted to other commercial and municipal purposes.

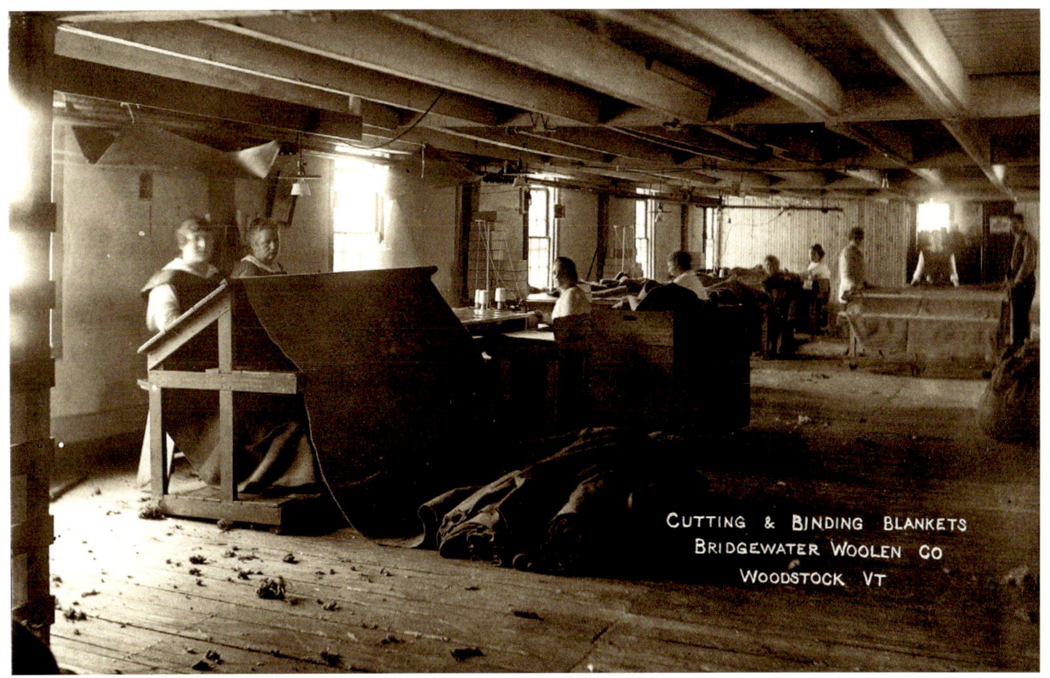

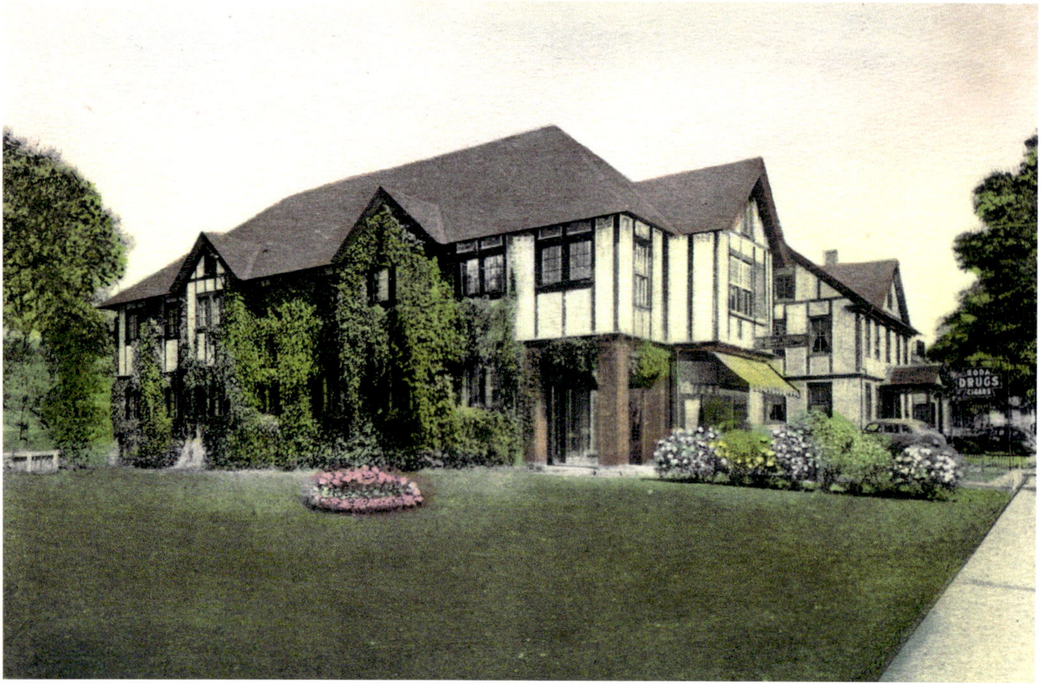

VERMONT NATIVE INDUSTRIES: That was the name of this establishment above, when the woolen mill was thriving. It was an attractive shop and office space for the woolen mill across the street. Piles of beautiful, soft and serviceable woolen blankets and other woolen items filled tables and shelves within this space during the Bridgewater Woolen Mill's productive years. History continues in this building today, below, as Mill Village Apartments breathes new life into the building.

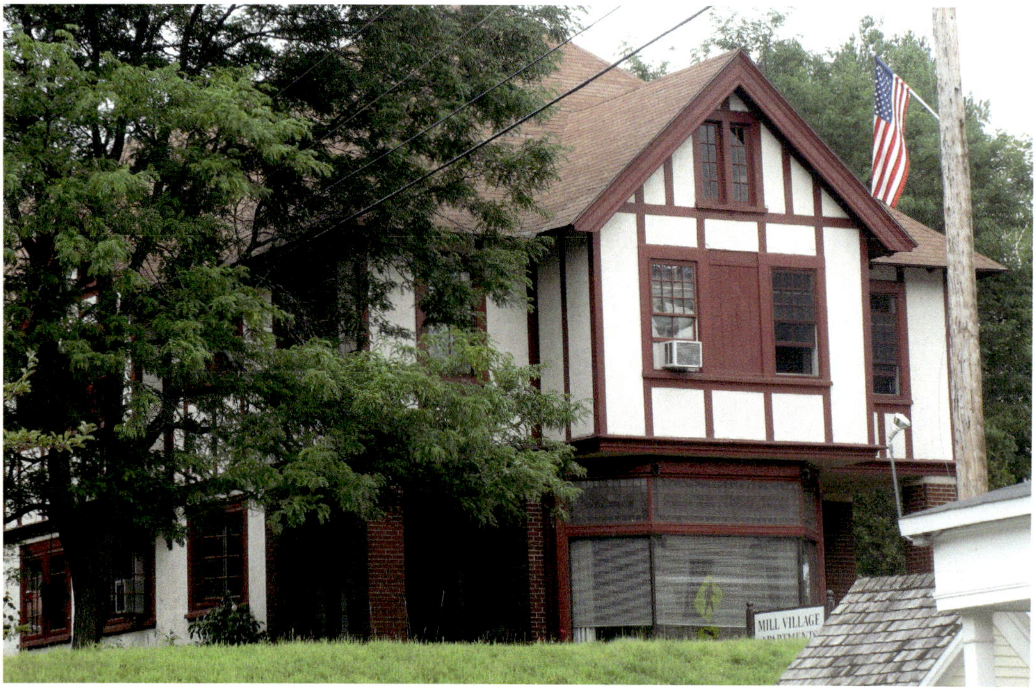

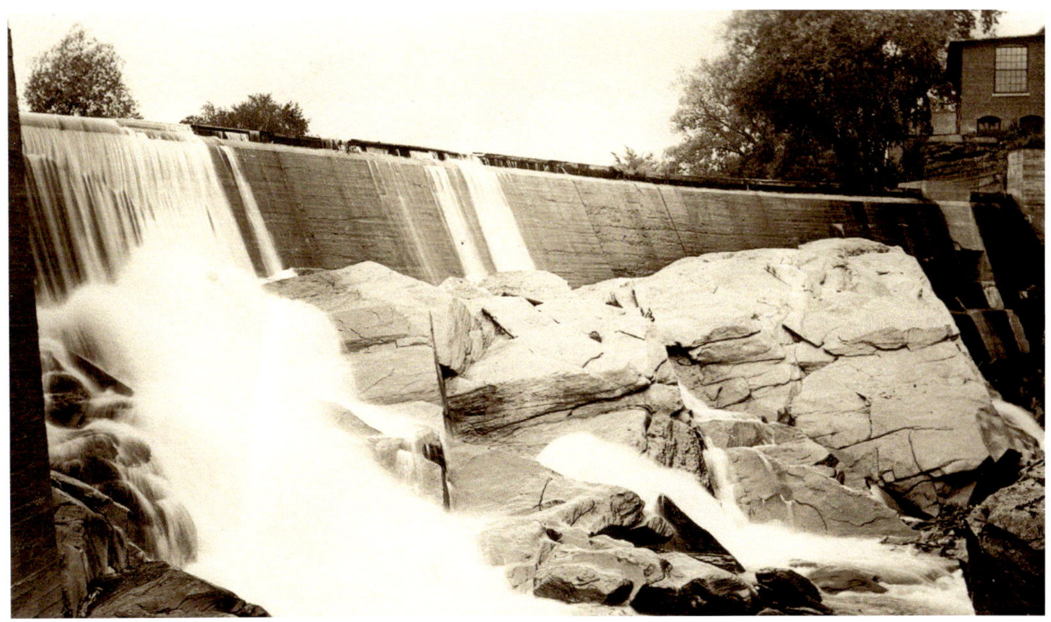

QUECHEE: Quechee is an unincorporated village in Hartford, Vermont. It was established in 1761 and contains the remains of several former mills sites.

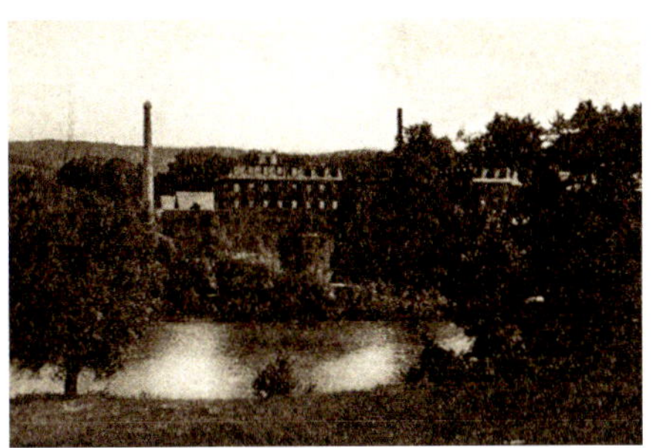

QUECHEE MILLS FALLS: Located at Quechee Mills, this manufacturing community thrived in the 1800s. J. C. Parker and Company, property now occupied by Simon Pearce Glass, shown at right, developed "shoddy," a fabric which incorporated new and old material. This 1929 image at top, shows the falls with a mill building behind. Dewey and Company set up just upriver from Quechee Village. The name of the Mills gave the community its name: Dewey's Mills; see the inset. The community of Dewey's Mills no longer exists due to a 1962 flood control project.

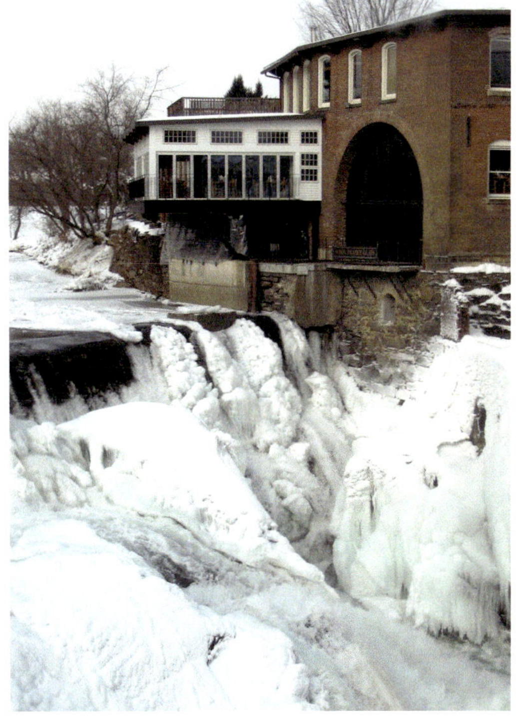

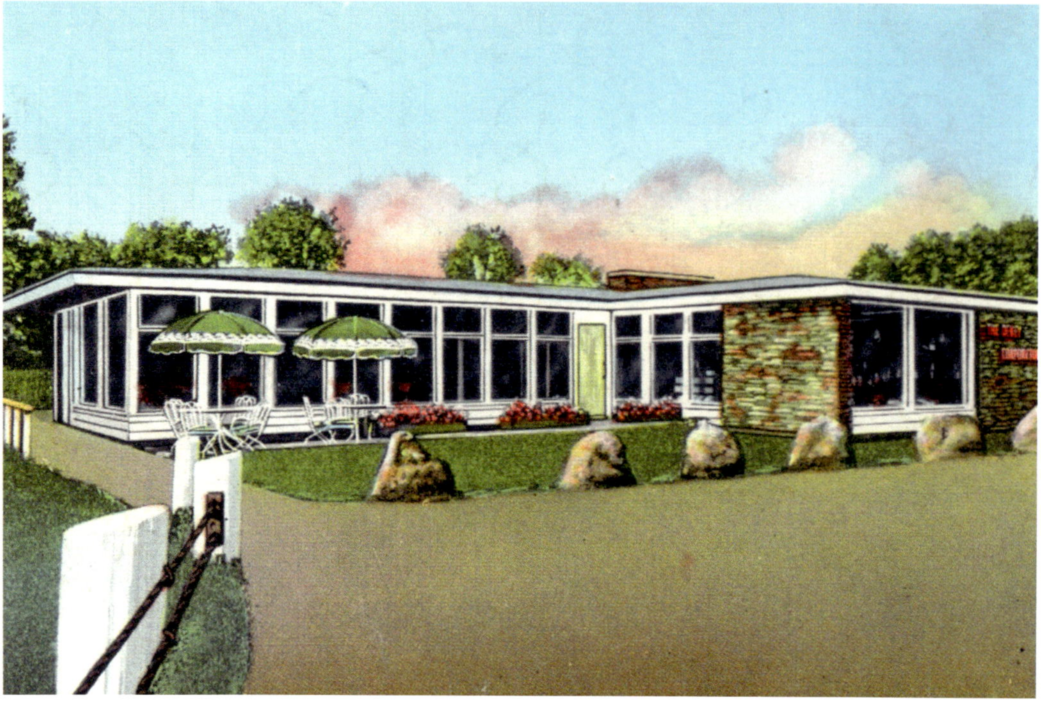

DEWEY'S MILLS SHOP: Built in the 1950s as a location where tourists and other shoppers could easily purchase products produced by Dewey's Mills. It is located on Route 4, at the edge of the canyon. This was not only convenient for people shopping, but encouraged travelers to park there and admire the gorge. It is a powerful site to this day and it's no wonder the chasm is nicknamed "Vermont's Little Grand Canyon."

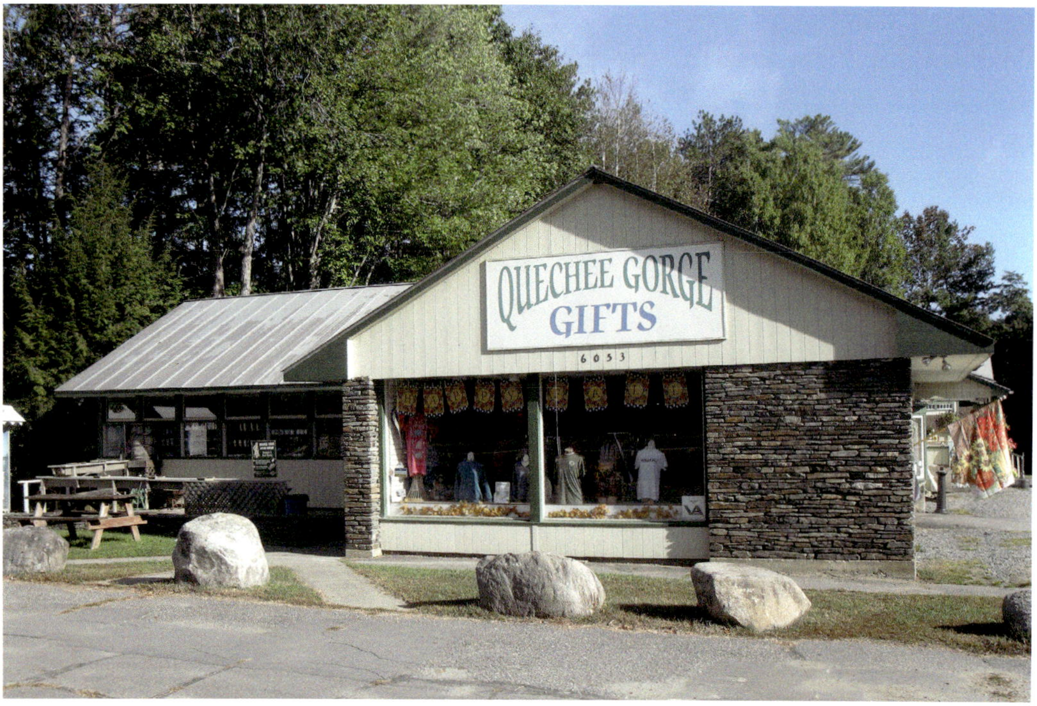

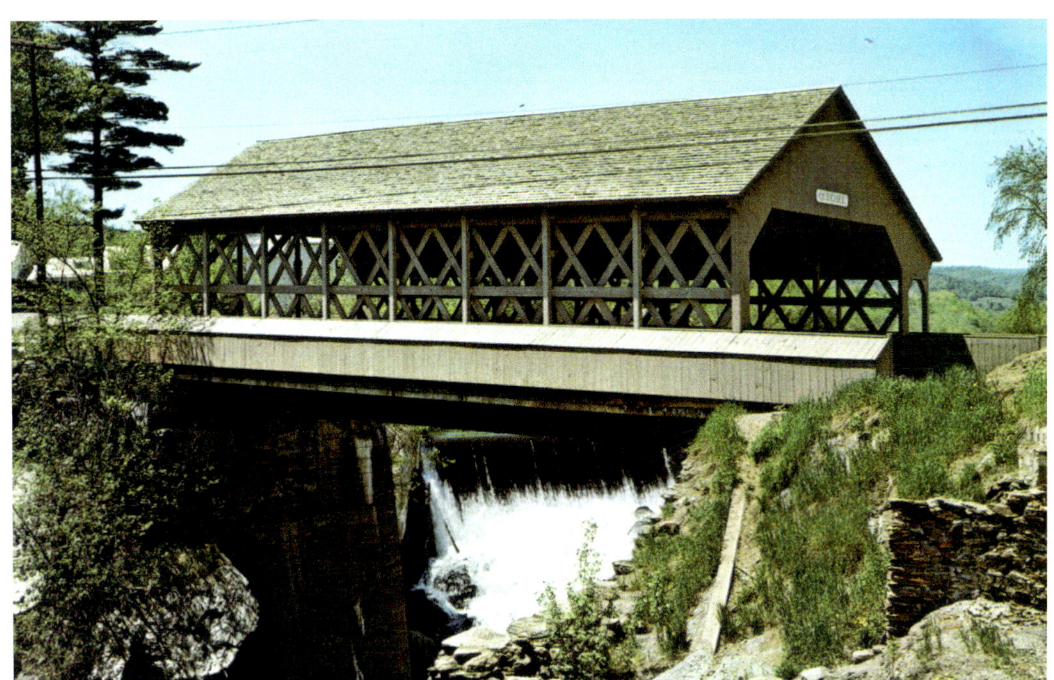

QUECHEE COVERED BRIDGE: This bridge, above, spans the Ottauquechee River adjacent to the mill complex still remaining in Quechee, where Simon Pearce Glass has an artisan studio and shop. Visitors can watch glass-blowing, pottery and weaving demonstrations there. A fine restaurant looks out over the Ottauquechee River and the falls. The covered bridge was originally built in 1970 at the site to handle increased traffic to the numerous mills in the area. It was entirely demolished by Tropical Storm Irene in 2011, below. It was rebuilt from the river bed up and reopened in 2012, see inset.

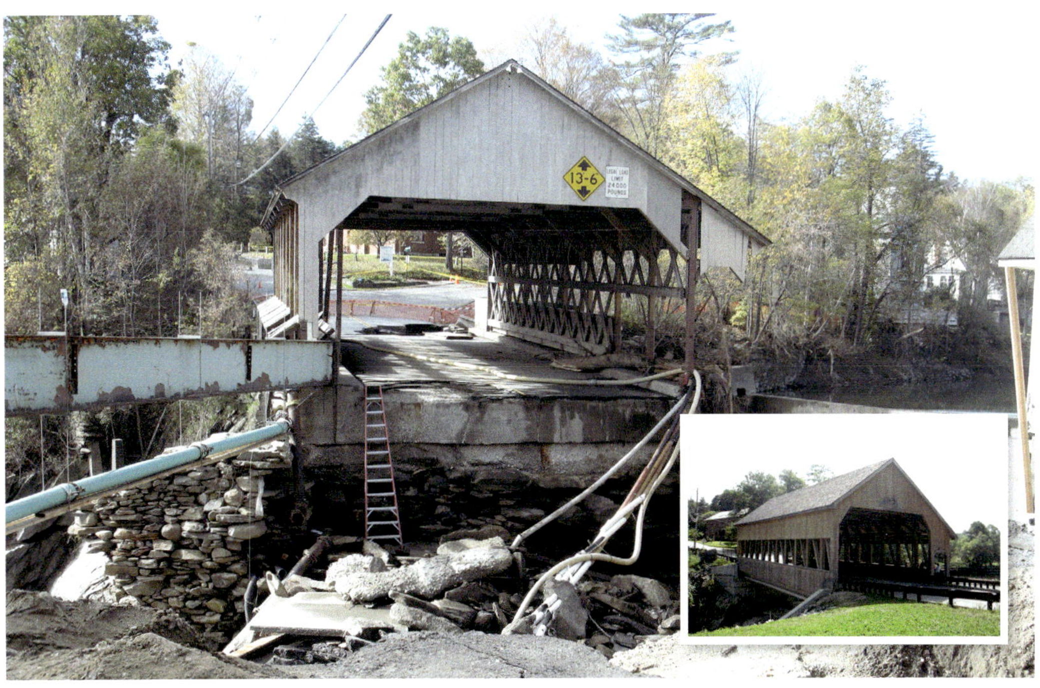

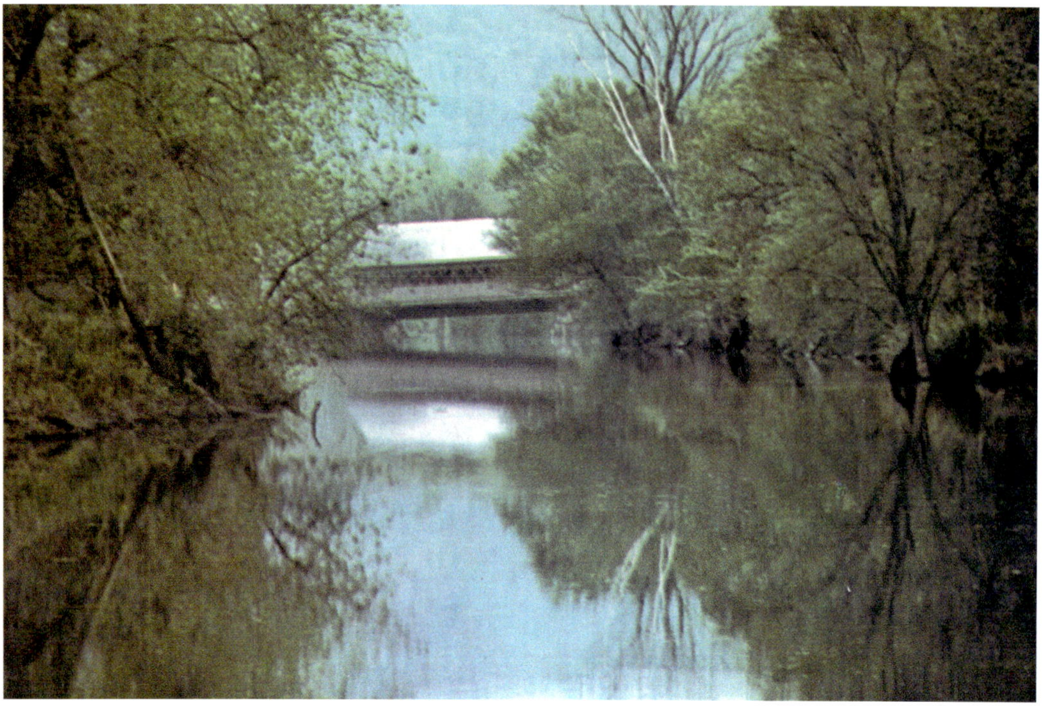

QUECHEE COVERED BRIDGE FROM AFAR: This image above, is captured in the 1900s from upriver on a serene summer day. The image, below, was taken just above the bridge and falls, on a stormy winter day, years later. These contrasting images show just how much the weather can affect the Ottauquechee River and surrounding landscape in Quechee, and indeed, all along the river's course.

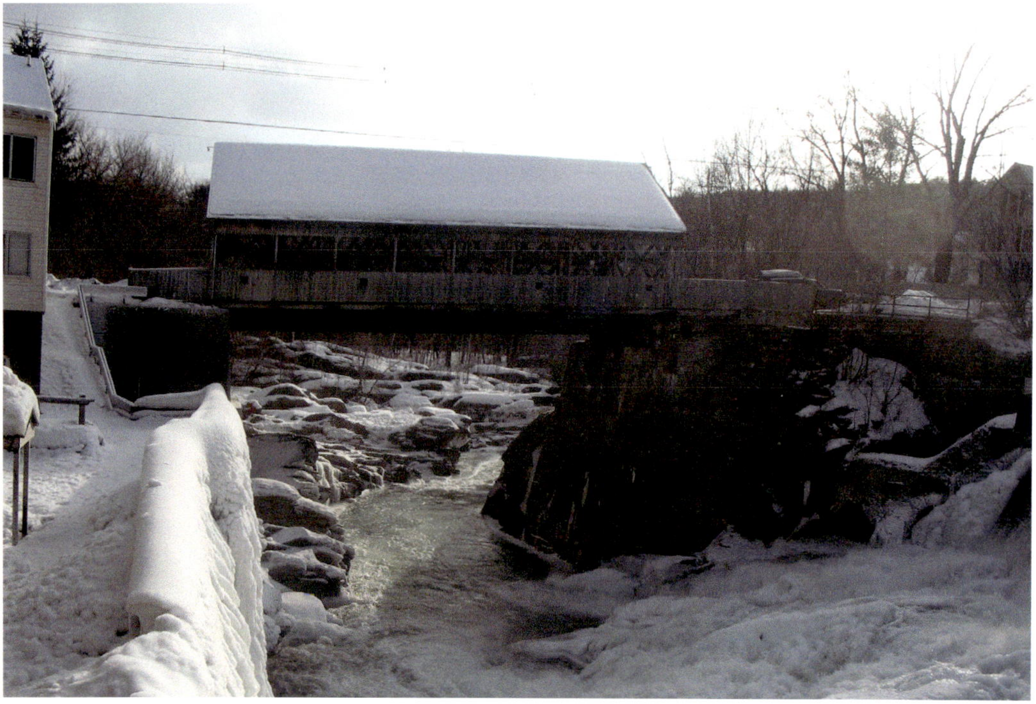

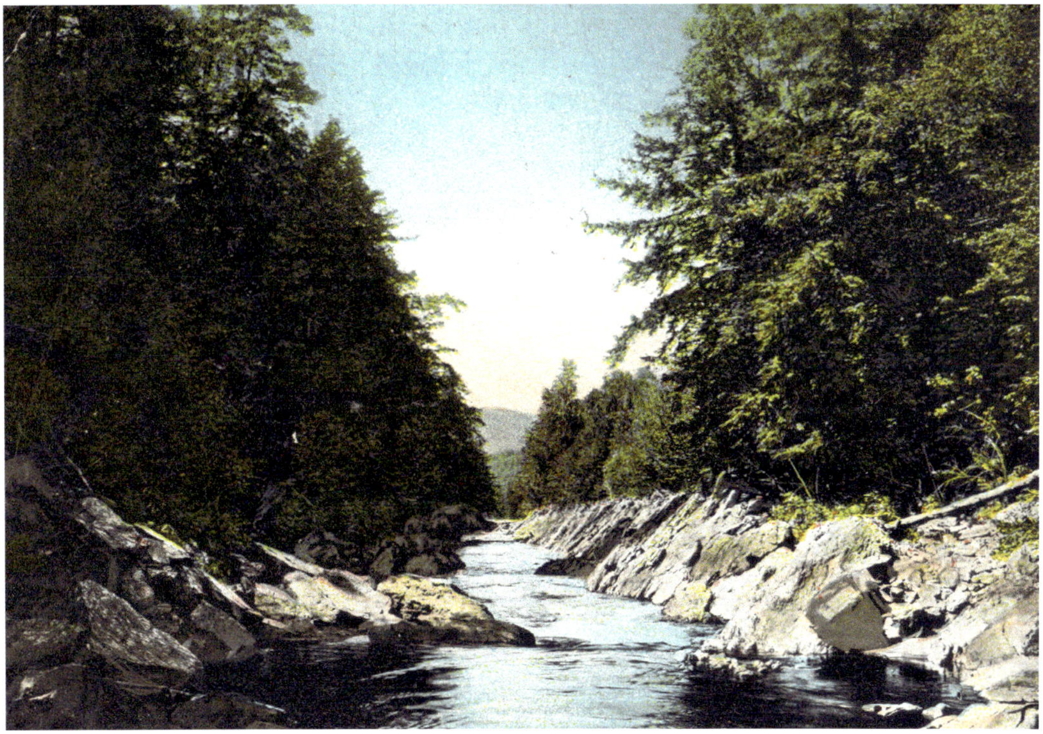

Quechee Gulf and Gorge:

This is a natural, very impressive ravine 165 feet deep, seen from the top down, below and from the bottom, above. A bridge crosses the gorge on US Route 4, where once a train trestle spanned the Ottauquechee River at that point. See the inset photograph taken when the trestle was first built in 1875 and tested for durability with a train engine and car. Quechee State Park is located close to the chasm.

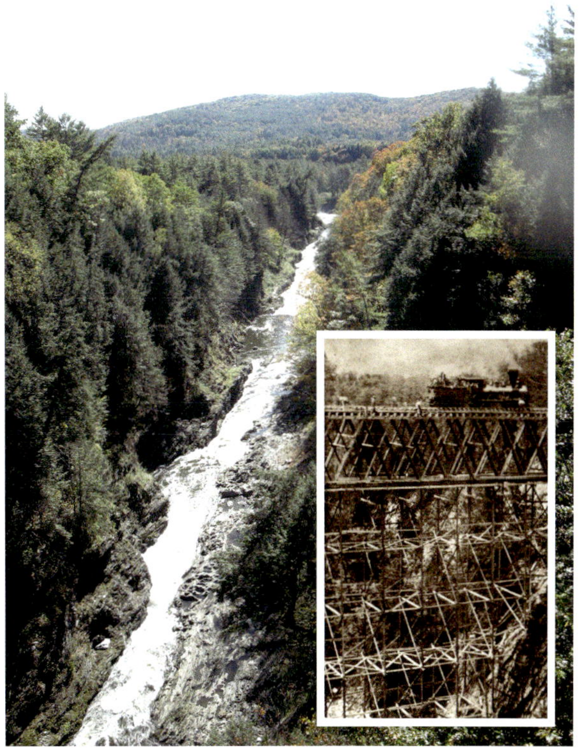

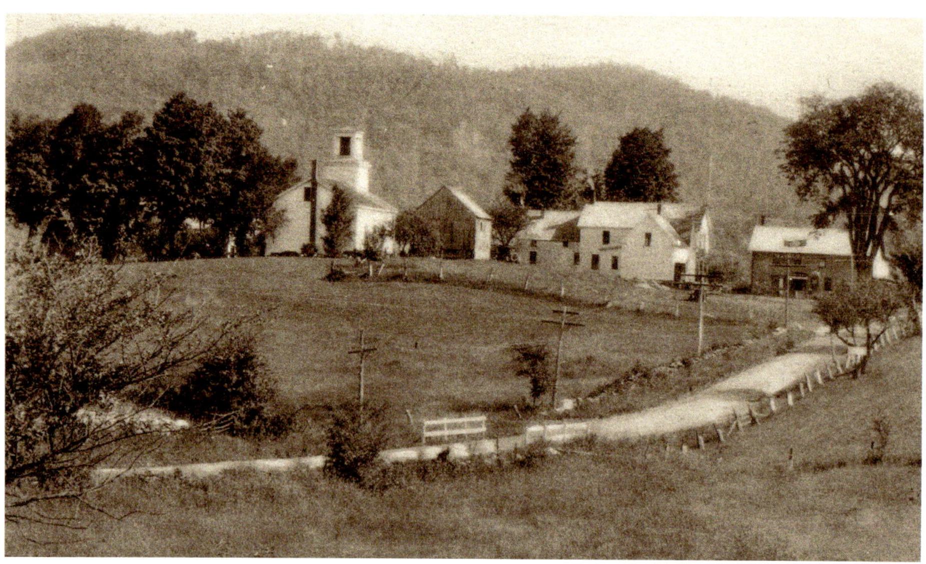

Plymouth: Originally named Saltash, Plymouth is close to two major ski areas: Killington and Okemo. The wool and dairy industry, copper, iron and even some gold mining, as well as the quarrying of marble, granite, limestone and soapstone, all figured prominently in the history and heritage of Plymouth. The rise and decline of each of these industries over time, has created a series of ghost towns scattered across the hills of Plymouth. Since then, the community is mostly residential, recreational and historic.

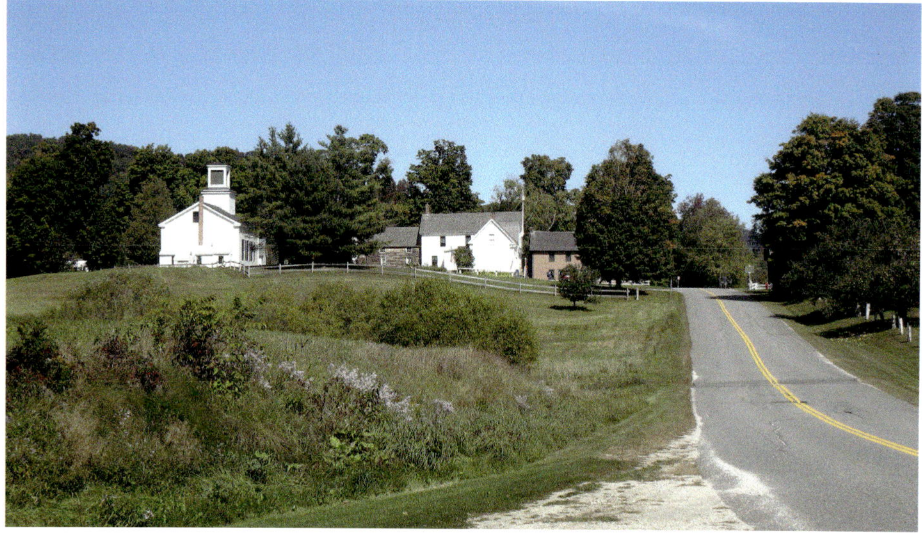

Calvin Coolidge Historic Site: Located at Plymouth Notch, the site remains much as it was during the thirtieth president's lifetime. The home Coolidge was born in, the one he lived in later on, the community church, general store, post office, school house and other village buildings have all been preserved. Even as president, Coolidge continued to vacation in Plymouth Notch. His remains rest in the cemetery located there.

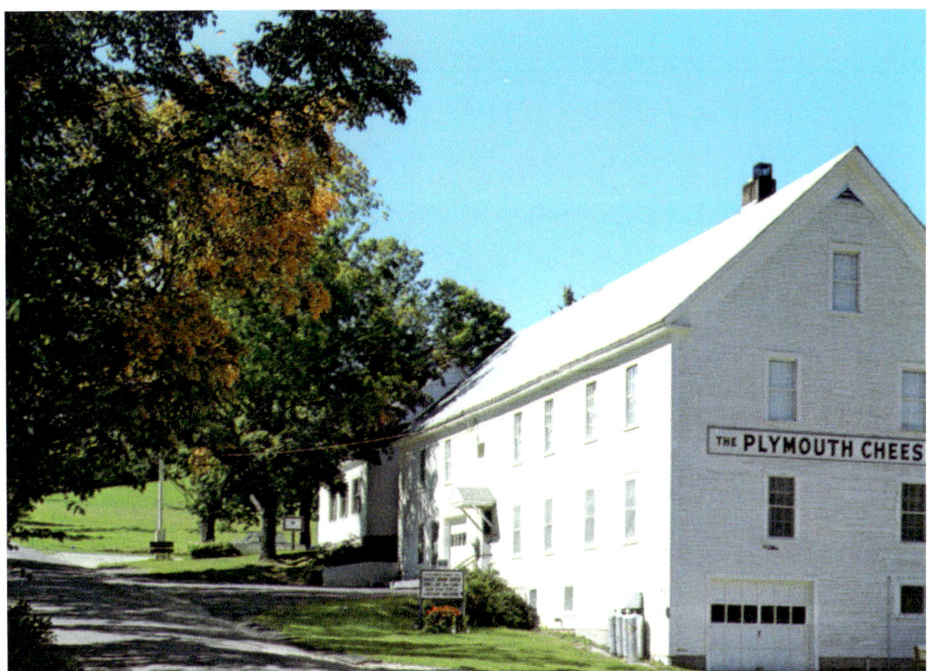

THE PLYMOUTH CHEESE FACTORY: Located on the hillside in the preserved village of Plymouth Notch. The Plymouth Cheese Factory was opened in 1890 in Plymouth, started by John Coolidge, father of President Calvin Coolidge. The cooperative made cheese at the site until the depression forced its closure in 1934. In 1960, Calvin Coolidge's son, also named John Coolidge, returned to Plymouth and re-opened the cheese factory. It was bought by the Vermont Division for Historic Preservation in 1998 and has operated there ever since.

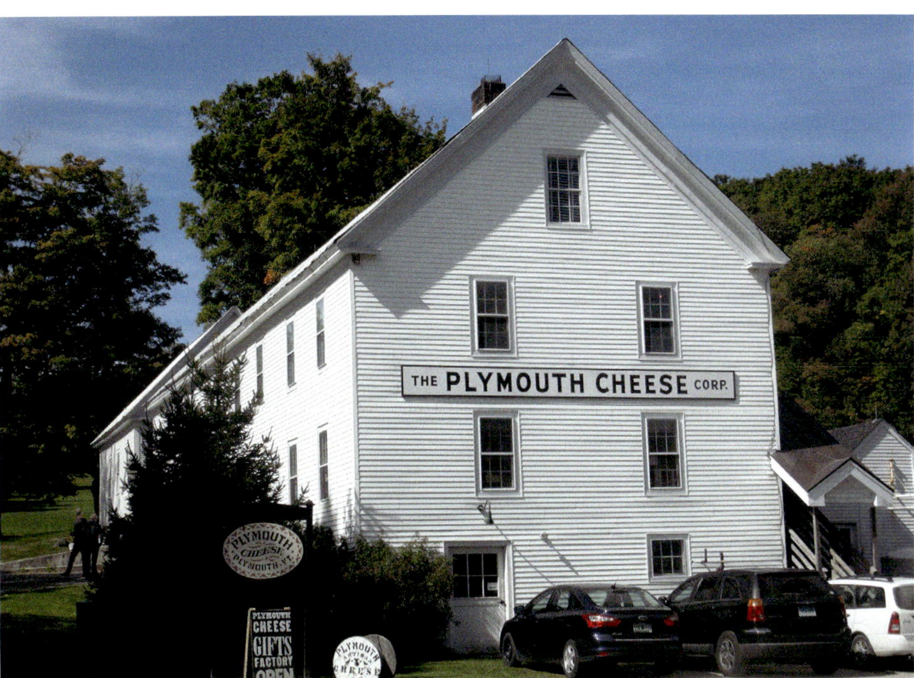

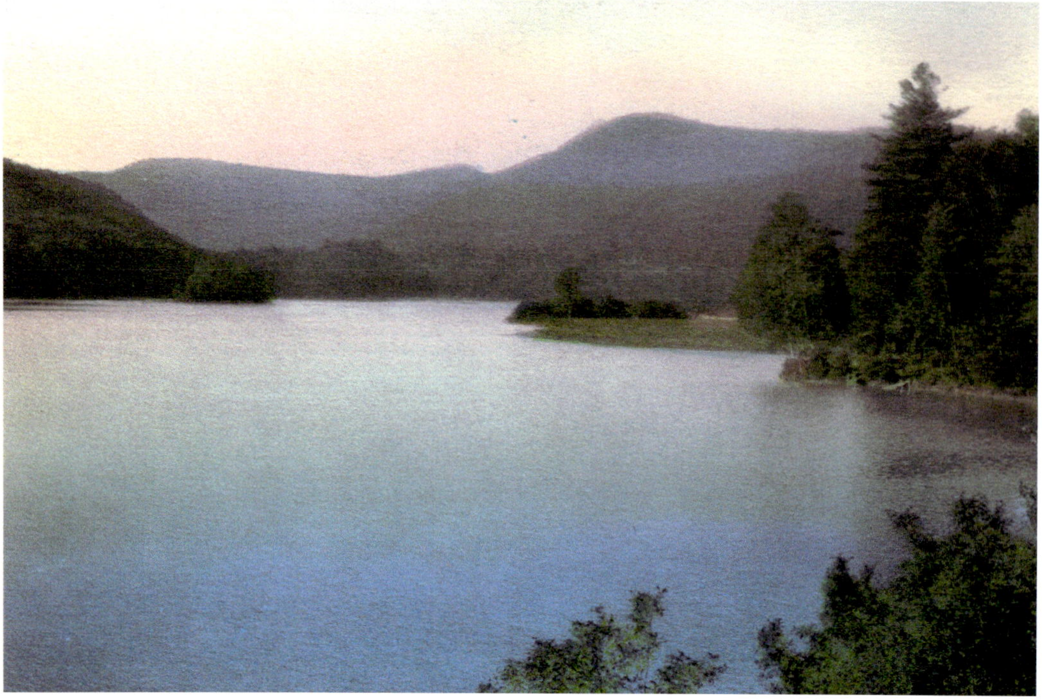

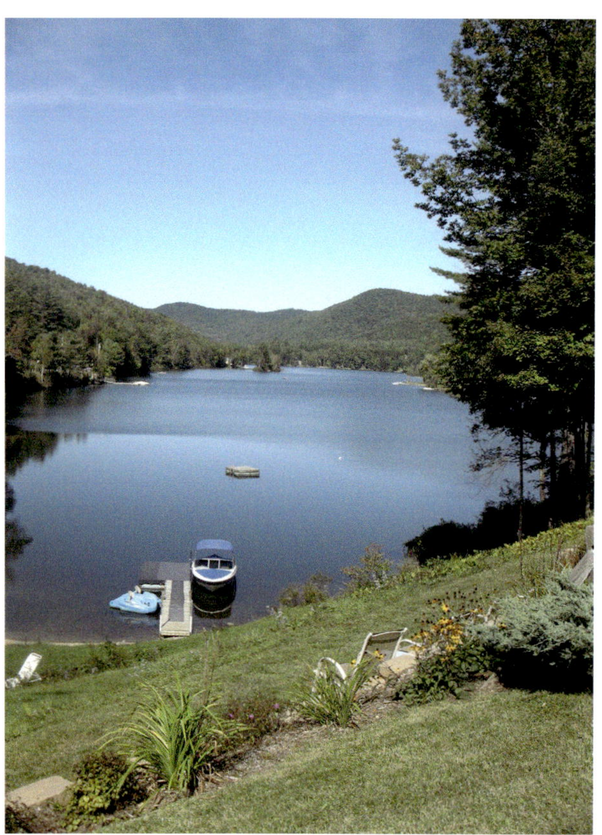

ECHO LAKE: Located in Plymouth, Vermont, it's a beautiful vacation and recreation destination. Echo Lake is three miles long and covers an area of 104 acres. The lake is easily accessible and is close to many historic sites in the area. The lush shores are unspoiled. A few camps, campgrounds, recreation areas and lodging sites dot the area.

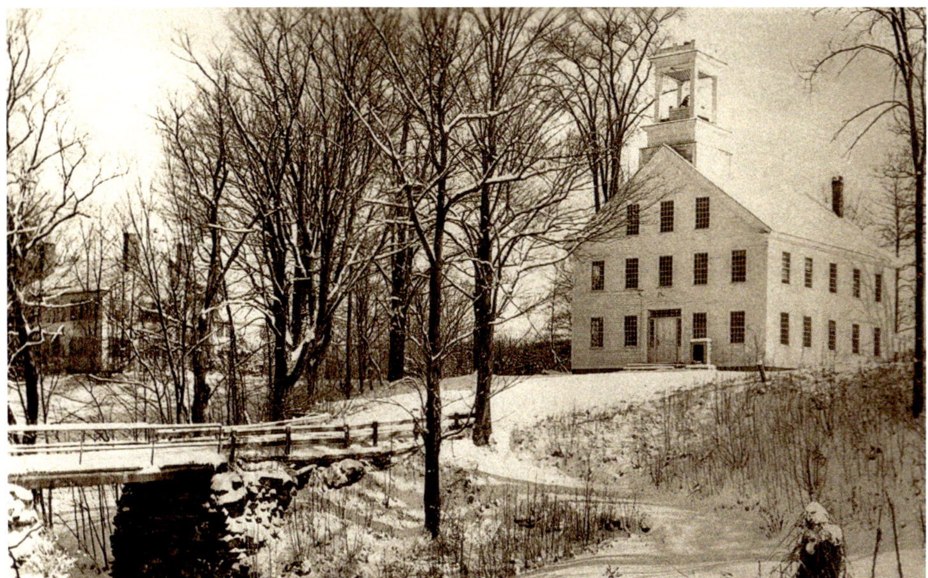

South Woodstock: Once called South Parish, this unincorporated village lies within, and south of, the town of Woodstock. It is nestled in the Kedron Valley and has a distinct personality and individuality of its own.

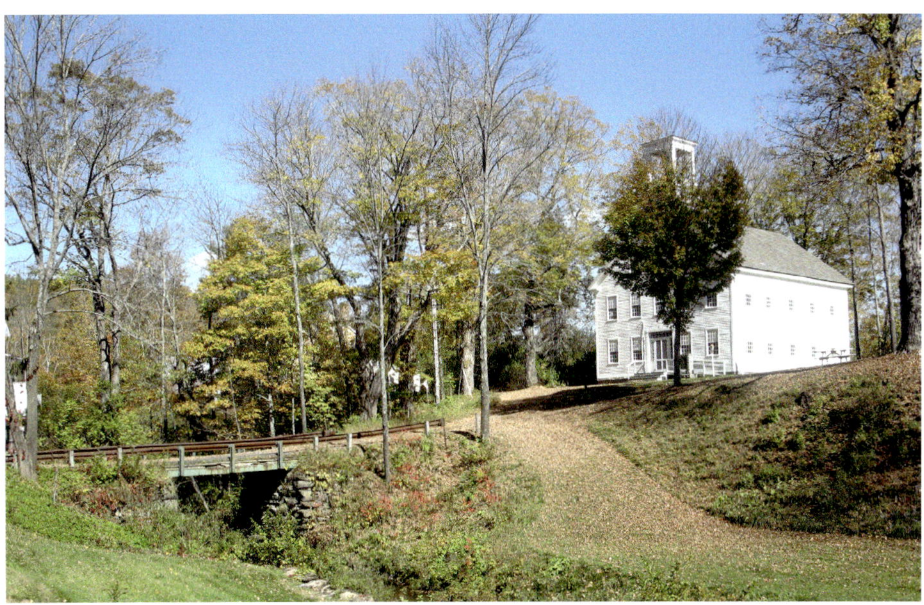

Green Mountain Perkins Academy: Built in 1848 and originally known as the Green Mountain Liberal Institute, then in 1869, the Green Mountain Perkins Academy. In 1898, the academy closed due to several factors, including declining enrollment. In 1956 the newly formed South Woodstock Historical Association restored the building and collected items relevant to the history of the school and the South Woodstock community. It is open to the public in July and August for limited hours.

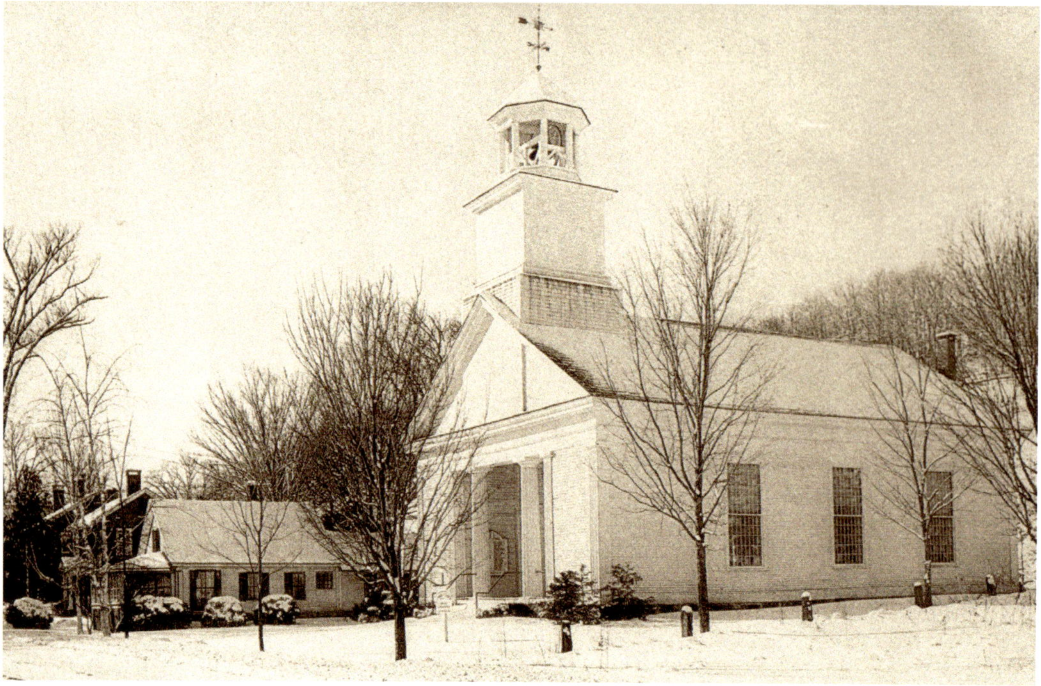

SOUTH CHAPEL: Built in the Greek Revival style by the chapel society in 1839. It is a well-maintained wood-framed, white clapboarded building with a recessed entrance graced with columns. An attractive octagonal belfry rises at the front. The church commands a site in the center of the South Woodstock Village. The above image dates from the early 1900s. As you can see below, the integrity has been maintained to this day.

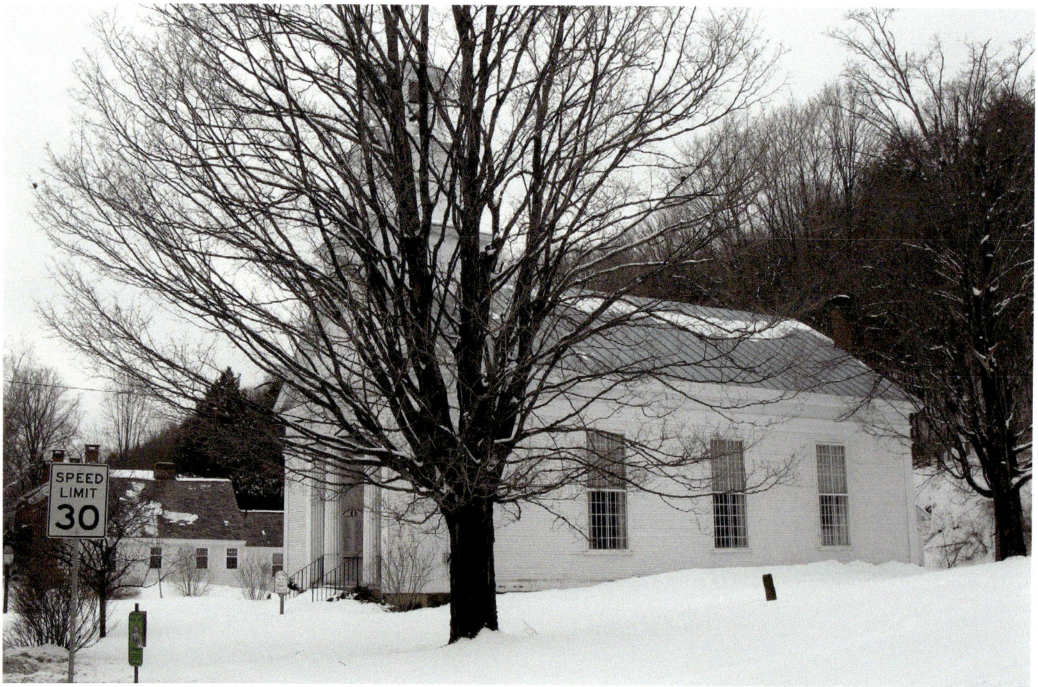

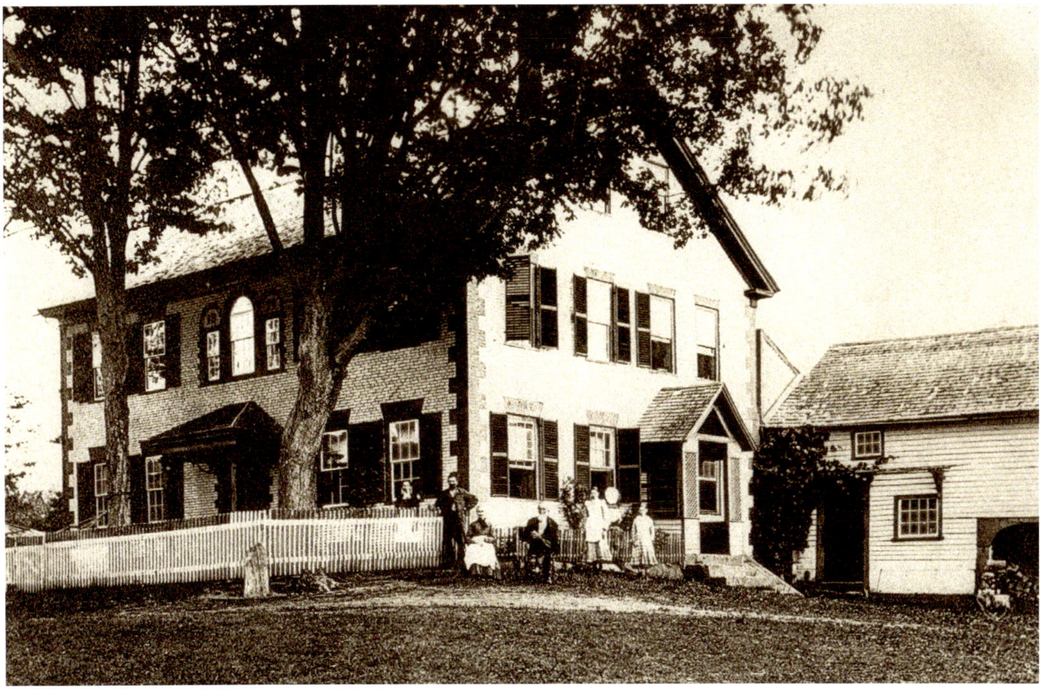

LOTTERY HILL FARM: Built on Lottery Hill with money won in the 1817 Louisiana Lottery. One resident, Carlos Adams, was a sheep farmer and a master violin maker. His instruments were sought after from near and far. He and his wife Luna and family lived in this Federal style brick home from 1872 to 1882, which remained in the family until 1939. The picture below is of the same house from the back showing a later addition.

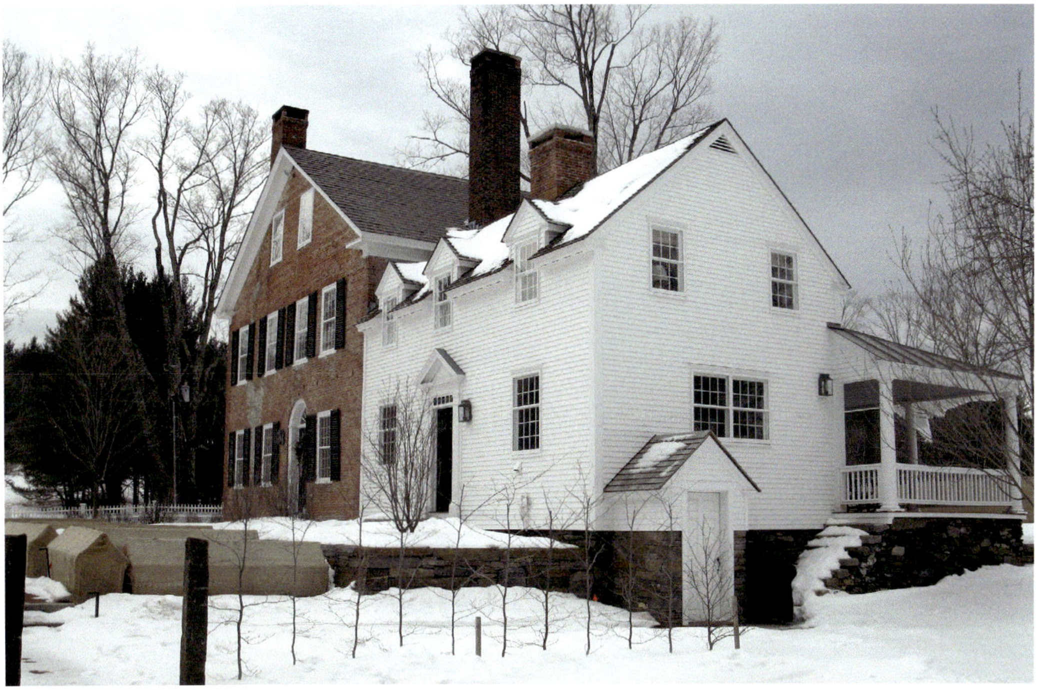

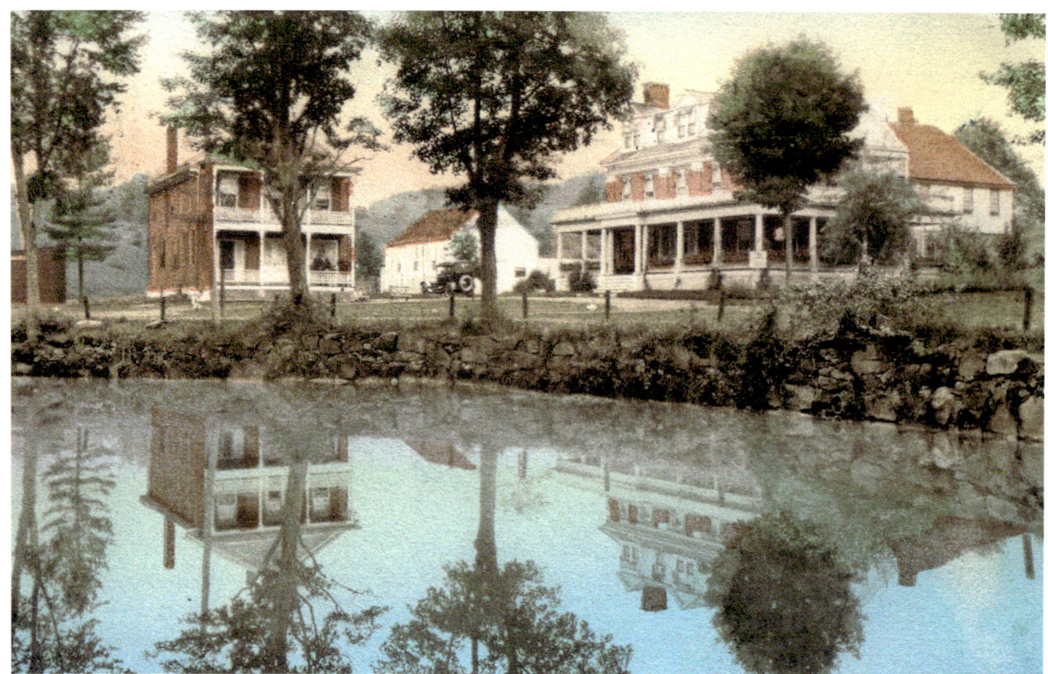

TAVERN AT SOUTH WOODSTOCK: Now known as the Kedron Valley Inn, this establishment has been a source of hospitality since 1828, nearly 200 years. During its long history, it's also been known as the National Hotel and the Colonial Inn. The tavern sits on eleven acres and offers a fine restaurant and lodging. A commodious porch with comfortable chairs overlooks the community center. The surroundings are historic and pleasantly vintage-feeling but the accommodations are completely up-to-date. A variety of recreational options are close by.

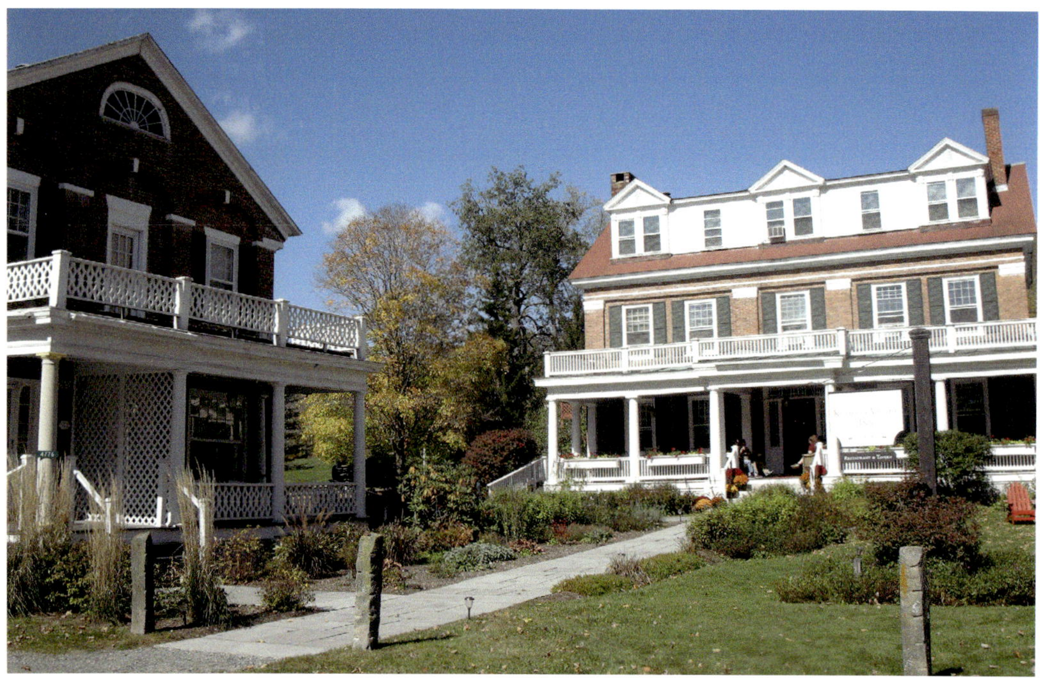

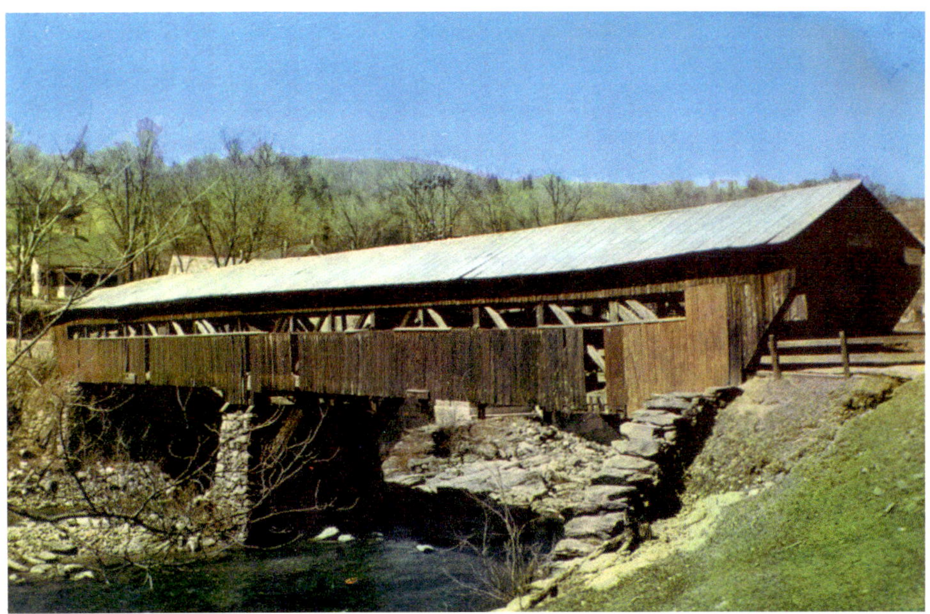

TAFTSVILLE: This hamlet east of Woodstock was named for the Taft family which owned and operated an iron factory on the Ottauquechee River in the 1800s. They also built the General Store which continues as the center of this community of less than 100 occupants.

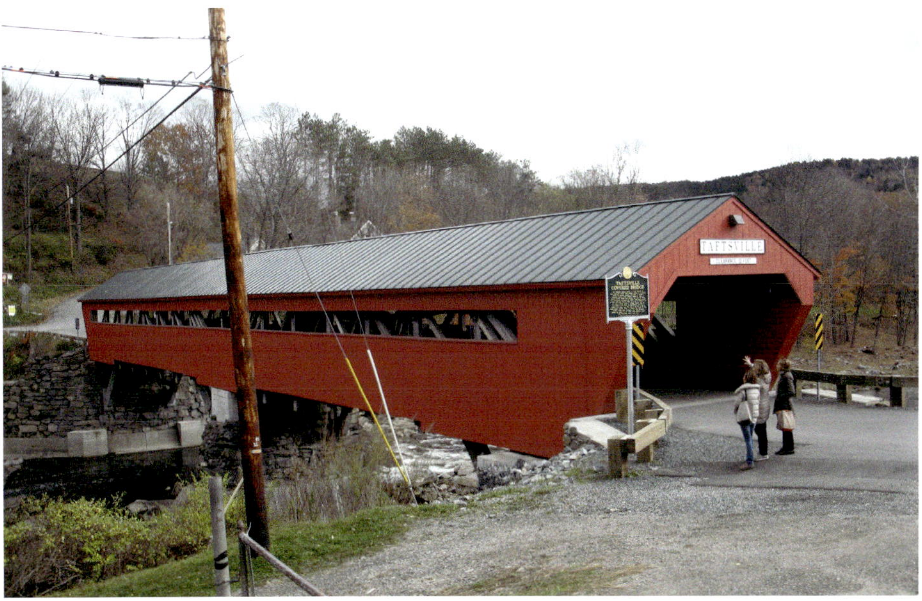

TAFTSVILLE COVERED BRIDGE: Built in 1836, it crosses the Ottauquechee River in the center of the hamlet. It is the second longest covered bridge in Vermont at 190 feet, and the third oldest in the state. The Kingpost truss and arch system bridge was badly damaged in September of 2011 due to tropical storm Irene, but was rebuilt again and back in operation by 2013.

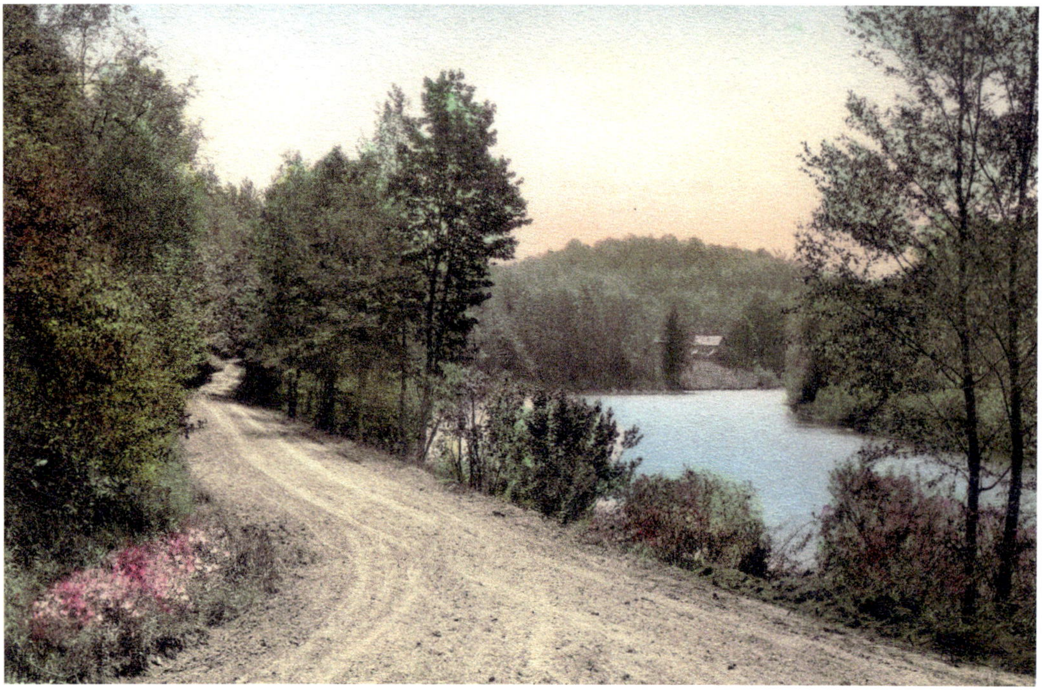

THE TAFTSVILLE ROAD: This road connects Old River Road in Woodstock with Route 4 in Taftsville. The road is paved on the Woodstock end, proceeds for a few miles along the Ottauquechee River and becomes unpaved as it continues to the Covered Bridge Road in Taftsville. There it emerges through the Taftsville Covered Bridge. The road is a really beautiful drive and if properly planned, can begin at Middle Covered Bridge in Woodstock and end at Taftsville Covered Bridge in Taftsville.

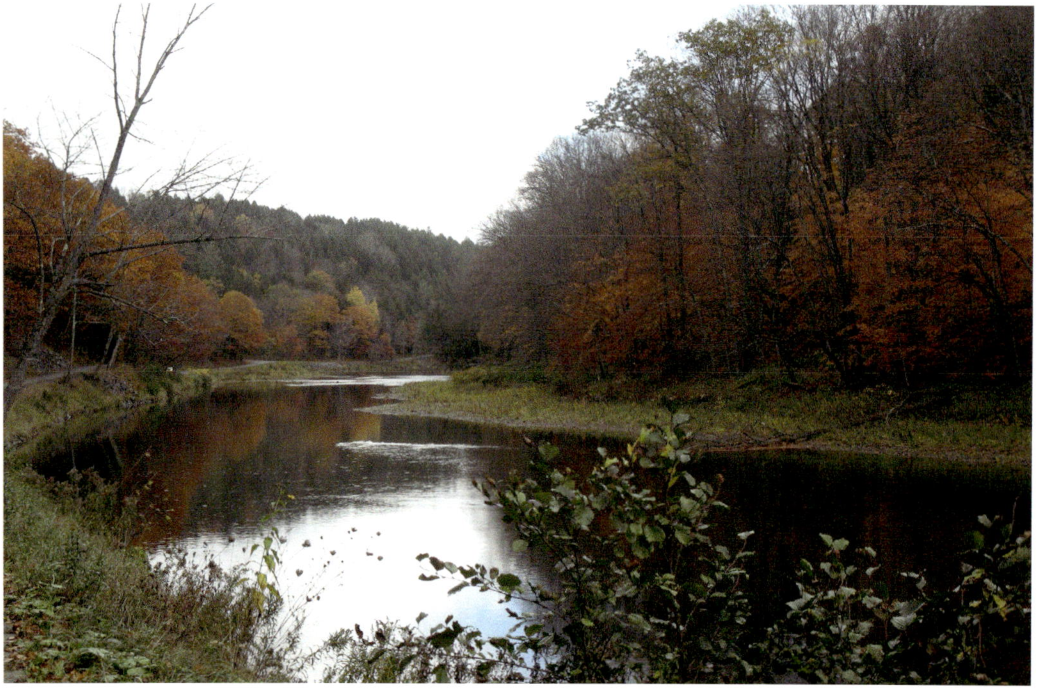

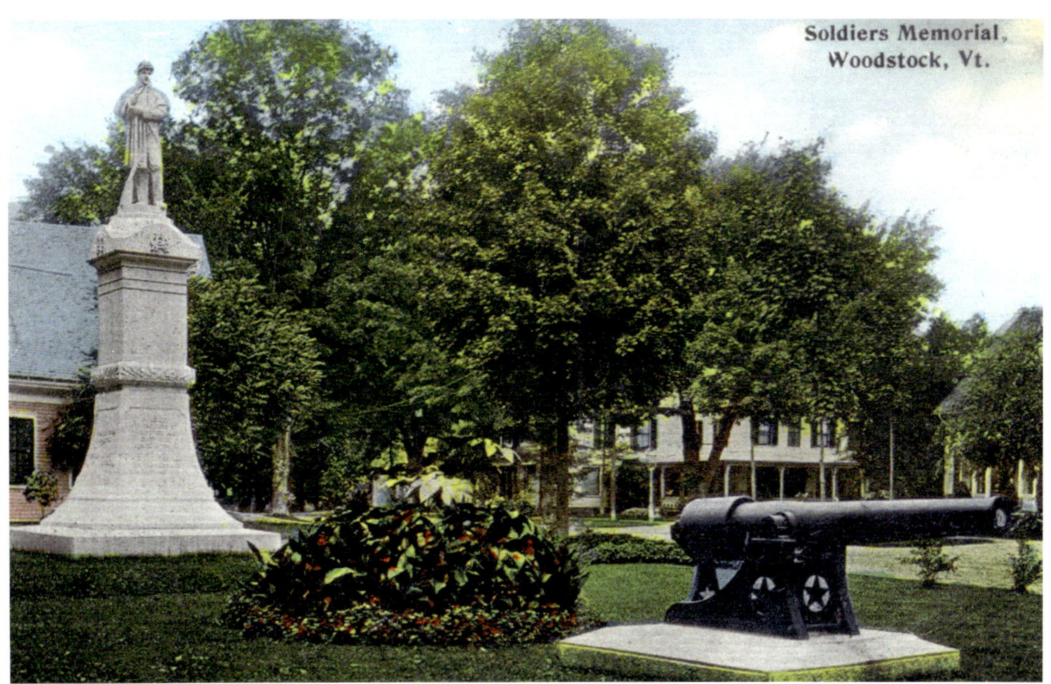

TRIBOU PARK AND THE SOLDIERS MONUMENT: Located at the intersection of Pleasant and Central Streets in Woodstock. The monument honors Civil War Veterans and was dedicated in 1909. For over one hundred years, a faithful granite soldier has vigilantly stood guard from his granite base, over the east end of Woodstock. Woodstock sent hundreds of soldiers to the Civil and other wars and many never returned home. I'd like to take this opportunity to say "Thank You!" to all veterans of all wars for the sacrifices they have made for the rest of us.

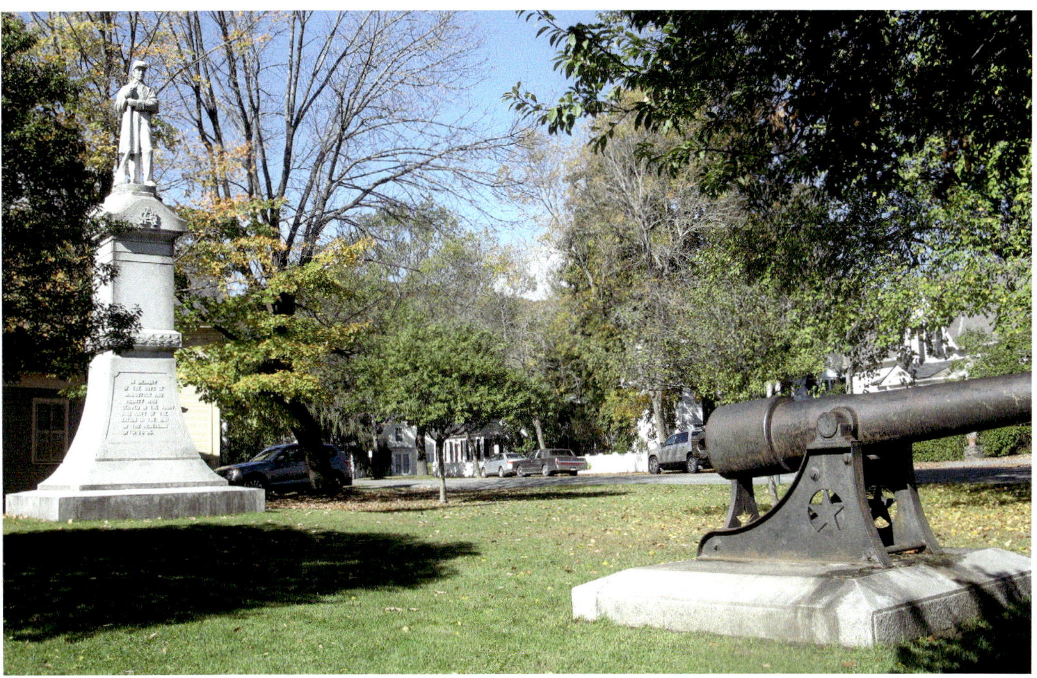

Acknowledgements

With gratitude forever to Pat Kenney, my husband, for so many things: frustrating research, company on road trips, great suggestions, endlessly fixing computer glitches; to my parents, Jack and Bettey Tobey, for introducing me to Woodstock as a young child and encouraging me to write; to my brother Jon Tobey, for helping me to capture some of the most elusive images and making sure I adhere to at least some of the rules of grammar; and to the Billings Family for enormous and gracious generosity and a wealth of local wisdom, memories and insight.

The following have helped to make this book a reality. Thank you all so much!

Jack Anderson, Assistant Windsor County Judge and historian
Gina Aurimna, North Universalist Chapel Society
Michael E. Brands, Town Planner & Administrative Officer, Woodstock
D. Michael Chamberlain, Windsor County Sheriff
Gail Devine, Director Woodstock Recreation Department
Robert J. Donnelly, Jr., Grand Secretary, Woodstock Masonic, Lodge #31, F & AM
Chip Evans, Gallery on the Green, Owner
The Flowers family for solving some tricky history mysteries
Geraldine Fowler, North Universalist Chapel Society
North Universalist Chapel Society
Erwin and Polly Fullerton, awesome record keepers
Courtney Lowe, Director of Sales and Marketing, Woodstock Inn
Reverend Norman N. MacLeod, St. James Episcopal Church
Mary McCuaig, South Woodstock Historical Society
Don Ramson, North Universalist Chapel Society
Paul Ramsey, Director of Operations, Woodstock Inn
Jonathan D. Robinson, Historian
Ruth Spencer, for keeping me company in Woodstock for a day
Sarah Stein at Simon Pearce Glassworks
Jon Sterling, Woodstock, Past Master, for research information and the photo of the Paul Revere bell
Renee L. Vondle, Assistant Zoning Administrator
Leigh Webb, Franklin, NH Historical Society President, for information regarding old railroads in New England, specifically turntables

Interesting Reading:

Woodstock Then & Now by Rhoda Teagle, Frederick Billings by Jane Curtis, Peter Jennison and Frank Lieberman
The History of Woodstock, Vermont 1890-1983
The Long Light of Those Days by Bruce Coffin, *Woodstock's Heritage* by Peter Jennison,
Country Towns of Vermont by Stillman D. and Barbara Radcliffe Rogers
Vermont Place Names, Footprints of History by Ethan Munroe Swift
Times Gone By, by Will & Jane Curtis and Frank Lieberman
The Woodstock Railroad by Edgar T. Mead
Small Towns by Margaret Merrill

With Appreciation to the Following Post Card Photographers:
G. B. Briggs, Howard Rutkowski, CW Allen and Leo Litwin